Environmental Law

by

Ronald J. Rychlak
and
David W. Case

Oceana's Legal Almanac Series:
Law for the Layperson

Oceana®
NEW YORK

OXFORD
UNIVERSITY PRESS

Oxford University Press, Inc., publishes works that further Oxford University's objective of excellence in research, scholarship, and education.

Published by Oxford University Press, Inc.
198 Madison Avenue, New York, New York 10016

Library of Congress Cataloging-in-Publication Data

Rychlak, Ronald J.
Environmental law / Ronald J. Rychlak, David W. Case.
p. cm. — (Oceana's legal almanac series : law for the layperson)
ISBN 978-0-19-973020-9 (hardback : alk. paper)
1. Environmental law—United States—Popular works.
I. Case, David Wayne. II. Title.
KF3775.Z9R93 2010
344.7304'6—dc22 2010000389

Note to Readers:

This publication is designed to provide accurate and authoritative information in regard to the subject matter covered. It is based upon sources believed to be accurate and reliable and is intended to be current as of the time it was written. It is sold with the understanding that the publisher is not engaged in rendering legal, accounting, or other professional services. If legal advice or other expert assistance is required, the services of a competent professional person should be sought. Also, to confirm that the information has not been affected or changed by recent developments, traditional legal research techniques should be used, including checking primary sources where appropriate.

(Based on the Declaration of Principles jointly adopted by a Committee of the American Bar Association and a Committee of Publishers and Associations.)

R.J.R.

To my father, my son, and my grandfather:
Joseph Rychlak

D.W.C.

To my father and my son:
Ronnie Jett Case

Table of Contents

CHAPTER 2:
THE AUTHORITY TO PROTECT THE ENVIRONMENT

CHAPTER 3:
AIR POLLUTION

CHAPTER 4:
WATER QUALITY

CHAPTER 5:
WETLANDS

CHAPTER 6:
TOXIC SUBSTANCES AND HAZARDOUS WASTES

CHAPTER 7:
THE NATIONAL ENVIRONMENTAL POLICY ACT

CHAPTER 8:
ENDANGERED SPECIES

CHAPTER 9: RESTRICTIONS ON DEVELOPMENT OF PRIVATE LAND

CHAPTER 10: THE GREENHOUSE EFFECT AND CLIMATE CHANGE

CHAPTER 11: PUBLIC ENVIRONMENTAL INFORMATION AND ENVIRONMENTAL ATTORNEYS

ABOUT THE AUTHORS

Ronald J. Rychlak

Professor Ronald J. Rychlak is Mississippi Defense Lawyers Association Professor of Law and Associate Dean for Academic Affairs at the University of Mississippi School of Law where he has been on the faculty since 1987. He is a graduate of Wabash College (BA, 1980, *cum laude*) and Vanderbilt University (JD, 1983, *Order of the Coif*). Prior to joining the faculty, Ron practiced law with Jenner & Block in Chicago, and he served as a clerk to Hon. Harry W. Wellford of the U.S. Sixth Circuit Court of Appeals.

Ron is an advisor to the Holy See's delegation to the United Nations and a member of the committee appointed by the Mississippi Supreme Court to revise that state's criminal code. He serves on the editorial boards of *The Gaming Law Review* and *Engage: The Journal of the Federalist Society Practice Groups*, and he is a member of the Mississippi Advisory Committee to the U.S. Civil Rights Commission. He also serves as the university's Faculty Athletic Representative.

Ron is the author or co-author of six other books, including *Real and Demonstrative Evidence: Applications and Theory* (1995, 2nd ed., 2003), and he has been published in *Notre Dame Law Review, UCLA Law Review, Boston College Law Review, Environmental Law* (Lewis & Clark Law School), *The Stanford Environmental Law Journal, The Fordham Environmental Law Journal, The Washington Post, The Wall Street Journal,* and several other periodicals and journals. He lives in Oxford, Mississippi with his wife, Claire, and their six children.

David W. Case

Professor David W. Case is Associate Professor of Law at the University of Mississippi School of Law where he has been on the faculty since 2007. He is a graduate of the University of Mississippi (B.A., 1985;

J.D., 1988, *cum laude*), Columbia University (LL.M., 1993), and Vanderbilt University (Ph.D., 2004). His Ph.D. is in Interdisciplinary Studies: Environmental Law, Management and Policy. Prior to joining the faculty, Professor Case was a Bridgestone Americas Fellow in Environmental Management at Vanderbilt University and a Research Associate with the Vanderbilt Center for Environmental Management Studies (VCEMS). David also previously practiced law with Ott & Purdy in Jackson, Mississippi, served as an attorney in the Civil Division of the U.S. Department of Justice in Washington, D.C., and served as a clerk to Hon. Rhesa H. Barksdale of the U.S. Fifth Circuit Court of Appeals.

David has published articles in the *Emory Law Journal*, the *Environmental Law Reporter*, the *Mississippi College Law Review*, the *Mississippi Law Journal*, the *University of Colorado Law Review*, the *University of Memphis Law Review*, the *Washington & Lee Law Review*, and the *William & Mary Environmental Law & Policy Review*, and several other book chapters and essays. He lives in Hernando, Mississippi with his wife, Catherine, and their four children.

ACKNOWLEDGEMENT: Professors Rychlak and Case gratefully acknowledge the invaluable research assistance of Megan Black and Lori Johnson, both third-year law students at the University of Mississippi School of Law, in the preparation of this book.

PREFACE

In 1987, when I first joined the faculty at the University of Mississippi School of Law, I was given the opportunity to teach environmental law. This was a young and exciting field of study, and I soon became enamored with it. In addition to the basic introductory course, I helped develop a course on coastal law, and I published several articles on environmental law topics. For a dozen years, I also taught environmental law to graduate engineering students, through the Jackson-Ole Miss Graduate Engineering Program (later to become a part of Jackson State University). It was in these classes, teaching bright students with no legal background about environmental law, that I came to realize the necessity of breaking down language barriers and talking about law—even complex matters of environmental law—in a manner that non-lawyers could understand. I had to do that in my course, and I hope that we have managed to do that in this book.

I was particularly happy when Oxford University Press agreed to let my former student and current colleague, David Case, co-author the book with me. David's determination to become a law professor led him to leave his law practice and earn a Ph.D in interdisciplinary environmental studies from Vanderbilt University (where I obtained my J.D.). David is now the anchor of the environmental law program at our law school.

There are, of course, many people to thank when one completes a task like this. Our secretaries, Niler, Mary, and Bernadette are always helpful. We also had two fine research assistants, Megan Black and Lori Johnson. Most importantly, though, we'd like to thank our families who give us support and put up with the demands that projects like this put on our time.

Despite the many people who have assisted us, any errors or omissions that remain in this final version, David and I blame on each other.

Ronald J. Rychlak

INTRODUCTION

Public concern for the environment has driven the development of environmental law in the United States for several decades. The serious risks to society posed by a polluted environment came to the forefront of the national public consciousness during the decade of the 1960s. Events such as the publication in 1962 of Rachel Carson's Silent Spring, which critiqued public health and environmental risks related to pesticide use, and several well publicized environmental disasters, such as the burning of the Cuyahoga River in Cleveland, Ohio and the massive Santa Barbara oil spill off the coast of California, energized public alarm over the perceived threats of industrial activities and pollution. By the end of the decade, environmental protection had become an important issue in national electoral politics. In response to the growing public concern over such issues as air and water quality, waste disposal, and threats to species and ecosystems, Congress enacted numerous major pollution control statutes and other environmental regulatory programs during the decades of the 1970s and 1980s.

Prior to the ascendancy of public pollution control legislation in the United States, common law nuisance litigation was the legal system's primary mechanism for resolving environmental problems caused by polluting activities. Industrial, commercial, agricultural, and municipal activities of all types and descriptions causing pollution of air, water, and land have been the subject of common law nuisance litigation in American courts since before the onset of the Industrial Revolution in the 1840s. However, nuisance law eventually came to be viewed as an inefficient and ineffective means of controlling large-scale problems associated with modern-day pollution. The inadequacies of common law actions in dealing with broad societal environmental concerns were a significant factor motivating the eventual development of the sweeping federal environmental programs and regulatory controls in place today.

These federal environmental regulatory programs are credited with substantial success over the years in reducing pollution, limiting the harmful impacts of human activity on the environment, and improving environmental quality around the nation. Nonetheless, public concern for the environment is higher than ever as the end of the first decade of the new century approaches. Both long-standing and relatively newer environmental challenges command the public's attention on a daily basis. Despite how far the nation has come in responding to environmental problems, much remains to be done to address such important issues such as global climate change, non-point source water pollution, ozone depletion, indoor air pollution, inefficient consumption of natural resources and energy supplies, and risks inherent in the manufacture and use of toxic chemicals. Environmental law is at the center of an ongoing national debate over how best to effectively and efficiently solve these critically important problems.

Widespread public concern for the environment leads to substantial awareness of and involvement with environmental issues by the average person. Tens of millions of people are members of environmental organizations, with most members of local groups. A study published in 2001 estimates that up to 30,000 local environmental groups were active in the United States at the dawn of the twenty-first century. Moreover, most major federal environmental statutes allow private citizens to bring a citizen suit against polluters or the government as a means of enforcing environmental laws. Individual citizens and environmental groups routinely take advantage of this opportunity for public participation in the field of environmental law. This combination of public awareness of and involvement with environmental issues and opportunity for public participation in the legal system makes environmental law of unique interest and importance to the average person.

This book provides an overview of environmental law presented in an understandable way for those who may be encountering this complex area of law for the first time. Through this book, the reader will gain an understanding of the major environmental regulatory statutes, including those addressing air and water quality, hazardous materials and wastes, pesticides and other toxic substances, wetlands preservation, and endangered species. The reader will also be introduced to the agencies responsible for implementing and enforcing these statutes. This book also covers the common law principles which are of continuing importance in environmental law and from which modern environmental law directly descends. The reader will further gain an understanding of environmental restrictions on private property development, the increasingly important issue of global climate change, and the ability of the public to obtain access to environmental information through community right to know laws and other environmental statutes.

CHAPTER 1: THE ENVIRONMENTAL AGENCIES

I. FEDERAL AGENCIES

Rachel Carson's *Silent Spring*, published in 1962, was the first book to bring the topic of environmental pollution to the public forefront. It dramatized the danger of pesticides and heightened public awareness about the environment. The first chapter, entitled "A Fable for Tomorrow," told of an American town which had once been thriving, but where plants, animals, and people were now all dying. The culprit was modern pesticides. In what she called "the other road," Carson argued for the development of pesticide policies based on the biological understanding of pests as living organisms. The then current approach, she argued, was "Stone Age" science, "born of the Neanderthal age of biology and philosophy" and it was "our alarming misfortune" that these "terrible weapons had been turned against the earth itself."

The environmental awakening spurred on by Carson and others came not only in the form of new laws and a new awareness in courts, but also with the opening of new departments in the government. In the 1960s, the federal government began establishing administrative agencies specifically designed to deal with environmental matters. To a significant extent, these agencies became responsible for protecting various aspects of our environment.

A. Environmental Protection Agency

The most important federal environmental agency is the United States Environmental Protection Agency (EPA). Its main objective is protecting the public health from environmental problems. The EPA accomplishes this in large part by enforcing and assuring compliance with environmental regulations.

The EPA is led by its Administrator, who is appointed by the President of the United States. The EPA is not a cabinet level agency, but the Administrator is normally given cabinet rank. The EPA employs 17,000 people across the country, with headquarters in Washington, D.C., ten regional offices, and more than a dozen labs. Each regional office is responsible for several states and territories. To get information about any given region, go to the EPA web page <http://www.epa.gov/epahome/state.htm>.

The EPA has a number of subdivisions that handle specific environmental issues and problems. They ensure that the federal environmental laws are implemented and enforced.

1. The EPA's Office of Enforcement and Compliance Assurance

The EPA's Office of Enforcement and Compliance Assurance (OECA) is responsible for making sure that those entities subject to regulation are in compliance with the relevant laws and regulations. In order to carry out this duty, the OECA applies regulatory enforcement mechanisms that include civil and criminal enforcement actions.

The OECA also assists businesses and communities with compliance training and guidance. It established national Compliance Assistance Centers for specific industries that are heavily populated with small businesses. These centers also assist businesses that face substantial regulation. The purpose of the centers is to provide comprehensive, easy-to-understand compliance information targeted to particular industries. Among these industries are: printing, metal finishing, automotive services and repair, small chemical manufacturers, and agriculture.

2. The Air Enforcement Division

The Air Enforcement Division (AED) of the EPA is responsible for judicial and administrative enforcement activities under the Clean Air Act (CAA) and the Noise Control Act. The AED's Mobile Source Program also enforces national motor vehicle fuel and emissions standards. The Stationary Source Program oversees major sources of emissions (like power stations), acid rain, and stratospheric ozone protection.

The AED provides technical, scientific, and engineering support; participates in and manages case negotiations; prepares litigation and settlement documents; and presents federal cases in administrative and court proceedings. The AED is the principal authority on all enforcement aspects of programs related to the CAA and is primarily responsible for enforcement-related rulemaking. In addition, the AED is responsible for reviewing citizen suits filed under the CAA.

3. The Water Enforcement Division

The Water Enforcement Division (WED) of the EPA is responsible for The Clean Water Act (CWA), the Safe Drinking Water Act, the Marine Protection, Research, and Sanctuaries Act, and the Oil Pollution Act. The WED also reviews citizen enforcement actions; participates in regulatory development; and develops national enforcement policies.

The WED works closely with other OECA offices, including the EPA's Office of Water, the EPA's Office of General Counsel, its regional offices, the states, and the Department of Justice on various water enforcement matters.

4. Hazardous Wastes and the Resource Conservation and Recovery Act Enforcement Division

Pursuant to the Resource Conservation and Recovery Act (RCRA), the role of the EPA's RCRA Enforcement Division is to oversee the national hazardous waste enforcement program. This division is responsible for protecting citizens from health risks caused by hazardous wastes. It also serves as a national clearinghouse for legal and technical advice, information, and data. This division takes enforcement actions against violators and oversees administrative and judicial appellate litigation.

5. The Toxics and Pesticides Enforcement Division

The EPA's Toxics and Pesticides Enforcement Division (TPED) handles case development, policy, and enforcement issues pursuant to the Federal Insecticide, Fungicide, and Rodenticide Act, the Toxic Substances Control Act, and the Emergency Planning and Community Right-to-Know Act.

The responsibilities of the TPED include coordinating national enforcement case initiatives; developing policy and guidance documents for case development and litigation; participating in regulatory workgroups; promoting supplemental environmental projects; supporting regions and states on regional and state cases; undertaking legislative work; and coordinating these activities with the states, OECA, the Department of Justice, and other federal agencies.

6. The Multimedia Enforcement Division

Despite the audio-visual image that that this name brings forth, the EPA's Multimedia Enforcement Division (MED) is actually focused on coordinating existing enforcement programs across multiple types of pollution. The MED fosters comprehensive approaches combining enforcement of all media in one case. The aim is effective overall management of environmental issues that is more cost-effective than bringing separate media-specific enforcement actions.

The multimedia approach is employed in three basic types of enforcement actions: 1) against single facilities, where entire industrial processes at a facility may be examined as a whole to determine compliance with all environmental laws; 2) against entire companies, where violations of different environmental laws occur at various facilities indicating ineffective corporate-wide management of environmental compliance; and 3) geographically based enforcement efforts arising from a comprehensive multimedia analysis of the environmental problems in a given area or industrial sector.

The MED promotes enforcement programs at the national, state, and regional level. It also provides legal and technical support for enforcement activities, coordination for national cases, contractual support for case development, and serves as an information clearinghouse for multimedia enforcement issues. It also coordinates enforcement efforts against companies that have violations at multiple facilities, revises EPA guidance documents, and improves coordination of penalty policies across different media programs.

7. The Federal Facilities Enforcement Office

The EPA's Federal Facilities Enforcement Office (FFEO) is responsible for making sure that federal facilities take actions necessary to prevent, control, and abate environmental pollution. The FFEO is comprised of two groups: the Site Remediation and Enforcement Staff and the Planning, Prevention and Compliance Staff. These two staffs help develop national policy and guidance related to compliance and enforcement issues confronting various federal facilities.

8. The National Enforcement Investigations Center

The EPA's National Enforcement Investigations Center (NEIC) conducts field investigations associated with highly complex technical and regulatory pollution problems. The NEIC lab is a center of expertise in forensic environmental chemistry. NEIC specialists assess, organize, and analyze information in order to prepare for investigations, settlements, negotiations, and trials.

NEIC experts advise EPA headquarters, regional offices, the Department of Justice, and U.S. Attorneys' offices regarding technical, regulatory, and financial issues that arise during case development, settlement negotiations, and litigation. NEIC personnel frequently serve as expert and fact witnesses during legal proceedings. One of the NEIC's specialties is analyzing an entity's financial records to determine its ability to pay proposed fines and/or cleanup costs.

9. The Criminal Investigations Division

The EPA's Criminal Investigations Division (CID) is responsible for criminal enforcement of federal environmental statutes. The CID investigates the polluters who pose the greatest threat to human health and the environment. Once upon a time, criminal cases tended to be restricted to willful violations. Today, many cases are brought based upon negligent activity by the defendant.

The CID provides training to its employees and other federal law enforcement agencies, U.S. Attorneys' offices, as well as state and local law enforcement and environmental agencies.

10. The Office of Administrative Law Judges

The EPA's Office of Administrative Law Judges (OALJ) is an independent office in the Office of the Administrator of the EPA. Administrative Law Judges (ALJs) conduct hearings and render decisions in proceedings between the EPA and regulated businesses, government entities, people, and other organizations.

ALJs preside in enforcement and permit proceedings as well as in proceedings involving alleged violations of environmental statutes. All ALJ decisions are subject to review by the Environmental Appeals Board. An ALJ's decision that disposes of a case becomes the final order of the EPA in 45 days if it is not overturned.

11. The Environmental Appeals Board

The EPA's Environmental Appeals Board (EAB) is an independent body created in recognition of the EPA adjudicatory proceedings as a mechanism for implementing and enforcing the environmental laws. It consists of four appellate judges appointed by the Administrator. The EAB is the final decision maker on administrative appeals under all major environmental statutes that the EPA administers. Decisions of the Board are final and may not be further appealed to the Administrator. The parties may, however, have statutory rights of appeal to federal court under the various environmental statutes.

The EAB's caseload consists primarily of appeals from permit decisions and civil penalty decisions. The EAB also hears petitions for reimbursement of costs incurred in complying with cleanup orders issued under the Comprehensive Environmental Response, Compensation, and Liability Act of 1980.

B. U.S. Army Corps of Engineers

The U.S. Army Corps of Engineers (the "Corps") provides engineering services for building and maintaining America's infrastructure. The duties of the Corps cover a wide spectrum, including: keeping channels open for navigation, protecting against floods, safeguarding the environment, generating hydropower, providing water to communities, managing recreation areas, and responding to disasters. The Corps has the responsibility of helping to care for these important aquatic resources. It oversees the dredging of America's waterways, and it helps minimize damage from disasters by devising hurricane and storm damage reduction infrastructure.

The Corps protects and restores the nation's environment including special efforts in the Everglades, the Louisiana coast, and along many of the nation's major waterways. The Corps is also cleaning sites contaminated with hazardous, toxic, or radioactive waste-material in an effort to sustain the environment.

Through its Civil Works program, the Corps carries out a wide array of projects that provide: coastal protection, disaster preparation, environmental protection and response, flood protection, hydropower, navigable waterways, recreational opportunities, and safe water supplies. The Corps seeks to achieve the best possible balance among these competing demands of economic growth, recreation, and sustainability.

1. Navigation and Commerce

The Corps plays a vital role in keeping goods moving by ensuring that water depths are sufficient for tows and barges to travel safely. The depth of a given river or waterway, and hence the amount of water flowing through it, can vary greatly. Through the construction, operation, and maintenance of a series of strategically placed locks and dams, the Corps is able to control water levels on the nation's major rivers, ensuring a consistent and safe depth. Of course, this does not come without environmental consequences.

Dredging is a major component of the Corps' efforts to protect navigation channels. Over time, the buildup of sediment and other material resulting from weather conditions and the natural flow of a river can reduce water depth to unsafe levels. The Corps regularly undertakes dredging projects to remove this material and ensure that rivers and inland ports remain navigable.

Dredging, of course, can have adverse environmental consequences caused primarily by the faster speed of the running water after dredging. This can lead to more movement of the sedimentation, causing it to be deposited and built up in new areas. The Corps evaluates the environmental impact of every project it undertakes on the nation's rivers. Dredging projects are usually carried out during "environmental windows" when they will have the least impact on sensitive species.

Each year the Corps also undertakes numerous projects to control erosion, restore aquatic ecosystems, and protect endangered species.

2. Recreation and Education

The Corps provides outdoor recreation, hosting nearly 385 million visitors a year at 4,300 recreation areas in 43 states. It hosts 33% of all freshwater lake fishing in the United States and 15% of freshwater boating. It also hosts about 200,000 fishing tournaments every year. Over 100,000 campsites are available at Corps-managed properties, and Corps parks include over 2,000 miles of trails. Corps parks are home to many special events including sailing regattas, arts and crafts festivals, and scouting activities.

As part of its ongoing effort to raise awareness about environmental issues, Corps park managers and rangers provide hundreds of environmental education programs every year, reaching more than three million people. Many of these educational events are offered in conjunction with recreational events, assuring greater participation.

3. Hydroelectric Power

The Corps is the largest operator of hydroelectric power plants in the United States. Its 75 hydropower projects provide 100 billion kilowatt-hours of energy annually. That is enough energy to serve more than 10 million households.

Hydropower plants do not burn fossil fuels, like coal and oil, and they provide an inexpensive source of power. They do, however, change the natural river environment, and they can adversely impact aquatic life. The Corps tries to find the right balance between society's needs and environmental concerns.

4. Water Supply

Many Corps lakes provide water for local communities, particularly in times of drought. The Corps has 117 water supply projects in 24 states and Puerto Rico, and they provide more than 3 trillion gallons of water for use by local communities and businesses. Corps reservoirs supply water to some of the nation's largest metropolitan areas including Atlanta, Dallas-Fort Worth, and Washington, DC.

The Corps also provides water to help farmers irrigate crops, particularly in western states. The Corps typically tries to maintain over eighteen trillion gallons of water available at 40 sites for irrigation and other uses.

5. Flood Control

More than ninety million acres of land in the United States are in areas at risk for flooding. A key function of Corps dams and lakes is to control water flow on rivers to prevent or reduce the impact of floods. Corps flood control reservoirs typically have a large area set aside where no water is routinely stored. During times of heavy rainfall or snowmelt, water can be stored in this area.

Over the years, the Corps also has built thousands of miles of protective levees and dikes to give communities additional protection against flooding. In addition, the Corps works closely with states and local communities to lessen the impact of potential flooding. Failure of the Corps properly to maintain the levees in and around New Orleans has been identified as one of the reasons for the flooding that followed Hurricane Katrina in 2005.

The Corps has recently begun to emphasize nonstructural flood control solutions rather than structural ones such as dams, levees, etc. Non-structural solutions involve modifying how floodplains are used or changing current uses to remedy potential flood hazards. A non-structural approach helps avoid changes to the floodplains that might have a negative effect on the environment.

6. Emergency Response

Each year Corps personnel respond to many presidential disaster declarations and numerous state and local emergencies, including floods, tornadoes, hurricanes, and earthquakes. Corps personnel move rapidly into an affected area to provide a wide range of vital services including: drinkable water; emergency power; search and rescue operations; emergency repairs to levees and other flood control projects; restoring public services and facilities; building temporary shelters; and assisting with long-term recovery and reconstruction.

7. Wetlands

The Corps heads the interagency task force responsible for identifying, prioritizing, and implementing projects to restore wetlands and to provide for the long-term preservation of wetlands. Each year more than 100,000 construction projects are undertaken in the United States that have the potential to affect wetlands and other aquatic resources. Through its regulatory program, the Corps strives to protect these resources, while allowing reasonable and necessary development projects to go forward.

Organizations undertaking projects that will have an unavoidable impact on aquatic resources must obtain a permit from the Corps. The Corps evaluates the positives and negatives of each project to determine what will best serve the public interest. For permitted activities that result in unavoidable losses of wetlands, the Corps usually requires replacement wetlands to offset those losses. The permit process is detailed in Chapter 5, "Wetlands," of this Almanac.

8. Ports and Harbors

The Corps is responsible for ensuring that ships can move safely and efficiently in and out of American harbors. Corps personnel oversee dredging to maintain channel depths at more than 1,000 harbors. One of the Corps' major focuses is to modernize and upgrade the nation's ports and harbors to keep pace with the growing traffic, as well as the increasing size of vessels in the world merchant fleet.

9. Coastal Protection

Many coastal areas in the United States are in peril from development, erosion, and pollution. The coasts are also regularly threatened and harmed by hurricanes and other major storms. The Corps is involved in a wide variety of projects aimed at protecting the coastlines from storm damage and erosion while at the same time preserving and restoring ecosystems. The Coastal Zone Management Act is discussed in Chapter 5, "Wetlands," of this Almanac.

Most coastal areas have either too much or too little sediment. Too much leads to blocked river channels and smothered reefs while too little leads to beach erosion and wetland loss. The regional management program is designed to move sediment from areas where it is harmful to areas where it can be beneficial. This initiative has fostered a series of projects across the country involving partnerships among federal and state agencies and private organizations aimed at developing regional approaches to the management of sediment.

C. United States Department of the Interior

The United States Department of the Interior (DOI) is the federal executive department responsible for the management and conservation of most federal land and the administration of programs relating to Native Americans, Alaskan Natives, and Hawaiian Natives. The DOI is administered by the Secretary of the Interior, which is a cabinet-level position. Several bureaus and agencies fall under the jurisdiction of the DOI, among the more important ones in terms of the environment are: the Bureau of Land Management, the Minerals Management Service, the National Park Service, the Office of Surface Mining, and the U.S. Fish and Wildlife Service.

D. United States Fish and Wildlife Service

The United States Fish and Wildlife Service (FWS) is the unit of the Department of the Interior dedicated to the management and preservation of wildlife. Its mission is working with others to conserve, protect, and enhance fish, wildlife, plants, and their habitats for the continuing benefit of the American people. The Service consists of a central administrative office with eight regional offices and nearly 700 field offices distributed throughout the United States. It manages 548 National Wildlife Refuges and 66 National Fish Hatcheries among other facilities.

The FWS has several units including the National Wildlife Refuge System, the Migratory Bird Program, the Federal Duck Stamp System, the National Fish Hatchery System, the Endangered Species Program, and the Office of Law Enforcement. For more information about the FWS and wetlands, see Chapter 5, "Wetlands," of this Almanac.

E. National Marine Fisheries Service

The National Marine Fisheries Service (MFS) is a division of the Department of Commerce, responsible for the stewardship of the nation's living marine resources and their habitat. MFS is responsible for the management, conservation, and protection of living marine resources within the United States' Exclusive Economic Zone (waters 3 to 200 miles offshore). MFS assesses and predicts the status of fish stocks, ensures compliance with fisheries regulations, and works to reduce wasteful fishing practices.

Under the Marine Mammal Protection Act and the Endangered Species Act (see Chapter 8, "Endangered Species," of this Almanac), MFS recovers protected marine species without unnecessarily impeding economic and recreational opportunities. With the help of the six regional offices and eight councils, MFS works with communities on fishery management issues and promotes sustainable fisheries by preventing lost economic potential associated with overfishing, declining species, and degraded habitats.

MFS also plays a supportive and advisory role in the management of living marine resources in coastal areas under state jurisdiction, provides scientific and policy leadership in the international arena, and implements international conservation and management measures as appropriate.

MFS has several units, including: the Office of Sustainable Fisheries, the Office of Protected Resources, the Office of Habitat Conservation, the Office of Science and Technology, the Office for Law Enforcement, the Office of International Affairs, the Aquaculture Program, and the Seafood Inspection Program.

F. White House Council on Environmental Quality

The Council on Environmental Quality (CEQ) coordinates federal environmental efforts and works closely with agencies and other White House offices in the development of environmental policies and initiatives. The CEQ was established within the Executive Office of the President by Congress as part of the National Environmental Policy Act (NEPA).

The CEQ's Chair serves as the principal environmental policy adviser to the President. The Chair assists and advises the President in developing environmental policies and initiatives. Through interagency working groups and coordination with other agencies, the CEQ works to advance the President's agenda. It also balances competing positions and encourages government-wide coordination, bringing federal agencies, state and local governments, and other stakeholders together on matters relating to the environment, natural resources, and energy.

The CEQ also oversees the Office of the Federal Environmental Executive and oversees federal agency implementation of the environmental impact assessment process, and acts as a referee when agencies disagree over the adequacy of such assessments. Under NEPA, the CEQ works to balance environmental, economic, and social objectives in pursuit of NEPA's goal of "productive harmony" between humans and the human environment. NEPA assigns CEQ the task of ensuring that federal agencies meet their obligations under the Act. NEPA is more fully addressed in Chapter 7, "The National Environmental Policy Act," of this Almanac.

II. STATE ENVIRONMENTAL AGENCIES

To implement federal and state legislation, most states have established their own departments of natural resources or environmental protection agencies. State environmental agencies may operate slightly differently from the federal EPA. Their mission first and foremost is to regulate and enforce state-adopted statutes. As a result, a large part of state-agency resources are used for monitoring, permitting, inspection, and enforcement.

State and environmental agencies can provide local technical assistance not available from EPA regional offices. State environmental agencies also often serve as good resources for training assistance. Some provide direct training assistance, while others maintain lists of approved or available service providers.

The best way to access state-agency websites is to search for the state Department of Natural Resources or Environmental Protection Agency. Searching websites provides an excellent source of background information, but personal contact is a good approach with state agencies.

Other state agencies such as departments of commerce and labor, occupational safety and health, or economic development can also be important sources of technical assistance for development and construction projects. They can also be located on the Internet.

CHAPTER 2: THE AUTHORITY TO PROTECT THE ENVIRONMENT

I. COMMON LAW REMEDIES

Today's environmental plaintiff has a myriad of federal legislation upon which to base a claim against a polluter. The Clean Water Act, the Resource Conservation and Recovery Act, and the Clean Air Act all provide for citizen suits, as do many other statutory schemes. In some cases, however, common law actions such as nuisance, negligence, trespass, and strict liability for abnormally dangerous activities provide more attractive features. What is the place of such laws in today's environmental litigation? To what extent, if any, have they been preempted by legislation? What are the potential dangers and pitfalls? This chapter attempts to answer these questions and provide guidance to those considering litigation.

A. Nuisance and Negligence

A cause of action designed to cover invasions of the plaintiff's property due to conduct wholly outside of that property has been available since virtually the dawn of the common law. Originally this cause of action may have had criminal as well as civil components. It evolved into what is today known as the tort of private nuisance. Nuisance may be defined as:

> That class of wrongs that arises from the unreasonable, unwarrantable, or unlawful use by a person of his own property, real or personal, or from his improper, indecent, or unlawful personal conduct, working an obstruction or injury to a right of another, or of the public, and producing such material annoyance, inconvenience,

> discomfort or hurt that the law will presume a consequent damage. *Young v. Weaver*, 202 Miss. 291, 32 So. 2d 202, 204 (1947).

Common law private nuisance actions still provide a viable alternative to the environmental plaintiff seeking to correct an environmental wrong. In many cases, a nuisance action provides procedural and substantive advantages to the plaintiff. The action can stand on its own or be appended to a complaint containing counts based on federal legislation.

The two basic components of a common law private nuisance claim are: 1) that the defendant acted with the intent of interfering with the use and enjoyment of the plaintiff's property; and 2) that a substantial and unreasonable interference with the plaintiff's use and enjoyment of his or her property did in fact result. Any lawful possessor of land who has been harmed has the ability (or "standing") to bring this type of suit. The "intent" that must be established is further explored below.

The main issue to be resolved in cases like this is whether the defendant has interfered with the plaintiff's enjoyment of his property. If this is established, and the plaintiff avoids common causation problems, the defendant has little in the way of affirmative defenses to relieve himself from liability. The plaintiff should be able to recover money damages, and in many cases he or she will be entitled to injunctive relief as well. A nuisance action should be considered in every environmental case.

The law further distinguishes between public and private nuisances. Unfortunately, there is a great deal of confusion between these two types of nuisances. This results from the overlap of these two doctrines in some areas and their divergence in other areas. A famous tort law scholar, Dean Prosser, once wrote that the common name given to public and private nuisance is "in the highest degree unfortunate."

A public nuisance may be described as an interference with the right of, or a threat to, the general public, such as a deep and dangerous hole in the shallow area of a lake used for swimming. A public nuisance is often defined by statute. A suit based on this theory usually is brought by a governmental entity as a civil action, but it is an offense against the state and may be criminally prosecuted. In some cases, it may also be pursued by a private plaintiff.

The traditional rule is that a private litigant can sue for damages based upon a public nuisance only when his or her injuries differ in kind from that suffered by the public at large. However, this requirement has more recently come under attack and has not been strictly enforced.

The modern trend is to eliminate the distinction between public and private nuisance in this area and to allow private individuals to institute legal actions whether the nuisance is private or public. Because the sovereign's suit is an exercise of police power, it is governed by strict liability; however, when a private litigant alleges a public nuisance, the plaintiff may have to establish some degree of culpability (negligence) by the defendant.

A private nuisance, on the other hand, is an unreasonable interference with the plaintiff's enjoyment of his or her property, such as the case where a farm creates an offensive odor that drifts over to the neighbor's property. An action for private nuisance is the typical common law approach for an individual litigant to remedy an environmental wrong that has harmed him. This cause of action can be based on many different types of interference with enjoyment of the land. The most common form of environmental nuisance is noise pollution. In order for noise pollution to be actionable, it must be more than annoying; it must be of such magnitude and intensity as to cause physical or psychological discomfort and annoyance to persons of ordinary sensibilities. Nuisance may also be found in dust, smoke, vibrations, odors, or an infinite variety of other pollutants, including toxins, which are carried to the plaintiff's property in the air, land, or water.

Despite numerous legislatively enacted causes of action, common law nuisance is the oldest and perhaps most useful legal theory for environmental plaintiffs. Often the environmental plaintiff is an individual or a small group, and the defendant is a large corporate entity. This imbalance of resources may make for a difficult uphill battle if the legal theory is based on expensive scientific evaluations. Thus many of the regulatory or statutory actions provided in environmental legislation are not favorable theories for a plaintiff. Instead, if the plaintiff can structure the suit to allege generally that the pollution looks bad, smells bad, and does bad things without getting mired in the scientific underpinnings, the plaintiff will be in the strongest position. The beauty of the simple common law nuisance, negligence, or trespass action is that it reduces the case to terms a lay person can understand: "You spilled it, it damaged me or my property, and you should pay."

A nuisance action may be available in cases where a statutory action would be barred because the defendant is in compliance with applicable regulations or statutes. Holding a permit for operation of an alleged nuisance does not, as a matter of law, constitute a defense against a nuisance action. Thus it has been held that a permit granted under the Clean Water Act does not shield the defendant from a common law nuisance suit. Similarly, compliance with zoning laws does not shield the defendant from a nuisance suit. Additionally, a nuisance claim might still be available after a statutory remedy is time barred. For instance, a five year statute of limitations applies to the Clean Water Act, but a nuisance action is not necessarily constrained by the same strict time limits.

Many environmental statutes have certain notice requirements which delay commencement of a suit. For instance, the Clean Air Act, the Solid Waste Disposal Act, and the Resource Conservation and Recovery Act all have 60-day notice requirements. In addition, unfamiliar legislation can lead to delays as counsel, judges, and jurors grapple with the statutory scheme. The relatively more familiar nuisance doctrine may lead to a quicker resolution of the problem. The timing in environmental litigation may be crucial; thus a nuisance suit, which often provides for a quicker remedy, may be the plaintiff's best alternative.

The remedy in a common law nuisance action can also be more attractive to an environmental plaintiff, because such claims can provide monetary as well as injunctive relief to the successful plaintiff, while many statutory actions provide only an injunctive remedy. Finally, a careful plaintiff's attorney evaluates the advantages and disadvantages of proceeding in state or federal court. If state courts provide a more favorable forum, a common law claim based on state law may be easier to keep there. If the case is to be litigated in federal court, nuisance counts may be litigated there under pendant jurisdiction.

1. Elements of the Case

The first component of a private nuisance, the defendant's intent, is typically required in private nuisance cases, but not in public nuisance cases. Originally, all nuisance cases (public and private) were decided under a strict liability standard. Plaintiffs, however, then realized that tort actions were easier to win under the strict liability doctrine of nuisance than under a negligence theory. If the defendant had created the nuisance in a negligent or reckless manner, and the plaintiff had also been negligent in some way, the negligence action might be barred by the doctrine of contributory negligence. However, the same suit brought under the strict liability theory of nuisance would not be barred. As Justice Benjamin Cardozo wrote: "It would be intolerable if the choice of a name [for the cause of action] were to condition liability."

Because of this problem, actions by private litigants to remedy private or public nuisances have evolved from the strict liability standard to an "intentionality" standard. This change has led some commentators to conclude that the tort of nuisance is virtually identical with the tort of negligence. Fortunately for the environmental plaintiff, this is not the case. In the first instance, the intent requirement is satisfied if the defendant creates or continues the nuisance with knowledge that harm to the plaintiff's interests are occurring or are substantially certain to follow. Thus "intent" does not mean that the defendant intends to interfere with the plaintiff's enjoyment of his land, or even that he negligently does so. When one understands this definition of intent, one can see that intent is a component of a nuisance action.

Moreover, when there is physical damage to the plaintiff's land, water, or improvements, even unintentional or accidental interferences are actionable. The rationale behind a fault-free standard for cases involving property is logical when one considers that the original reason for requiring intent was to prevent plaintiffs from avoiding the rules concerning contributory negligence. It is rare when the plaintiff's contributory negligence affects this type of nuisance case. As other commentators have noted, it may be proper to require people who have taken another's property for their own purposes to pay for that property, no matter how faultless or socially useful their conduct may have been. As such, when dealing with property rights, it is reasonable to speak in terms of strict liability.

In order for an interference with land to constitute a nuisance, the invasion of the plaintiff's interests must be both substantial and unreasonable. Substantial simply means a significant harm to the plaintiff. Thus minor interferences of short duration do not amount to nuisance. The harm, however, is not limited to physical harm or injury. The standard for determining whether the harm is substantial is determined by looking to the senses of a "normal person in the community." When the invasion affects the physical condition of the plaintiff's land, the substantial or significant nature of the interference is not in doubt. Thus for the typical environmental plaintiff in a nuisance suit, this requirement should not pose a significant barrier.

The interference with the plaintiff's interest must also be unreasonable in order for a nuisance to be declared. This does not mean that the defendant's *activities* must be unreasonable, only that the *burden* on the plaintiff is unreasonable. The reasonableness of the burden is determined by the jury (or judge if there is no jury). There is no hard and fast controlling rule; the use under one set of facts might be reasonable and unreasonable under another. In order for the nuisance to be actionable, however, it must be of such magnitude and intensity as to cause actual physical discomfort and annoyance to persons of ordinary sensibilities.

Once that is established, even if the defendant is using the utmost care in operating the complained of activity, if the plaintiff's property is burdened unreasonably, an action for nuisance is appropriate. Accordingly, if the environmental plaintiff's property has been burdened, none of the elements of nuisance should be difficult to establish.

After the plaintiff has established that the defendant has substantially and unreasonably interfered with the plaintiff's use, enjoyment, and value of his property, the burden shifts to the defendant to establish that its use was reasonable or the interference inconsequential. This burden is a particularly difficult one to carry. The defendant is not excused simply because the offensive conduct is necessary, modern, or efficient. Nor is the defendant excused because it is unable to obtain better equipment due to events beyond its control. Moreover, if the plaintiff's land is imposed upon, it may be almost impossible to prove that the defendant's use is reasonable. Thus it will be difficult for the defendant to carry this burden if the plaintiff establishes a *prima facie* case.

State statutes often define certain activities as nuisances. Several states statutorily define nuisance as a place where lewdness, assignation, or prostitution takes place or where controlled substances are found. Other times statutes provide guidelines for conduct, but do not declare that violations constitute public nuisances. Compliance with statutory guidelines do not shield the defendant from a common law nuisance suit; however, violation of such statutes by the defendant can make the plaintiff's case much easier. If the legislature has declared that a certain activity is a nuisance, courts invariably defer to that determination. Thus it is wise to inspect the statutory scheme for legislatively determined nuisances. If the legislation regulates or prohibits certain activity, without labeling it a nuisance, evidence of the violation is still relevant in determining whether the activity constitutes a nuisance. Accordingly, a careful review of the state's statutory scheme is very important in nuisance cases.

2. Causation Problems

Despite its many advantages, there are certain drawbacks associated with common law nuisance. The greatest difficulty encountered by plaintiffs has typically been proof of causation. All of the common law tort doctrines require the plaintiff to establish a causal link between the defendant's wrongdoing and the plaintiff's injury. With a still evolving body of scientific knowledge concerning toxic effects, this can pose a significant problem to the environmental plaintiff. Careful planning and preparation are needed when evaluating this aspect of a nuisance case.

Miller v. National Cabinet Co., a New York case from 1960, is not a nuisance case, but it illustrates the causation problem typical of common law doctrines. In that case, the widow of a furniture finisher sought workmen's compensation after her husband died from leukemia. She claimed that the leukemia had been brought on by her husband's exposure to benzene in the workplace. Although the Workmen's Compensation Board awarded benefits, the court overturned the Board and denied benefits because there was no evidence of causation. At the hearing only one doctor had identified any causal relationship between benzene and leukemia, and his opinion was very guarded. This was insufficient for the plaintiff to carry her burden.

The *Miller* case had three distinct causation problems. First, there was insufficient evidence to establish that benzene exposure could lead to leukemia in humans. The plaintiff had no epidemiological evidence, nor was there any evidence from animal studies on this point. This, of course, was due in large part to limited scientific knowledge. Today we know that benzene can lead to leukemia but in 1960 the evidence was lacking.

The second causation problem for Mrs. Miller was in establishing that benzene exposure had caused Mr. Miller's leukemia. Even if it had been established that benzene could cause leukemia, it would not necessarily follow that Mr. Miller contracted his disease that way. Finally, Mr. Miller had been exposed to benzene while working for five different employers. Accordingly, there was a problem in determining which defendant's benzene (if any) had caused the leukemia.

The first causation problem, establishing a link between the specific pollutant and the injury suffered by the plaintiff, poses a problem whenever the injury is not immediately apparent. Thus if the alleged nuisance involves noise from a neighboring plant, it should not be hard to prove that this interferes with the plaintiff's sleep. However, when the claim is that a certain chemical has created some type of chronic health problem, the jury does not have a common body of knowledge upon which to draw, and scientific evidence is needed. This likely requires expert witnesses well versed in the relevant scientific field. Problems are most likely to arise when the scientific knowledge is limited or subject to dispute.

The 1985 *Agent Orange* litigation illustrates such a problem. The plaintiffs in that case relied mainly on animal studies and "industrial accidents" to prove causation. The defendants, however, were able to win on summary judgment by producing conflicting epidemiological studies. The court found that the studies relied upon by plaintiffs' experts were nonprobative and formed an insufficient basis for an expert's opinion. The court said that the "only useful studies having any bearing on causation" were epidemiological studies. While not all courts demand epidemiological evidence, it may well be true that the burden of proof is more scientific than legal.

Against this background, how is the environmental litigant to approach a case? Preparation is the key. The following points should be considered: carefully examine the expert, the expert's credentials, and the basis for the expert's opinion. The expert should have licenses, certifications, and memberships in relevant recognized scientific or medical organizations. The opinion should be based on recent peer-reviewed publications and leading texts. The expert should also be familiar with conflicting studies and theories. Additionally, litigants must understand that legal causation may differ from causation in the expert's profession. This issue must be addressed with the expert, and he or she must understand the language needed to meet the prerequisites of legal causation.

Once the plaintiff has established that exposure to the element at issue can lead to the problem complained of, the next causation issue is whether that exposure caused this plaintiff's condition. (As *Miller* illustrates, this element is necessary when the plaintiff is seeking money damages. When the plaintiff seeks only injunctive relief a lesser showing may be sufficient.) The plaintiff's medical records must be carefully reviewed to determine whether the problem complained of existed prior to exposure. The litigants should also consider the plaintiff's work history or other opportunities for exposure to harmful pollutants. If possible, the expert should personally examine the plaintiff and perform any necessary tests or experiments so that the opinion can relate to this specific plaintiff's problem.

The final causation issue is linking the defendant with the pollutant. Often this evidence is easy for the plaintiff to produce, or it is available through discovery. For instance, if the nuisance is dust from a cement company, it should not be hard to establish that the dust comes from the defendant's cement company. If there is only one source for the pollutant, as is often true with toxic substances, this linkage should not be hard to establish. If the plaintiff has been exposed to the pollutant by more than one source, the court may turn to some type of apportioning, or joint and several liability.

It is unlikely that all of these causation problems will be present in every case. For instance, there may be no claim relating to physical injury.

In such a case, many of the scientific problems are avoided. In other cases (such as a benzene exposure case today) the "scientific causation" is not in doubt. Moreover, some more recent cases seem to require less in the way of proof of causation. For instance, equitable relief often can be based on threatened rather than actual harm. In every case, however, the plaintiff has the initial burden of establishing both the defendant's fault in causing the nuisance and the harm suffered by the plaintiff.

B. Trespass

When discussing trespass, most people think of a person who intrudes on the property of another. When it comes to environmental law, however, trespass may be applied to a contaminant or some other substance that intrudes on the property of another. Thus if chemicals are seeping from one property to another, the second landowner may have a trespass action against the first landowner.

Trespass is closely related to nuisance and easily confused with it. Trespass is a direct physical invasion or intrusion of the plaintiff's land by the defendant, the defendant's agent, or an object that the defendant has caused to be deposited on the land. The general rule is that a landowner is entitled to an injunction directing the removal of a trespassing object on his or her property. The fact that the aggrieved owner suffers little or no damage from the trespass, that the wrongdoer acted in good faith and would be put to disproportionate expense by the removal of the trespassing structures, or that neighborly conduct as well as business judgment would require acceptance of compensation in money for the lands appropriated ordinarily are unacceptable reasons for denying an injunction. Rights in real property cannot normally be taken from the owner at valuation, except under power of eminent domain. Only when there is some estoppel due to an unnecessary and prejudicial delay on the part of the plaintiff, or a refusal on the plaintiff's part to consent to acts necessary to bring the trespass to an end, will an injunction be refused.

This traditional approach has come under some recent attack. Since an injunction is an equitable remedy, it is only granted after the relative hardships are considered. Courts are free to adjust equitable remedies as needed. Thus if the harm can be minimized without shutting down the defendant's operations, at least for a period of time sufficient to permit the defendant to attempt to correct the problem, that remedy would be appropriate. See *Boomer v. Atlantic Cement Co.,* (N.Y. Apps. 1970), discussed below in the injunctive relief section.

C. Strict Liability

Strict liability is a legal doctrine that makes some persons responsible for damages their actions or products cause, regardless of any "fault" on their part. To recover under this doctrine, the landowner must demonstrate that a condition or activity qualifies as abnormally dangerous and is in fact the cause of the environmental injury. Many common activities have been decreed abnormally dangerous, including collecting large quantities of water in hydraulic power mains, storing gas in large amounts, and transmitting high-powered electricity under city streets.

Courts sometimes struggle in determining when something rises to the level of abnormally dangerous, and liability generally also attaches for extraordinary, abnormal, exceptional, and non-natural activities or conditions. Courts have applied strict liability to cases involving contamination from oil wells, leaking fuel tanks, radioactive emissions, oil well drilling, crop dusting, blasting, and more.

Strict liability for environmental contamination became a fact with the 1980 enactment of the Comprehensive Environmental Response, Compensation, and Liability Act (CERCLA), and similar state laws imposing strict liability for the release of hazardous substances. Since that time, awareness of the widespread nature and risks of environmental contamination and the need for strong tools to remedy those conditions have permeated the public consciousness, the business community, and the courts. As a result, strict liability for environmental contamination under various federal and state statutes has become widespread.

In recent years, some courts have become reluctant to apply common law strict liability, which imposes strict liability for abnormally dangerous activities. Apart from cases involving blasting and a few other historic applications, the current trend is to reject the expansion of strict liability in favor of negligence as the dominant tort theory. Nevertheless, the trend in environmental contamination cases appears to be the opposite, with strict liability being the norm.

D. Defenses

A defendant might claim a prescriptive right to carry out the activity in question. This would prevent the landowner from obtaining relief in court. A prescriptive right is somewhat akin to a statute of limitations that prohibits legal action by the landowner after some point in time, but with the prescriptive claim there is no statue. For this to apply, the plaintiff would have to knowingly acquiesce to the nuisance for a lengthy period of time. Two factors make this very unlikely. First, the plaintiff would have had to knowingly condone, for a very long period of time, a condition about which he or she probably would have objected. Additionally, the condition would have had to continue at the same level for that period of time. If there had been an increase in the intensity of the nuisance, the period would begin running anew. It would be a rare case indeed when the defendant could successfully plead this defense.

The defense of latches might also be raised by environmental defendants. Latches, however, is a creature of equity and does not hold great doctrinal promise for those who claim they should be allowed to take another's property without compensation. Courts ruling on environmental matters have not, in general, looked favorably on this defense. While the environmental plaintiff should take care not to "sit on his rights," latches should not pose a significant problem in most cases.

Defendants also may argue that the plaintiff has "come to the nuisance." This argument stems from the old legal axiom that he who voluntarily places himself in a situation whereby he suffers injury will not prevail. An example would be where the plaintiff has purchased a home near a factory that he now claims is a nuisance. The majority rule is that this will not bar the plaintiff from asserting a nuisance cause of action for the continued use or operation. This rule is based on the theory that pure air and comfortable enjoyment of property are as much rights belonging to the owner as the right of possession and occupancy. In those jurisdictions that allow this defense, the crucial question is whether the plaintiff was aware of the nuisance when he "came to it."

A defendant might also try to avoid liability by shifting blame to a prior owner of the nuisance. In the case of a private nuisance, the familiar principle of *caveat emptor* dictates that responsibility for the offending condition is transferred between parties to the sale of land on which it exists. Thus the owner can not successfully assert this defense. If a party has created a *public* nuisance on certain property, and that property has since been turned over to and accepted by a new party, not only may the new party find itself liable for continuing to operate a public nuisance, the original owner can also be held responsible for having created it.

In any event, it is obvious that the defendant accused of operating an environmental nuisance has little in the way of defenses to that charge. He or she must, instead, concentrate on defeating the plaintiff's claim. This places the environmental plaintiff in a very strong position. If the plaintiff can prevail on his theory, it is unlikely that an affirmative defense can excuse the defendant.

E. Remedies

The ultimate hope of a successful plaintiff, of course, is to have the court find in his or her favor. What the court orders following its determination is the remedy. Usually it involves a legal remedy (money), an injunctive order, or a combination of the two.

1. Money Damages

Once the plaintiff has established the defendant's fault and the harm suffered by the plaintiff, he or she is entitled to a remedy. The plaintiff may prefer a nuisance remedy over a statutory one because a nuisance action can provide monetary relief to the successful plaintiff, while many statutory actions provide only an injunctive remedy. The primary focus of state and federal environmental legislation is to prevent or abate pollution by regulation rather than by providing damages to injured persons. Compensation of pollution victims has been incidental to the accomplishment of this primary purpose. While this may be an appropriate way to protect the environment, it may not be a favorable approach for the environmental plaintiff who has been harmed and seeks compensation.

Legal damages are aimed at restoring the plaintiff's losses by giving him or her money. Damages for temporary injuries from neighboring nuisances generally consist of the reduction of usable or rental value of the property for the time the condition existed, together with special damages, such as loss of business, damage to crops or animals, or damages to structures. If the damage to the plaintiff's property is permanent, the appropriate measure of his loss is the reduction in the property's market value.

In addition, the landowner is entitled to recover such special damages as he may be able to prove. These damages are separate, distinct, and independent of the depreciation of the value of the property or of the depreciation of the rental or usable value of the property. Included in this category of special or incidental damages are annoyance, discomfort, inconvenience, and sickness. There may be others. Accordingly, a damage award in a nuisance or negligence suit should be sufficient to satisfy the aggrieved plaintiff.

Punitive damages are given not just to compensate the plaintiff for his or her loss, but to punish the defendant's wrongdoing. In order to be entitled to punitive damages, the plaintiff usually must establish either a willful and intentional wrong or gross negligence.

2. Injunctive Relief

When the injury to the plaintiff is of a continuing nature, money damages may not be sufficient to correct the wrong, and the plaintiff may seek an injunction either to shut down the nuisance or to impose conditions on the defendant which will lessen the impact on the plaintiff's right to enjoy his or her property. The plaintiff may be entitled to injunctive relief even before any actual injury has been suffered.

In *Boomer v. Atlantic Cement Co.*, (N.Y. Apps. 1970), neighbors of a large cement plant brought action for injunctions, alleging injury to property from dirt, smoke, and vibration emanating from the plant. At trial, the plant was held to constitute a nuisance, but the injunction request was denied. The Court of Appeals first noted the traditional rule that "where a nuisance has been found and where there has been any substantial damage shown by the party complaining an injunction will be granted." The Court, however, ultimately declined to enter an injunction. After noting that "to follow the rule literally in these cases would be to close down the plant at once," the court instead awarded the payment of permanent damages to the plaintiffs. Dissenting Judge Jason pointed out that this remedy, in essence, gave the defendant power to condemn adjoining properties.

In fashioning this remedy, the *Boomer* court was obviously aware of the hardship an injunction would cause the defendant. It noted that the dust problem was "universal wherever cement is made," implying that it would be too much to ask this one plant to solve the problems plaguing an industry. Although it was not discussed to any great extent in the appellate opinion, the main reason that the trial judge had declined to issue an injunction seems not to have been undue hardship to the defendant, but rather the important role that the plant played in the local economy.

The modern approach to injunctive remedies in nuisance cases, as reflected in *Boomer*, comes down to a balancing of the equities. Factors such as good faith, technological feasibility, and importance of the activity to the local economy all play an important part in that process. The plaintiff can, however, have an impact on this balancing.

In the case of *Renkin v. Harvey Aluminum*, (1963), plaintiffs sought to have the defendant better control gasses that were escaping from its aluminum plant. The plant was using hoods to trap the gases, but approximately 20% of the gases were escaping. The plant was a major employer in the area, and new equipment would be expensive, but the plaintiff established that other aluminum plants in the country were using a more advanced process. Since there was an injunctive remedy available that was short of closing down the plant, the court ordered installation of the better hoods. This better process was technologically feasible, and the cost was not prohibitive.

The lesson to be derived from these cases, then, is that the environmental plaintiff who is seeking injunctive relief should be aware that the court might balance the equities before granting injunctive relief. If the defendant's activities are important to the local economy, or if there are other justifications for the defendant's actions, injunctive relief might not be available. However, if the plaintiff is aware of a way for the defendant to carry on its activities without continuing the nuisance, that information should be brought to the attention of the court, because the defendant may be ordered to use this less offensive procedure.

3. Mootness

In some cases, a successful plaintiff may not receive any remedy. This is most likely to be the case if the matter at issue has become moot. Consider, for instance, a critical habitat that is threatened by the construction of a bridge. A successful plaintiff might expect the court to order the project stopped when the judge is persuaded that the project threatens the habitat. If, however, the habitat has been completely destroyed before the case is resolved, the judge may find the point moot and decline to stop the project since there would be no benefit to the environment from doing that. (Of course, a litigant who intentionally rendered a case moot by destroying habitat or doing something similar could be found in contempt and sanctioned in some other way.)

II. FEDERAL LEGISLATION

In addition to common law causes of action, several federal statutory schemes have provisions that can be used by individual litigants to enforce their rights.

A. Citizen Suits

Numerous federal statutory schemes authorize the use of "citizen suits" to protect environmental concerns. The Clean Water Act (CWA); the Safe Drinking Water Act; the Clean Air Act (CAA); the Resource Conservation and Recovery Act; the Comprehensive Environmental Response, Compensation, and Liability Act; the Surface Mining Control and Reclamation Act; the Endangered Species Act; and the Emergency Planning and Community Right-to-Know Act all expressly authorize citizen suits for injunctive relief to compel compliance with the respective Acts. Many environmental groups have taken advantage of this right to bring about compliance with the environmental statutes.

There are three different types of citizen suits. A private citizen can bring suit against a citizen, corporation, or government body for engaging in conduct prohibited by a particular federal statute. For example, a citizen can sue a polluter under the CWA for illegally dumping waste into a waterway. A private citizen can also bring suit against a governmental agency for failing to perform a nondiscretionary duty. Thus a private citizen could sue the EPA for failing to set clean air standards as required by the CAA. Finally, citizens may sue for an injunction to abate an imminent and substantial endangerment involving the generation, disposal, or handling of waste, regardless of whether the defendant's conduct violates a statutory prohibition. (This third type of citizen suit is similar to the common law tort of public nuisance.) In general, these laws entitle plaintiffs who bring successful citizen suits to recover reasonable attorney fees and other litigation costs.

Citizens may only bring citizen suits in federal court if they have standing to sue. To establish standing, the courts require proof that the plaintiff has suffered an injury in fact, meaning an invasion of a legally protected interest which is concrete, particularized, and actual or imminent, not conjectural or hypothetical. (The standing doctrine is discussed in greater detail below.) There must also be a causal connection between the injury and the defendant's conduct. Finally, it must be likely, as opposed to merely speculative, that the injury will be redressed by a favorable decision.

Most of these federal statutes have notice provisions that must be complied with before suit is filed. Typically, the plaintiff is required to notify the defendant 60 days before filing suit. In theory, this gives the defendant the opportunity to correct the problem without resort to litigation. In many cases, this notice period simply gives the parties time to brace for court.

B. The Scope of Federal Power

Under the U.S. Constitution, the federal government has limited authority. The Tenth Amendment of the Constitution provides: "[T]he powers not delegated to the United States by the Constitution, nor prohibited by it to the States, are reserved to the States respectively, or to the people." As such, the Tenth Amendment explicitly allows states to keep and exercise their inherent powers. Federal legislation is only legitimate if it is in some way authorized by the Constitution.

The Commerce Clause (Article 1, Section 8, Clause 3 of the U.S. Constitution) provides that "The Congress shall have power . . . To regulate commerce . . . among the several states." Three broad categories of activity that Congress regulates under this authority are: 1) use of the channels of interstate commerce, 2) instrumentalities, persons, or things in interstate commerce, and 3) those activities that substantially affect interstate commerce. Where a federal statute is not sufficiently related to interstate commerce, it will be overruled.

Due to its authority under the Commerce Clause, Congress may preempt state laws regulating private citizens and businesses, provided it can establish that the regulated activity affects interstate commerce. The federal government may wholly preempt state regulation regarding activities that fall within its constitutional authority. Dispute, however, exists as to the extent of powers granted to Congress by the Commerce Clause.

The Commerce Clause is often paired with the Necessary and Proper Clause of the Constitution, and the combination is used to take a broad, expansive perspective of these powers. Other scholars deny that this is the proper application of the Commerce Clause, and they give the clause a more restrictive reading. A court may invalidate legislation enacted under the Commerce Clause if the court concludes that there is no rational basis for a finding that the regulated activity affects interstate commerce or there is no reasonable connection between the regulations and the legitimate federal interest in interstate commerce.

Most federal laws employ an approach under which a federal agency establishes minimum national standards that states may either implement themselves or leave implementation to federal authorities. The Clean Air Act, the Clean Water Act, the Safe Drinking Water Act, and federal hazardous waste legislation all require the EPA to set minimum national standards, while authorizing delegation of authority to administer these programs to states. In states that fail to receive program delegation, the laws are administered by federal authorities.

Congress may condition the receipt of federal funds on state participation in federal environmental programs, which is a proper use of Congress's spending power and consistent with the Tenth Amendment so long as the conditions bear some relationship to the purpose of the federal spending. Thus the Clean Air Act's denial of federal highway funds to states that fail to meet national air quality standards has been found to be constitutional.

A few constitutional issues have arisen in conflicts over environmental federalism. First, states have argued that some federal environmental regulations impermissibly infringe on state sovereignty in violation of the Tenth Amendment. Few federal environmental laws are vulnerable to Tenth Amendment challenges because most offer states a choice between regulating an activity according to federal standards or having state law preempted by federal regulation.

In 1995, the Supreme Court held that Congress's regulatory authority under the Commerce Clause extended to intrastate activities only when those activities substantially affected interstate commerce (*United States v. López*, (1995)). The *López* case spawned a set of challenges to federal environmental regulations. Arguments that some federal environmental laws exceeded Congress's authority by regulating noncommercial activity that was wholly intrastate have been rejected by most courts because of the potential cumulative impact of even localized environmental damage.

Another source of constitutional limitations on federal authority is the Eleventh Amendment, which makes states immune from suits for damages in federal court. (*Seminole Tribe of Florida v. Florida*, (1996)). This limits the ability of environmental groups to sue states that are alleged to be polluting.

Finally, courts have used the so-called Dormant Commerce Clause to strike down state laws. In general, the Commerce Clause itself—absent action by Congress—restricts state power; the grant of federal power implies a corresponding restriction of state power. In other words, Congress maintains the direct power to either permit a state action invalidated by a court or to preempt (otherwise constitutional) state action because it directly interferes with interstate commerce. This second limitation has come to be known as the "dormant" Commerce Clause because it restricts state power even though Congress's commerce power lies dormant.

C. Federal Preemption

With extensive federal environmental legislation, one logical question is whether common law actions have been preempted by federal law. The Supremacy Clause of the U.S. Constitution provides:

> This Constitution, and the Laws of the United States which shall be made in Pursuance thereof, and all Treaties made, or which shall be made, under the Authority of the United States, shall be the supreme Law of the Land; and the Judges in every State shall

> be bound thereby, any Thing in the Constitution or Laws of any State to the Contrary notwithstanding.

If a state or local law substantially interferes or conflicts with federal laws, the state or local laws will be held invalid. As such, defendants often claim that state tort laws have been preempted by federal law. Courts rarely agree.

When analyzing preemption challenges regarding an area of law traditionally occupied by the states, courts apply a presumption against preemption. Environmental health and safety laws are strongly associated with the state, so the presumption strongly favors the validity of state and local environmental laws, and common law causes of action survive federal legislation. The Supreme Court, for instance, has recognized the continuing validity of nuisance actions for water pollution cases, despite arguments that they have been preempted by the federal Clean Water Act.

Federal preemption of state law depends on congressional intent. Congress can preempt state law in two ways: either expressly or through implication. Absent an express provision specifically stating legislative intent to preempt, a court will not find express preemption. Since virtually no federal environmental statutes expressly preempt common law actions, the question to be resolved is whether the Act in question is inconsistent with the application of state law. Implied preemption exists only to the extent that it is impossible to comply with both state and federal law or where the state law stands as an obstacle to the accomplishment of the full purposes of Congress.

The Clean Water Act is an all-encompassing program of water pollution regulation, designed to establish a comprehensive long-range policy for the elimination of water pollution. The program is based on permits and effluent limitations on the discharge of pollutants into waters of the United States. In addition to state and federal roles in regulating the effluent limitations established in the permits, there is a provision for citizen suit enforcement of the Act. The citizen suit section contains a so-called "savings clause" covering suits outside the Act:

> nothing in this section shall restrict any right which any person (or class of persons) may have under any statute or common law to seek enforcement of any effluent standard or limitation or to seek any other relief (including relief against the Administrator or a state agency).

This clause is at the heart of three Supreme Court decisions which define the role of common law nuisance in light of federal environmental legislation. Similar provisions appear in other major federal legislation.

D. Judicial Review of Government Decisions

Despite common law and legislatively created causes of action related to the environment, certain legal doctrines can affect the ability of a plaintiff to bring or a defendant to defend an environmental case.

1. Standing

Standing (*locus standi*) is the term for the ability of a party to demonstrate to the court's satisfaction that there is a sufficient connection between it and the harm caused by the action at the heart of the litigation. In other words, not everyone is entitled to bring suit for every wrong. The plaintiff must have a legitimate stake in the outcome. The standing doctrine holds that a plaintiff cannot bring a suit challenging the constitutionality of a law unless he or she can demonstrate that the plaintiff is (or will imminently be) harmed by the law. The party suing must have something to lose. Otherwise, the court will dismiss the case without considering the merits of the claim of unconstitutionality.

The standing requirement emanates from Article III of the U.S. Constitution, which requires that courts hear only cases or controversies. Standing limits the docket to justiciable issues so as to prevent courts from becoming forums for airing generalized grievances. A plaintiff's mere allegation of a sincere interest in an area affected by environmental degradation does not constitute an injury-in-fact.

Whether a plaintiff has standing turns on three different tests: 1) Is there an injury-in-fact, so as to establish a "case or controversy?" 2) Is the claimed injury within the "zone of interests," so that the claimants are within a class that Congress intended to benefit when it passed the underlying law? 3) Should prudential principles be used by the court to deny standing because the judicial remedy would not redress the claimed injury or it is not ripe?

Standing requirements have caused some major environmental organizations to expand their membership and even develop general membership for the first time. In this way, they can be assured of always having an affected member in an area where there is a potential threat to the environment. Some judges and scholars, wanting to expand the ability of courts to protect the environment, have argued that trees should have standing.

2. Reviewability

It seems unusual to most people, but not all issues are decided in a courtroom. Agencies, like the EPA, conduct hearings and render opinions. Sometimes agency decisions can be appealed to a court, but sometimes they are final. It all depends upon the statutory scheme.

In the early days of American environmental law, it was not clear whether environmental laws would be judicially reviewable. Then came thc case of *Calvert Cliff's Coordinating Committee v. Atomic Energy Commission*, (U.S. 1971). It would overstate the case only slightly to say that *Calvert Cliffs* launched environmental law in the United States. The relationship between effective environmental programs and judicial review has been nearly linear.

Today it is well accepted that judicial review applies following administrative determination of environmental issues. There may be a need to first exhaust administrative remedies by taking the controversy to the relevant agency panel, but after that result is in, the issue may be reviewed in court. Prior to *Calvert Cliff's*, however, it was not clear that courts had jurisdiction to review environmental decisions.

The next question, logically, is what level of deference the court should give to the administrative agency. This can vary from statute to statute and even from issue to issue. Typically, courts view administrative agencies as being expert in their field. Thus when the issue is environmental in nature, a court would likely apply a deferential standard of review and be less likely to overturn the EPA. On the other hand, if the issue involves the interpretation of a statute, the court is the expert, and the EPA would not receive much deference.

CHAPTER 3:
AIR POLLUTION

I. THE AIR POLLUTION PROBLEM

Air pollution has been a significant concern since the Industrial Age of the late nineteenth century. American cities especially experienced the negative environmental consequences of the Industrial Revolution. During the twentieth century, the largest U.S. cities grew into giant, heavily populated metropolitan areas and industrial air pollution became a highly visible and ubiquitous problem. Most major industries are sources of air pollution, as well as many other diverse sources such as automobiles, trucks, planes, buses, motorboats, lawnmowers, gas stations, dry cleaners, construction sites, and fireplaces. Air pollution can cause serious property damage, including discoloration and corrosion of buildings, statues, and monuments. Air pollution also can kill trees and crops and destroy urban vegetation. Air pollution reduces visibility in cities and national parks and can even interfere with aviation.

The most serious concerns associated with air pollution, however, are threats to public health. Common airborne pollutants such as ground-level ozone and particulate matter cause respiratory problems, especially for children, the elderly, and people with asthma or heart or respiratory diseases. Air pollution can increase fatality rates from lung diseases such as pneumonia and diphtheria as well as increase nasal, throat, and bronchial illnesses. Some chemical airborne pollutants such as benzene or vinyl chloride are highly toxic and can cause many serious adverse effects, including birth defects, cancer, lung damage, or brain and nerve damage. In cases of severe exposure, breathing airborne toxic pollutants can even cause death.

On October 26, 1948, a large cloud of air pollution formed above the town of Donora, Pennsylvania. Pollutants emitted from the industrial town's factories had become trapped between a layer of warm air residing above a cool air mass. The pollution cloud remained above Donora for four days killing twenty people and numerous animals and causing over half of the town's 12,000 residents to fall ill. Four years later, in 1952, a similar instance of severe air pollution killed over 3,000 people in London, England. This episode became known as London's "Killer Fog." The smog was so dense that guides carrying lanterns were required to walk ahead of buses in order for them to safely operate.

Such extreme incidents generated considerable public attention to the serious health risks posed by air pollution. Governments began to take initial steps to address problems caused by industrial air pollution and urban smog from motor vehicle exhaust. The first state air pollution agency was created in Oregon in 1952. Because of severe smog problems associated with the state's over abundance of automobiles, California followed suit in 1959. The first federal legislation involving air pollution was the Air Pollution Control Act of 1955, which provided funds for federal research in air pollution. The first federal government regulation of air pollution was the Clean Air Act of 1963, which established a federal program within the U.S. Public Health Service and authorized research into techniques for monitoring and controlling air pollution. This was followed by the Air Quality Act of 1967 which expanded federal government activities in the regulation of air pollution.

However, both the 1963 and 1967 Acts put primary responsibility on state governments to adopt and enforce state ambient air quality standards consistent with advisory federal criteria on air quality. These early efforts by the federal government to encourage the states to control air pollution in the United States were seen as a failure. The interstate character of air pollution makes it an extremely difficult problem for state or local jurisdictions to control. Air pollution does not respect municipal, state, or international boundaries. Pollutants can be carried for extremely long distances by wind. Thus an urban area with serious smog problems caused by industrial air emissions and a high density of motor vehicle exhaust can end up causing pollution hundreds of miles away, including in remote areas such as national parks and wilderness areas. Further, by the late 1960s, policy makers came to the realization that any serious effort to control air pollution in the United States would require imposing significant controls on the automotive and oil industries. States were perceived as reluctant to do this given the risks of losing industry jobs and tax revenues to other states with more lenient laws. As public awareness and concern over the serious dangers posed by air pollution increased during the late 1960s, Congress eventually came to the conclusion that comprehensive federal control was needed to combat these problems.

In 1970, therefore, Congress passed the Clean Air Act of 1970, which represented a dramatic change in the federal government's role in addressing the problem of air pollution. The 1970 Act authorized the development of comprehensive federal and state regulations to limit emissions of air pollutants from both stationary (industrial) sources and mobile sources (primarily motor vehicles). That same year, Congress created the Environmental Protection Agency (EPA) and gave it the primary role in carrying out the responsibilities of the new Clean Air Act. Among other things, the 1970 Act authorized the EPA to establish National Ambient Air Quality Standards (NAAQS) to protect public health and welfare and to regulate emissions of hazardous air pollutants. Major amendments were added to the Clean Air Act by Congress in 1977 and then again in 1990. These amendments substantially increased the responsibility and authority of the federal government to implement and enforce regulations reducing air pollutant emissions.

II. THE CLEAN AIR ACT

A. National Ambient Air Quality Standards for "Criteria" Pollutants

The basic objective of the Clean Air Act is relatively simple. The EPA is to determine national ambient air quality standards for the most common air pollutants. The standards set by the EPA seek to determine an allowable level of outdoor, or ambient, concentrations of these air pollutants sufficient to protect human health and the environment. Once the EPA has established standards, then the Clean Air Act requires the states to decide how to specifically control local pollution sources so as to meet that standard. Although the basic idea is simple, the process of establishing standards and deciding how to implement them at the local level is extremely difficult and often controversial.

The Clean Air Act requires the EPA to issue "air quality criteria," based on the "latest scientific knowledge" for air pollutants that "cause or contribute to pollution which may reasonably be anticipated to endanger public health or welfare." The Act further requires the EPA to create and achieve NAAQS in every state in order to address the public health and welfare risks posed by each such "criteria" air pollutant. Thus far, the EPA has identified and issued NAAQS for the following six "criteria" air pollutants:

- *Particulate matter*—solids or liquids in various sizes, including the very fine dust, soot, smoke, and droplets formed from chemical reactions produced by burning fuels such as coal, wood, or oil;
- *Sulfur oxides*—corrosive, poisonous gases produced when fuel (such as coal or oil) containing sulfur is burned (principally by utility power plants, industrial boilers, and residential heating);

• *Nitrogen oxides*—produced by the burning of fuel at very high temperatures which oxidizes nitrogen in the air (principally by vehicles and combustion plants);

• *Carbon monoxide*—a colorless, odorless, poisonous gas produced by the incomplete burning of carbon in fossil fuel combustion processes, such as the internal combustion engines that drive cars and trucks or utility and other industrial boilers;

• *Ground-Level Ozone*—the primary ingredient of smog formed when nitrogen oxides and volatile organic compounds (VOCs—released by vehicles burning gasoline, petroleum refineries, chemical manufacturing plants, and other industrial facilities) chemically react in the atmosphere during periods of intense sunlight; and

• *Lead*—a heavy metal that can be released directly into the air as suspended particles through the burning of leaded gasoline or by industrial sources such as lead smelters, waste incinerators, utilities, or manufacturing processes.

NAAQS are divided into "primary" and "secondary" standards. "Primary" standards are based upon the protection of people and public health. The Act requires primary standards to be based on ambient air quality criteria that, "allowing an adequate margin of safety, are requisite to protect the public health." "Secondary" standards are intended to protect public welfare, such as environmental and property damage (such as prevention of damage to crops or trees or deterioration of buildings or infrastructure). The air quality criteria used by the EPA are supposed to reflect "the latest scientific knowledge" useful in identifying the effects on public health and welfare to be expected from the presence of the criteria air pollutant in question in the ambient air.

As discussed previously, the Clean Air Act imposes responsibility on the states to determine precisely how to achieve the NAAQS for each criteria pollutant within their borders. Each state is required to prepare and to periodically update a State Implementation Plan (SIP) adequate to assure that each air quality control region within the state comes into compliance (attainment) with the NAAQS by a specified date. A SIP is a collection of the regulations, programs, and policies that the state will utilize to determine how to control the numerous existing sources of a criteria pollutant in the state in order to meet the NAAQS for that pollutant. The states are required to involve the public and industries through hearings and opportunities to comment on the development of each SIP. If a state fails to prepare a SIP, or if the SIP prepared by the state is deemed inadequate, the EPA is required to prepare a

Federal Implementation Plan (FIP) for that state that ensures the NAAQS will be met.

The EPA designates any part of the country that does not meet the NAAQS for a criteria pollutant as a "nonattainment" area for that specific pollutant. As of August 2008, approximately 132 million Americans lived in counties that exceeded the NAAQS for ground-level ozone. At that same time, approximately 88 million Americans lived in counties that exceeded the NAAQS for particulate matter pollution. Designation as a nonattainment area requires creation of a SIP imposing strict limitations on the construction of new or modified sources (such as new manufacturing plants or factories or installation of new equipment at existing businesses) of that criteria pollutant. The SIP must also incorporate strict pollution controls intended to move the region toward compliance, which might include such requirements as a ban on some sources of the criteria pollutant, vehicle inspection and maintenance programs, use of high occupancy vehicle (HOV) lanes, or reformulated fuels for vehicles. New stationary (industrial) sources of the criteria pollutant moving into the area will be required to meet the toughest emissions standards possible, known as the Lowest Achievable Emission Rate (LAER). Existing stationary pollution sources may be required to retrofit their technology to comply with higher emissions standards known as Reasonably Achievable Control Technology (RACT).

The EPA classifies geographic areas with air quality that is cleaner than the NAAQS for a specific criteria pollutant as an "attainment" area. Attainment areas are subject to "prevention of significant deterioration" (PSD) programs to maintain the air quality in that area. PSD programs require major new stationary pollution sources moving into the area to utilize emissions standards known as Best Available Control Technology (BACT). Such new sources also must demonstrate that the added pollution they will bring will not cause the area to exceed the NAAQS for the criteria pollutant in question. Air quality control regions can be, and frequently are, in nonattainment for one of the criteria pollutants but not for others.

B. Toxic Air Pollutants

The 1990 amendments to the Clean Air Act established a separate control system for hazardous or toxic air pollutants, the exposure to which is considered to pose a particularly severe danger to public health. Toxic air pollutants are known to cause or are suspected of causing cancer, birth defects, reproduction problems, and other serious illnesses. As the notorious mid-twentieth century incidents in Donora and London aptly demonstrate, severe levels of exposure to some toxic air pollutants are known to cause death. Similarly, the more recent 1984 tragedy in Bhopal, India, in which an accidental release of methyl isocynate from a Union Carbide chemical plant killed over 3,000 persons and severely injured scores of thousands of others, highlights the extremely serious risks posed by toxic air pollutants. Thus because the risks of exposure to these pollutants are significantly higher, the Clean Air Act takes a much different approach to their regulation than for "criteria" pollutants.

The Clean Air Act contains an initial list of 189 toxic air pollutants to be regulated by the EPA. The Act requires the EPA to identify categories of industrial sources for these listed pollutants. For these industrial categories, the EPA must establish either technology-based standards and controls or performance-based standards for reducing toxic emissions from "major" and some smaller (known as "area") industrial sources of these pollutants. The technology-based standards are required to achieve the maximum degree of reduction in emissions by use of the "Maximum Achievable Control Technology" (MACT). In many cases, the EPA does not impose a specific control technology for an industrial category, but instead sets a performance level based on technology or best practices already in use by low emitting sources in that industry. If a technology-based control standard is utilized, an individual company is required to install the specific pollution control equipment or devices selected by that standard. If, on the other hand, a performance-based standard is employed, an individual company is free to decide for itself how it will reduce its toxic air emissions so long as it meets the level of emissions allowed by the regulation.

Toxic air pollutants come from many sources, including factory smokestack emissions, motor vehicle exhaust, refineries, gas stations, incinerators, paper mills, dry cleaners, and printing shops. The EPA has established technology-based or performance-based toxic emissions standards for many of these industrial categories and has also issued regulations relating to development of cleaner-burning fuels and more efficient engines in an effort to reduce releases of toxic air pollutants from motor vehicle exhaust.

C. Mobile Sources of Air Pollutants

Motor vehicles currently contribute over 75% of nationwide carbon monoxide emissions, and approximately half of nationwide smog-forming nitrogen oxide and volatile organic compounds (VOC) emissions and toxic air pollutant emissions. To address these emissions, the Clean Air Act authorizes the EPA to regulate both the content of fuels burned by cars, trucks, and buses and the emissions standards for new vehicles. Thus the EPA has utilized its Clean Air Act authority to issues rules requiring the elimination of lead from gasoline, to require certain metropolitan areas with the worst ground-level ozone pollution to use reformulated gasoline that reduces emissions of toxic air pollutants and pollutants that contribute to smog, to reduce the sulfur content of gasoline, and to encourage the development and sale of alternative fuels other than gasoline and diesel (such as biodiesel, ethanol, natural gas, and electricity). The EPA has also issued rules to require passenger vehicles, including SUVs, minivans, vans, and pickup trucks, and diesel trucks and buses to meet higher tailpipe emissions standards, and to require reduced emissions by "non-road" equipment such as locomotives and marine vessels, recreational vehicles, and lawn and garden equipment.

D. Reducing Acid Rain

When certain types of air pollutants mix with moisture in the air, acid precipitation is formed such as acid rain, acid snow, or acid fog or mist. Dry forms of acidic pollution in the air can cause the formation of acid gas and acid dust. When acid precipitation or dry acid gases or particles fall to earth, the result can be environmental damage to property, trees, and vegetation, human health problems, and harm to animals or aquatic life. Sulfur dioxide and nitrogen oxides are the principal air pollutants that cause acid precipitation or acid gases or dusts. Over two-thirds of sulfur dioxide emissions are caused by power plants burning coal or heavy oil. The vast majority of nitrogen oxide emissions are from power plants, cars, buses, trucks, and other forms of transportation, or industrial and commercial boilers.

Some of the largest contributors to the acid rain problem were utility companies responding to the air pollution control requirements of the Clean Air Act of 1970. Because of the stricter control of local air pollution brought about by the new law, during the 1970s many electric utility companies built tall smokestacks that could project pollution plumes high enough in the upper atmosphere to carry the pollution hundreds, even thousands, of miles away. This avoided the regulatory effects of the 1970 Act at a local level, but caused serious acid rain problems in the eastern United States and in parts of Canada. More than 175 smokestacks higher than 500 feet were constructed following the enactment of the 1970 Act. This practice was outlawed in the 1977 amendments to the Clean Air Act. In the 1990 amendments, Congress created a nationwide program to directly reduce the sulfur dioxide and nitrogen oxides emissions that had created an interstate and international acid rain problem.

The 1990 amendments to the Clean Air Act created a market-based cap and trade approach to achieve these emissions reductions. The first step in the acid rain program was a permanent cap on emissions by electric power plants nationwide. Within 10 years, sulfur dioxide emissions from electric power plants were required to be reduced by 10 million tons per year from 1980 levels. Emissions of nitrogen oxides had to be reduced by approximately 2 million tons per year from 1980 levels. The second step in the acid rain program was implemented in two phases. The first phase began in 1995 and applied only to the 110 highest emitting power plants in twenty-one Midwest, Appalachian, and Northeastern states. The second phase went into effect in 2000 and applied to all large coal-burning power plants in the nation as well as some smaller plants. The government allocated pollution allowances to these sources based on their past emissions and fuel consumption. Each allowance was worth one ton of emissions released from the plant's smokestack. Plants are only permitted to release emissions equal to the amount of allowances issued to them. If a plant has a need to release more emissions than it has allowances for, it must either trade allowances by buying them from another power plant that has them to sell or it must use technology or other methods to control its emissions.

The Clean Air Act imposes substantial monetary penalties on plants that emit more pollutants than are covered by their allowances. The acid rain program requires power plants to install monitoring systems to track the amount of sulfur dioxide and nitrogen oxides emissions they are is releasing and to report such information to the EPA four times per year. The Clean Air Act's acid rain program is considered successful thus far. As of 2005, emissions covered by the program had been reduced 41% below 1980 levels.

E. Other Interstate and International Air Pollution Problems

States attempting to address non-compliance with NAAQS for criteria pollutants within their borders may sometimes be unable to do so because of pollution blowing in from other areas. As discussed earlier, air pollutants emitted at the local level can be transported by the wind and weather hundreds or thousands of miles and contribute to pollution in downwind states. Thus the Clean Air Act has numerous provisions designed to combat emissions from one state that contribute to public health and welfare problems in downwind states. Each state's SIP is required to contain provisions to prevent sources of criteria pollutant emissions within its borders from contributing significantly to air pollution problems in downwind states that are failing to meet NAAQS. If a state has not addressed this issue in its SIP, the EPA can require it to do so. If the problem remains unaddressed, the EPA can create a FIP to address the problem. Downwind states also have the right under the Clean Air Act to petition the EPA to set emissions limits for specific sources of pollution in upwind states that are significantly contributing to air quality problems in the downwind state.

The Clean Air Act also authorizes the creation of interstate commissions to develop regional strategies for dealing with significant interstate air pollution problems. A well known example is the Ozone Transport Commission, a group of east coast states from Maine to Virginia and the District of Columbia that work together to form a regional strategy to reduce ground-level ozone. Similar regional commissions have been formed to reduce pollutants that create air pollution that causes reduced visibility in national parks and wilderness areas, such as the Grand Canyon, Yosemite, and the Great Smoky Mountains National Park.

F. Stratospheric Ozone Layer Protection

In the stratosphere (upper atmosphere), ozone occurs naturally and creates a protective layer shielding the earth from a portion of the sun's ultraviolet (UV) radiation. Too much UV radiation has the potential to cause skin cancer and eye damage (such as cataracts) and can also damage crops and other vegetation. The stratospheric ozone layer, therefore, protects human health and the environment by filtering out these harmful UV sun rays. This form of beneficial ozone should be distinguished from ground-level ozone, a pollutant that causes serious health and environmental problems and, as discussed earlier, is one of the "criteria" pollutants regulated under the Clean Air Act.

In the 1970s, scientists became concerned that certain types of widely used chemicals were capable of destroying the beneficial stratospheric ozone layer. The ozone-destroying chemicals of largest concern were chlorofluorocarbons (CFCs), commonly used as aerosol propellants in consumer products such as hairsprays and deodorants and as coolants in refrigerators and air conditioners. In 1978, Congress banned CFCs as propellants in most aerosol uses. In the 1980s, however, scientists monitoring the stratospheric ozone layer began to observe evidence of the layer's depletion. Studies have shown that a five-percent loss of stratospheric ozone has occurred between 1978 and 1997. An ozone "hole" in the South Pole region appears each Antarctic winter (summer in the United States) and is often larger in size than the continental United States. In 1987, the United States joined over 190 countries in signing the Montreal Protocol, an international agreement aimed at limiting the production and use of chemicals that destroy stratospheric ozone.

The 1990 amendments to the Clean Air Act required the EPA to establish a program to phase out production and use of ozone-destroying chemicals. By 1996, production of many such chemicals had ceased in the United States, including CFCs, halons, and methyl chloroform. The EPA has established rules regarding the use of these chemicals, such as the requirement that special equipment be used to prevent release of refrigerant chemicals into the air when air conditioning systems are recharged. The Clean Air Act also encourages the development of substitutes for ozone-destroying chemicals and the reformulation of products and processes to avoid their use. Despite these steps, stratospheric ozone layer destruction will continue for many years because of the level of chemicals already in the stratosphere and because additional chemicals will continue to arrive over the next few years. Estimates are that it will be about 60 years before the damage to the stratospheric ozone layer is fully repaired.

G. Permits and Enforcement

Another major change to the Clean Air Act accomplished by the 1990 amendments was creation of an operating permit program for larger stationary (industrial and commercial) sources of air pollutant emissions. Operating permits are legally enforceable documents that permitting authorities issue to air pollution sources after the source has begun to operate. The operating permit program streamlines the way federal, state, and local authorities regulate air pollution by consolidating all air pollution control requirements into a single, comprehensive "operating permit" that covers all aspects of a source's year-to-year air pollution activities. The permit clarifies what a polluting facility (source) must do to control air pollution, including how much of a particular pollutant the facility is allowed to release and what steps the operator is required to take to reduce the pollution.

The EPA authorizes states to issue operating permits. However, the EPA can take over the issuance of permits in a particular state if it is determined the state is not performing its job of carrying out the Clean Air Act requirements in a satisfactory manner.

The 1990 amendments to the Clean Air Act also substantially increased the EPA's authority to enforce violations of the Act. The Act significantly increased the range of civil and criminal sanctions available to the EPA to penalize companies that do not comply with their obligations. If the EPA determines a violation has occurred, the agency can issue an order requiring the violator to comply, issue an administrative penalty order (use EPA administrative authority to force payment of a penalty), or bring a civil judicial action (sue the violator in court).

H. Greenhouse Gas Emissions

A decade into the 21st century, countries around the world are considering how to best approach the problems of climate change associated with the emissions of greenhouse gases (GHGs), such as carbon dioxide and methane. (These issues are discussed further in Chapter 10, "The Greenhouse Effect and Climate Change," of this Almanac.) Although the Clean Air Act was not designed to address the problems of GHGs, there is a strong possibility that the Act may be utilized in the future for the purpose of reducing such emissions. In the 2007 case of *Massachusetts v. EPA*, the U.S. Supreme Court held that the Clean Air Act's sweeping definition of "air pollutant" includes any physical or chemical substance which can be emitted into the ambient air. Thus GHGs qualify as "air pollutants" under this definition. The Court further held that the EPA was required by the Act to determine whether or not emissions of GHGs cause or contribute to air pollution which may reasonably be anticipated to endanger public health or welfare, or whether the science is too uncertain to make a reasoned decision.

In response to the Court's ruling, in April 2009, the EPA issued a proposed finding that six GHGs—carbon dioxide, methane, nitrous oxide, hydrofluorocarbons, perfluorocarbons and sulfur hexafluoride—contribute to air pollution that may endanger public health or welfare through the threat of climate change. This is known as an "endangerment finding" under the Clean Air Act. Following issuance of the proposed finding, the EPA initiated a 60-day public comment period and eventually received and considered more than 380,000 comments on the issue. On December 7, 2009, the EPA announced its final "endangerment finding" that GHGs threaten the public health and welfare of the American people. This finding does not, however, impose any requirements or obligations on industry or other entities under the CAA to reduce GHGs. Instead, this final endangerment finding creates the authority under the CAA for the EPA to move forward with creating regulations designed to reduce emissions of GHGs. This regulatory process will take anywhere from a few to several years before regulation of GHGs under the Act can begin.

Further, Congress may eventually decide to pre-empt any coverage by the CAA to GHGs in favor of comprehensive legislation directly addressing issues relating to climate change. Indeed, both President Obama and EPA Administrator Lisa Jackson emphasized their preference for comprehensive legislation to address this issue at the time both the proposed and final endangerment findings were issued by the EPA. Thus it will be some time before it is known whether the CAA will be actually utilized to address emissions of GHGs.

III. INDOOR AIR POLLUTION

The health effects of smoking had long been a concern, but the evidence of a link between smoking and health problems were inconclusive. By the late 1940s, however, evidence began to emerge showing the association between cigarette smoking and shorter life expectancy.

In 1964, the Surgeon General officially announced the health related dangers posed by smoking. This spurred more press on the subject, and eventually all cigarette packages had to carry a warning about the adverse health effects of smoking.

The tobacco industry had faced its first lawsuit alleging negligence and breach of warranty in 1954. Between 1954 and 1994, private citizens filed at least 813 unsuccessful tort actions against tobacco companies. These suits proved unsuccessful because there had not yet been a scientifically reliable causal connection associating cigarette smoking with cancer. Without this link, plaintiffs could not show that their health-related damages were foreseeable to the defendants.

In addition to causation problems, the contributory negligence of plaintiffs (by continuing to smoke despite knowing the risks) left courts unwilling to hold the tobacco companies liable. By the mid-1990s, however, the landscape was changing. In *Cipollone v. Liggett Group, Inc.*, (3d Cir. 1990), the plaintiff claimed, and the court agreed, that nicotine addiction can supply the causation element necessary for a tort cause of action. During the trial, plaintiff Cipollone revealed a confidential study prepared by the Phillip Morris Research Center called "Motives and Incentives of Cigarette Smoking." The study contained a statement telling the company to "think of the cigarette as a dispenser for a dose of nicotine." As a result of this and other industry wrongdoing, the trial judge found evidence of a conspiracy between the three major tobacco companies that was "vast in its scope, devious in its purpose, and devastating in its results."

A. Second Hand Smoke

The smoke that comes off the end of a burning cigarette, cigar, or pipe along with the smoke that is exhaled by the smoker make up what most individuals refer to as secondhand smoke, or "environmental tobacco smoke" (ETS). A 1972 U.S. Surgeon General's report first noted the possible threat to non-smokers from ETS. The issue was addressed again in Surgeon Generals' reports in 1979, 1982, and 1984. The 1986 Surgeon General's report resulted in three important conclusions concerning ETS.

First, involuntary smoking is a cause of lung cancer and other diseases in healthy nonsmokers; second, the children of parents who smoke compared with children of nonsmoking parents have an increased frequency of respiratory infections, an increase in respiratory symptoms, and slightly smaller rates of increase in lung function as the lungs mature; third, the separation of smokers and nonsmokers within the same airspace may reduce, but does not eliminate, the exposure of nonsmokers to passive smoke.

The EPA has since labeled secondhand smoke as a Class A carcinogen and has reported that secondhand smoke "is a human lung carcinogen, responsible for approximately 3,000 lung cancer deaths annually in U.S. non-smokers."

In 2004, the Centers for Disease Control ("CDC") released a study indicating that minimal exposure to smoke can increase the risk of heart attacks, even for non-smokers. In 2006, the U.S. Surgeon General's office released a new report on ETS: *The Health Consequences of Involuntary Exposure to Tobacco Smoke*. That report concluded that there was no risk-free level of ETS exposure. This report provided a comprehensive review of studies examining the effectiveness of separate smoking sections and ventilation systems and concludeed that "[t]hese studies clearly demonstrate that secondhand smoke exposure can be eliminated with a smoking ban... However, the findings also indicate the need for full compliance with such bans because incomplete compliance will lead to continued exposure."

Many other studies have failed to find a link between ETS and health problems, but many studies do show adverse health impacts from ETS exposure. Perhaps most importantly, more than 80% of Americans now believe secondhand smoke is harmful to non-smokers.

B. The Tobacco Settlement

As its defenses began to weaken (because non-smokers were not usually limited by contributory negligence), the tobacco industry became an even bigger target for tort claims. With scientific evidence of causation, a group of trial attorneys developed a theory to permit state governments, as opposed to individual smokers, to file suit. The idea was that the tobacco companies should reimburse the states for Medicaid expenditures on behalf of smokers who developed cancer or other health problems. Working with state attorney generals, and perhaps with the threat that criminal charges might be pressed against them, this group convinced the tobacco companies to sign the "Master Settlement Agreement."

This agreement required the industry to pay $243 billion over 25 years, and then approximately $18 billion per year in perpetuity which is supposed to fund a charitable foundation that will support the study of programs to reduce teen smoking and substance abuse and the prevention of diseases associated with tobacco use. (According to some, the money actually "goes directly into state government coffers and is spent largely for the benefit of non-smokers.") Despite the enormous monetary award granted to the states, the settlement did not preclude or limit future lawsuits brought by individual smokers. Perhaps even more importantly, by agreeing to it, the tobacco companies gave governmental agencies all the evidence they needed to put even greater restrictions in place.

C. Smoking Bans

Long before cities and towns began enacting smoking bans, many private businesses voluntarily designated smoke-free areas. By 1991, more than 85% of private businesses had some type of smoking policy. The Surgeon General's 2006 report, *The Health Consequences of Involuntary Exposure to Tobacco Smoke*, prompted additional employers and businesses, including major hotel chains, to adopt voluntary smoke-free policies.

While voluntary smoking policies remain common, mandatory smoke-free policies are becoming the norm. Because secondhand smoke is viewed as a danger to public health, states and municipalities can regulate smoking under their police power, which allows them to "make laws protecting the public health." As of July 2008, 748 municipalities in the United States had 100% smoke-free bans. Twenty-one states and the District of Columbia banned smoking in stand-alone bars. In many states, however, casino gaming floors are exempted from the smoking regulations.

1. Economic Impacts

Many bar and restaurant owners argue that smoking bans lead to an approximate 30% or greater decline in sales. Such a reduction in demand not only affects the business entities, it also impacts employment and state revenue. On the other hand, many studies suggest that smoking bans do not have serious adverse economic impacts on business.

Banning smoking may significantly increase the number of non-smokers who visit a business, which could result in an overall gain of patrons.

In New York City, according to the city's Department of Finance, restaurant sales tax receipts increased during the year following the implementation of a city-wide smoking ban. The concentration of various ETS pollutants in an indoor space also varies greatly, depending on the number of smokers, their pattern of smoking, the volume of the space, the ventilation in the room, the effectiveness of the air distribution, the rate of removal of ETS from the indoor air by air cleaners, deposition of particles onto surfaces, and surface adsorption and re-emission of gaseous components. Thus science that indicates a problem in one area might not be a problem in a different area.

Anti-smoking advocates have strongly opposed the "separate and ventilate" approach. They argue that there is no "risk-free level of exposure to secondhand smoke" and that current air cleaning technologies cannot eliminate all of the chemicals released in ETS. Even if current technology cannot remove all ETS from the air, this approach does show good faith on the part of the business, and it may persuade lawmakers not to risk the economic consequences of a full smoking ban in businesses. It may also prompt further technology that works better than today's ventilation systems.

2. Litigation

Non-smokers have increasingly used the courts in an attempt to force businesses to restrict smoking as well as to receive compensation for complications caused by ETS exposure at work. So far, the courts have generally left the issue of smoking in the workplace in the hands of employers, subject to applicable statutory requirements. Courts have, however, upheld claims made under the common law duty to provide a safe workplace and, even more recently, workers' compensation statutes. The successful claims usually have had a combination of two elements. First, the non-smoking employee was hypersensitive to ETS or suffered from a pre-existing medical condition that was worsened by ETS in the workplace. Second, the employer refused to take any action to help accommodate the hypersensitive employee.

a. The Americans with Disabilities Act

The Americans with Disabilities Act (ADA) requires businesses to make reasonable accommodations for people suffering from disabilities. Not long after the ADA's adoption, commentators and scholars began to examine whether the ADA could be used to protect smoke-sensitive individuals.

In light of the ever-expanding understanding of the public health benefits of smoking bans, some commentators now argue that the ADA "can and should be used to ban smoking in most indoor public places in the United States."

The ADA defines a disability as "a physical or mental impairment that substantially limits one or more of the major life activities." Since breathing is a major life activity, an individual with a breathing problem like asthma would likely be covered by the act. Not everyone with an upper respiratory problem would however be covered. The disability must substantially limit the major life activity of the individual in order to be protected by the ADA. Courts have repeatedly held that such limitations cannot be merely potential or hypothetical, but must be actual and imminent. Accordingly, only those disabled non-smokers who are substantially, actually, and imminently affected by ETS would be covered under the ADA.

Plaintiffs have argued that the reasonable accommodation standard of the ADA requires places of public accommodations to ban smoking completely because of the threat to their health presented by ETS exposure. While it seems that businesses might have to accommodate a non-smoking individual covered under the ADA, a complete ban on smoking would not necessarily be required.

The ADA provides an exception if the modification imposes an undue burden on the business. The undue burden analysis weighs several different factors including the financial or administrative impact of the accommodation. A complete smoking ban in a business could have a potentially severe financial impact on the business, and the administrative costs of enforcing the complete ban might make it unreasonable. However, as bans become more and more common, such arguments are likely to carry less weight.

b. Occupational Safety

Although 70% of all workers are covered by some smoke-free policy, food and beverage service employees are the least protected workers. In fact, bar and tavern workers are typically exposed to levels of ETS four to six times higher than other workplaces. Most states have occupational health statutes that protect workers' rights to a safe and non-hazardous work environment. These statutes naturally lend themselves to litigation involving ETS exposure.

For example, in *Palmer v. Del Webb's High Sierra* (1992), the Nevada Supreme Court was forced to decide whether a casino worker claiming to suffer from a disease caused by ETS was entitled to compensation under the Nevada Occupational Disease Act (NODA). For twenty years, the plaintiff was employed at the defendant's casino as a pit boss. The pit areas he managed had noticeably high levels of ETS and the casino encouraged smoking by providing free cigarettes and numerous ashtrays. Palmer claimed that the casino's smoking policies violated state law and his "disease caused by inhaling tobacco smoke exhaled by others in the work place" was compensable under NODA.

In reading the occupational disease statute, the court reasoned that the legislature intended for there to be a connection between the kind of job and the kind of disease. It concluded that the occupational disease must arise out of the employment and be related to the nature of the employment at hand. The court refused to recognize tobacco smoke as being related to the nature of the employment, stating: "It is apparent to us that despite its common place in bars and casinos, environmental tobacco smoke is not incidental to the character of these businesses, and is not a natural incident of these businesses." The court used the illustration of coal mining and black lung disease, stating that coal dust, the cause of black lung disease, is incidental to the character of coal mining because mining coal necessarily creates coal dust. Tobacco smoke, on the other hand, "is not part of the nature or character of a bar or casino business." The court further noted that while tobacco smoke may be more heavily associated with casinos and bars than with other businesses, the levels of ETS vary greatly and depend on numerous factors that are specific to individual businesses.

The *Palmer* court was also concerned that ETS exposure can occur in numerous places outside the workplace. The court said: "secondary smoke is a hazard to which workers, as a class, may be equally exposed outside of the employment." The court went on to say that although the Nevada legislature had not done so, it was "free to declare that any person who contracts some secondary smoke related disease at work is eligible for occupational disease compensation." Thus the state legislature could easily provide avenues of relief for employees affected by ETS in the workplace if it so chose.

Of course, *Palmer* may reflect the thinking of an earlier era. In *Mullen v. Treasure Chest Casino, LLC* (5th Cir. 1999), the plaintiff/employees sued a casino citing defective and improperly maintained air-conditioning and ventilation systems. Over three hundred workers were stricken with occupational respiratory illnesses, and they sought certification to bring a class action suit. The court ruled that the elements of numerosity, commonality, typicality, and adequacy of representation were all satisfied to allow for a class to be certified. By allowing the casino workers complaining of an occupational disease like this to form a class action lawsuit, the court appears to have accepted the premise underling the ETS suit filed by casino employees.

The bottom line seems to be that businesses must be aware of applicable occupational safety statutes and undertake efforts to protect workers and customers. These efforts should include proper ventilation, smoke-free areas, and accommodations on a case-by-case basis for extra-sensitive customers and employees.

CHAPTER 4:
WATER QUALITY

I. THE CLEAN WATER ACT

From the nation's hundreds of rivers, lakes, and wetlands to its thousands of miles of coastal shoreline, Americans are fortunate to enjoy an abundance of water resources. As a nation, Americans value these resources for their natural beauty; for the many ways they help meet human needs; and for the fact that they provide habitat for thousands of species of plants, fish and wildlife.

Prior to 1972, America's water resources were rapidly declining. Many of the nation's waterways were unsafe for recreational activities, such as fishing and swimming. Soil was eroding due to agricultural runoff, resulting in a large quantity of phosphorus and nitrogen being deposited into the water. People were concerned about the safety of their seafood and their drinking water.

In response to public concern, Congress passed the 1972 amendments to the Federal Water Pollution Control Act (known as the Clean Water Act or CWA). Today, the CWA is the cornerstone of water quality protection in the United States. It uses a variety of regulatory and nonregulatory tools to reduce pollutant discharges into surface water, to finance municipal wastewater treatment facilities, and to manage polluted runoff. These tools are used to achieve the broad goal of restoring and maintaining the chemical, physical, and biological integrity of the nation's waters so that they can support "the protection and propagation of fish, shellfish, and wildlife and recreation in and on the water."

The CWA established the goals of eliminating releases into water of high amounts of toxic substances, eliminating additional water pollution by 1985 and ensuring that surface waters would be safe for human sports and recreation by 1983. The CWA was designed to accomplish its objectives by: maintaining strict standards on water quality; offering financial aid to state and local governments; and protecting wetlands and other aquatic habitats through its permit process. The result has been a dramatic improvement in the quality of America's water.

The CWA gives the EPA authority to set effluent limits on an industry-wide (technology-based) basis and on a water-quality basis that ensures protection of the receiving water. The CWA requires anyone who wants to discharge pollutants to first obtain a National Pollutant Discharge Elimination System (NPDES) permit. Otherwise, any discharge will be considered illegal. The NPDES Permit Program is carried out through the cooperative efforts of federal, state, local, and tribal governments. The EPA is empowered to let state governments perform many of the permitting, administrative, and enforcement duties. In states that have been authorized to implement CWA programs, the EPA retains oversight responsibilities. In addition, the EPA has established partnerships with other federal agencies, drinking water utilities, and non-profit organizations to assist in the implementation of EPA standards.

The EPA's Office of Water Management has developed a NPDES Watershed Strategy under which six areas must be addressed to improve water quality: 1) coordination with state water protection programs; 2) streamlining the NPDES permit process; 3) developing state-wide monitoring strategy and requirements; 4) revising and updating national accountability measures; 5) encouraging public participation in developing watershed protection plans and identifying local environmental goals; and 6) bringing enforcement actions against violators.

A. The National Pollutant Discharge Elimination System

The CWA permit system controls direct discharges into navigable waters. The term "navigable waters" has been defined broadly as "the waters of the United States." This includes nameless creeks and wetlands even if they are not connected to any river or lake. Groundwater, such as that found in underground aquifers, is not directly covered by the CWA.

Direct discharges or "point source" discharges are from sources such as pipes and sewers. The CWA defines a "point source" to mean:

> any discernible confined and discrete conveyance, including but not limited to any pipe, ditch, channel, conduit, well, discrete fissure, container, rolling stock, concentrated animal feeding operation, or vessel or other floating craft, from which pollutants are or may be discharged.

Point sources include industrial facilities, such as manufacturing, mining, oil and gas extraction, and certain service industries. A failed septic tank for a neighborhood can be a point source. Bulldozers and dump trucks engaged in filling wetlands can also be point sources. Even military airplanes dropping bombs into the ocean have been held to be point sources.

Nonpoint source (NPS) pollution, unlike pollution from industrial and sewage treatment plants, comes from many diffuse sources. NPS pollution is caused by rainfall or snowmelt moving over and through the ground. As the runoff moves, it picks up and carries away natural and man-made pollutants, finally depositing them into lakes, rivers, wetlands, coastal waters, and even underground sources of drinking water. NPS pollution is not regulated by the same permit system that controls point source pollution.

1. The Permit Program

The NPDES Permit Program is the mechanism by which the CWA ensures that there are no unauthorized discharges of pollutants into the nation's waters. The CWA requires wastewater dischargers to obtain a permit before any discharge. NPDES permits contain industry-specific, technology-based and/or water-quality-based limits, and establish pollutant monitoring and reporting requirements. The permit establishes pollution limits and specifies monitoring and reporting requirements.

NPDES permits regulate household and industrial wastes that are collected in sewers and treated at municipal wastewater treatment plants. They also regulate industrial sources and concentrated animal feeding operations that discharge into other wastewater collection systems, or that discharge directly into receiving waters.

A facility that intends to discharge into the nation's waters normally must obtain a permit before initiating a discharge. A permit applicant must provide quantitative analytical data identifying the types of pollutants present in the facility's effluent. The permit then sets forth the conditions and effluent limitations under which a facility may make a discharge. If a regulated facility fails to comply with the provisions of its permit, it may be subject to enforcement actions.

Effluent limitations in permits are usually expressed numerically. Permits may also contain compliance schedules and other stipulations relating to enforcement. NPDES permits are transferable to a new owner. The EPA and the state, however, can revoke any permit or reissue it with modifications if there is an alteration in the permitted activity and for various other reasons.

An NPDES permit may also include discharge limits based on federal, state, or tribal water quality criteria or standards that are designed to protect designated uses of surface waters, such as supporting aquatic life or recreation. These standards, unlike the technological standards, generally do not take into account technological feasibility or costs. Water quality criteria and standards vary from location to location, depending on the classification of the receiving body of water. Most states follow EPA guidelines that propose aquatic life and human health criteria for many of the priority pollutants.

Under the CWA, the term of a permit may not exceed five years. Early on, the EPA suffered a backlog of permit renewal applications, resulting in permits not being issued and every discharge therefore constituting a violation. To avoid this problem, the Administrative Procedure Act (APA) provides that upon application, the old permit will not expire until the agency has made a final determination. Therefore the permits which might have expired do not expire as long as a renewal application has been filed.

2. Permit Standards

The CWA governs discharges to "navigable waters" with the NPDES permit program, which sets permissible levels of pollution discharge based upon available technology (as opposed to the Clean Air Act, which—at least in theory—is "technology forcing"). Depending upon the type of discharge, a certain level of technology must be applied.

Pollutants regulated under the CWA include "priority" pollutants, consisting primarily of various toxic pollutants; "conventional" pollutants, which include things like total suspended solids (TSS), fecal coliform, oil and grease, and pH; and "non-conventional" pollutants, which would be any pollutant not identified as either conventional or priority. The CWA regulates both direct and indirect discharges.

Permits will not be issued unless four conditions are met: 1) there is no practical alternative that will have a less adverse impact, 2) no violation of any applicable federal, state, or local law will take place, 3) there will be no significant adverse impacts, and 4) all reasonable mitigation measures will be employed. In issuing a permit, the EPA's primary objective is to avoid potential impacts to the extent practicable. Compensation for restoration of resources (such as buying credits in a wetland bank) is a last resort. Finally, both EPA and the Corps require *cumulative* impacts in a particular area to be considered.

Although individual permits considered alone may not have an adverse impact, the combination of all the permits may have a cumulative impact on the wetland that is not acceptable.

EPA guidelines for permit issuance focus on two major criteria: the "practical alternatives" test and the "water dependency" test. Under the "practical alternatives" test, a permit should not be issued if a practical alternative to the proposed activity exists that would have a less adverse effect on the aquatic environment. The "water dependency" criterion asks whether water use is a critical component of the activity. When an activity is considered non-water-dependent, practical alternatives are assumed to be available unless specifically shown to be otherwise. The applicant bears the burden of demonstrating that no such alternative location is available. ("Available" means that another location to serve the same basic purpose reasonably could be obtained.)

The Clean Water Act is primarily concerned with technology-based standards. These standards rely on the ability of technology to reduce the amount of pollutants in industrial effluent. They are based on engineering criteria. When it comes to required treatments under the NPDES permit program, one usually thinks of treatment at the end of the pipeline. The EPA may, however, also require "in process" technologies.

a. Best Practicable Control Technology Currently Available

Conventional pollutants must be treated by the Best Practicable Control Technology currently available (BPT) before being discharged into the waters of the United States. Conventional pollutants are those contained in the wastewaters of homes, businesses, and industries. Conventional pollutants are commonly found in human waste, laundry and bath water, and sink disposal deposits. They may include fecal coliform and organic substances comprised of hydrocarbons, fats, oils, waxes, and/or high-molecular fatty acids.

BPT is defined as the average of the best performers in industry. In other words, this standard requires point sources to use good technology, based upon technology already being used in the relevant industry. There is a cost concern, but BPT is not expected to be cheap. Congress knows that it is expensive to treat conventional discharges. For cost to invalidate a BPT standard, it must be "wholly disproportionate" to benefits. Since the standard is based upon technology already in use, this seems unlikely.

How does the EPA identify the "best performers" in a given industry so that it can calculate BPT? In general, the EPA says that it looks to those companies that use its preferred technology. If a whole industry is backwards, the EPA may look to other, similar industries.

In order to calculate the average of the best performers in an industry, the EPA has to define the industry. This leads to the issue of BPT subcategorization. Many issues can arise here. For instance, consider all of the restaurants in town as an industry. Suppose now that fast-food restaurants wanted to be considered as a sub-category. Alternatively, what if Italian, Mexican, and Greek restaurants each want separate sub-categorization for their cuisine? How would a fast-food Mexican restaurant be categorized?

Restaurants are not usually at issue under the CWA, but the point is that the EPA can break an industry down in many ways. As a general rule, the EPA creates new subcategories only when members of that subcategory are so fundamentally different that they cannot practicably achieve the industry average. Courts usually defer to the EPA on this issue.

b. Best Available Technology

The CWA requires the EPA to establish a list of toxic pollutants, also called priority pollutants. These pollutants are categorized as either 1) organic—e.g., pesticides, solvents, polychlorinated biphenyls ("PCBs"), and dioxins; or 2) metals—e.g., lead, silver, mercury, copper, chromium, zinc, nickel, and cadmium. Priority pollutants are particularly harmful to plant and animal life. When it comes to toxins, the CWA calls for a standard that is stricter than the one it applies to conventional pollutants.

Permits for the discharge of priority pollutants are based upon Best Available Technology (BAT). Rather than being based upon the average of the best performers in industry, BAT is based upon the technology used by the best single plant in the field. This can be very expensive, but it is possible for costs to invalidate the regulations if they are way out-of-line.

In setting the BAT, the EPA can pick and choose—one facility may have a treatment that is best for pollutant A, and another facility might be best for pollutant B. The EPA can use the two standards and make them binding on *all* companies. As with BPT, the EPA can identify and use a preferred technology from a related industry.

It is worth noting that discharges containing toxins are held to BAT standards, but there are "gray area" pollutants, which may or may not be considered toxins. As such, BAT may apply or BPT may apply.

c. Best Conventional Technology

Best Conventional Technology (BCT) is for conventional pollutants. It is an advancement on the BPT standard. The idea is that the average of the best performers in any industry can be stagnant. In other words, the BPT standard may allow polluters to discharge greater quantities of conventional pollutants than would be the case if the industry were "pushed" a bit. BCT is designed to provide that push.

BCT is supposed to be cost effective. It is expected to remove "cheap" waste. The EPA must do a cost/benefit analysis before setting a standard based on BCT. Regarding diminishing marginal returns (the cost/benefit call), case law suggests that great discretion is left to EPA.

BCT can be required by EPA to force polluters to clean up beyond what BPT requires, without going all the way to BAT. BCT supplements BPT. They both still exist; the EPA can set standards based on either. If the added cost of going to BCT is greater than the benefit derived from doing that, the technology required under BCT may be the same as that required under BPT.

d. New Source Performance Standards

New Source Performance Standards (NSPS) apply to new construction. Major sources of conventional water pollution are required to install the best technology, even if it is not widely used in the industry (and therefore would not be required under either BPT or BCT). Inasmuch as NSPS is supposed to be the best technology, it is usually similar to BAT, though it is not applicable only to toxic pollutants. In fact, NSPS is often more strict than BAT.

There is a cost component to NSPS, but it is not true cost/benefit analysis. Costs have to be way out-of-line to void NSPS. If a new plant is built to meet NSPS standards, it is exempt from routine revisions (such as updates required under BPT due to advances in technology) for 10 years.

e. General or Area Permits and Exemptions

Under section 404 of the CWA, the Corps may issue individual permits or it may regulate entire categories of activities through the use of general permits issued on a state, regional, or nationwide basis. General permits are allowed for activities that are similar in nature, that have minimal adverse environmental effects if performed separately, and that have minimal cumulative adverse effects on the environment. The use of a general or area permit approach allows the EPA to focus on the problems for specific regions, but forces the agency to reexamine the issue at least every five years, which is preferable to granting an exemption which will probably never again be examined.

The CWA contains a few exemptions. Section 402 of the CWA provides that in certain circumstances the EPA may issue a permit for the discharge of a pollutant, notwithstanding a general prescription of discharges found elsewhere in the CWA. This gives the EPA flexibility in framing the permit to achieve a desired reduction in pollutant discharge. When numerical effluent limitations are infeasible, the EPA may issue comments with conditions designed to reduce the level of effluent discharges to acceptable levels.

Section 404(f)(1) of the CWA exempts certain activities from section 404 regulation. For instance, no permit is required for discharges from normal farming, silviculture, and ranching activities. Other exempt activities include maintenance of serviceable structures such as dikes, dams, levees, riprap, and causeways; construction or maintenance of farm or stock ponds and irrigation ditches; maintenance of drainage ditches; construction of temporary sediment basins at a construction site; and construction or maintenance of farm, forest, or mining roads.

Totally new activities such as construction of farm roads, construction of farm or stock ponds or irrigation ditches, and minor agricultural drainage, are all exempt by statute, as is discharge of dredged material for the purpose of maintaining drainage ditches. All of these exemptions are self-executing. In other words, they do not require an administrative holding that the statute does not apply.

Under section 404(f)(2), these new projects can lose their exempt status if all of the following conditions exist:

1. A discharge of dredge or fill material in the navigable waters of the United States;

2. The discharge is incidental to an activity having as its purpose the bringing of an area of navigable waters into a use to which it was not previously subject, and;

3. The flow or circulation of the navigable waters may be impaired or the reach of such waters may be reduced.

A landowner who intends to make substantial investments in acquisition or improvement of land may lawfully proceed with exempt activity, with no permit being required. The problem is that should the activity later be determined to be not exempt due to section 404(f)(2) or for some other reason, the Corps or the EPA will issue a cease and desist order, and the owner may lose the investment that he or she put into the project. Accordingly, it has become common for landowners to seek "no-jurisdiction" determinations from the Corps prior to starting work. This provides some level of assurance that the activities will be seen as having been undertaken in good faith.

f. Water Quality Standards

Unlike the Clean Air Act, the CWA does not set national ambient water quality standards to be met in each water body nationwide. There are no uniform national standards for water quality. Instead, states classify the waters within their jurisdictions, varying state by state and region by region. Acceptable levels of pollutant discharge depend upon the size of that water body, the number of other dischargers to that water body, and the state administration.

When it comes to toxins, however, the CWA requires the EPA to set standards to regulate the amount of pollutants in effluent by considering six factors: (1) the toxicity of the pollutant, (2) its persistence, (3) its degradability, (4) the usual of potential presence or affected organisms in waters, (5) the importance of the affected organisms, and (6) the nature and extent of the toxic substance's effect on the organisms. The agency is required to set the effluent standards at a level sufficient to ensure environmental protection with "an ample margin of safety." These are health-based standards, not predicated on existing technology.

The CWA also imposes water-quality standards for receiving water bodies whenever the EPA administrator determines that technology-based discharge limits have failed to achieve the water quality designated for that particular water body. Section 304 of the CWA requires the EPA to adopt water-quality criteria and guidelines for effluent limits, pretreatment programs, and administration of the NPDES permit program. Individual NPDES permits in these areas include more stringent limits.

A water-quality standard has two parts. The first is the designated use of the water body. For instance, the state may declare a particular water body fit for agriculture, for industrial purposes, for recreation, as a public water supply, or for some other use. The second part of the water-quality standard is the water-quality criteria necessary to meet the designated use. Pursuant to the CWA, the EPA publishes recommended acceptable concentrations of pollutants based upon the latest scientific knowledge.

3. Publicly Owned Treatment Works

Publicly Owned Treatment Works (POTWs) are treatment plants for municipal sewage —the used water supply of a community, including waterborne waste from residences, businesses, and industry. In some cases it may also contain storm water runoff and surface water or groundwater.

The national pretreatment program (CWA Section 307(b)) controls the indirect discharge of pollutants to POTWs by "industrial users." Facilities regulated under this section must meet certain pretreatment standards. The goal of the pretreatment program is to protect municipal wastewater treatment plants from damage that may occur when hazardous, toxic, or other wastes are discharged into a sewer system and to protect the quality of sludge generated by these plants.

Pretreatment standards for the sources that send their water to POTWs are set by EPA based on technology. For conventional pollutants, the polluter usually must treat the wastewater to a BPT level. For toxic wastes, treatment usually must be done to the BAT level. Some firms may, however, qualify for variances (even for toxic discharges). The EPA can set the standard, then exempt specific dischargers that are atypical to the industry.

If the secondary polluter's waste is too polluted, the POTW can refuse to take its waste water. Three possible problems might exist: 1) chemicals in the waste water might harm the POTW process; 2) chemicals in the waste water might render the sludge at the POTW valueless; or 3) chemicals in the waste water might pass through and contaminate other bodies of water. If any of these three outcomes is likely, the pollutants are "incompatible," and they cannot be sent to a POTW.

If, on a nationwide average, more of the pollutant "passes through" the POTW than would be taken out by BAT from a direct discharger, the pollutant is incompatible and it may not be sent to a POTW. The polluter must first pre-treat the water (on a BAT standard). This is true even if, for an individual polluter, the POTW does the full job. In other words, the individual polluter must comply with the pretreatment standard even if the water coming out of its POTW is clean.

4. Dredge and Fill Permits (Wetlands)

Under the CWA, any discharge of dredged or fill materials into "waters of the United States," including wetlands, is forbidden unless authorized by a permit issued by the U.S. Army Corps of Engineers (Corps). Essentially, all discharges of fill or dredged material affecting the bottom elevation require a permit from the Corps. These permits are an essential part of protecting wetlands. Wetlands are vital to the ecosystem in filtering streams and rivers and providing habitat for wildlife. Chapter 5, "Wetlands," of this Almanac deals with wetlands in greater detail.

Anyone proposing to discharge dredged or fill material to navigable water is required to obtain not only a section 404 permit from the Corps but also a Water Quality Certification under section 401. The section 401 certification is a statement that there is reasonable assurance that the proposed activity will not violate the applicable state surface water-quality standards. This certification may include specific requirements to ensure adequate environmental protection.

B. Nonpoint Source Pollution

Nonpoint source (NPS) pollution includes water pollution that does not come from a drain pipe or other point source. This would include things like:

- Excess fertilizer, herbicide, and insecticide from agricultural lands;
- Oil, grease, and toxic chemicals from urban runoff;
- Sediment from improperly managed construction sites, crop and forest lands, and eroding stream banks;
- Acid drainage from abandoned mines; and
- Bacteria and nutrients from livestock and faulty septic systems.

While permits can be used to control point source pollution, nonpoint source pollution is less susceptible to that type of regulation.

1. In General

It is very difficult to establish parameters or treatment facilities for NPS pollution. Accordingly, EPA has tried to develop Best Management Practices (BMP) to guide activities that can result in NPS pollution. Section 208 of the CWA directs states to develop pollution treatment plans for both point source pollution and NPS pollution. This planning process is supposed to estimate the growth of and needs for municipal sewage treatment; to inventory point source pollution; to identify NPS pollution sources; to estimate the economic, social, and environmental impact of the plans; and to designate appropriate agencies to implement them. Through a variety of programs, states assist and encourage producers to use best management practices to reduce or prevent instances of NPS pollutants migrating into waters.

The only part of the CWA that directly covers NPS pollution relates to the total maximum daily load for water bodies that are out of compliance with pollution levels. When water bodies are too polluted, they are placed on the Total Maximum Daily Load list. They are then restricted for all types of pollution, including non-point source pollution.

2. Storm Water Discharges

The CWA requires the EPA to establish a program to address storm water discharges, and in response the EPA promulgated the NPDES storm water permit application regulations. Storm water discharge associated with industrial activity means the discharge of storm water from a conveyance which is directly related to manufacturing, processing, or raw materials storage areas at an industrial plant. The regulations require that facilities with the following storm water discharges apply for an NPDES permit: 1) a discharge associated with industrial activity; 2) a discharge from a large or medium municipal storm sewer system; or 3) a discharge which EPA or the state/tribe determines to contribute to a violation of a water quality standard or which is a significant contributor of pollutants to waters of the United States.

As part of storm water permits, facilities are often required to implement pollution prevention plans. This reflects the EPA's desire to prevent pollution at the source, before it causes environmental problems.

Storm water pollution prevention plans should identify potential sources of pollution that may reasonably be expected to affect the quality of storm water discharges associated with industrial activity from the facility. The plans should also describe and ensure the implementation of practices that reduce the pollutants in storm water discharges.

Communities with problems related to the control of combined sewer overflows are required to take immediate and long-term remedial actions. This includes making sure that the sewer systems are operating properly and receiving regular maintenance. In addition, a public notification requirement ensures that the public receives prompt notification of the health and environmental impact of such overflows.

C. The Oil Pollution Act

The Oil Pollution Act (OPA) is an effort to expand the prevention, preparedness, and response capabilities of the federal government and industry over oil discharges. Oil spills pose serious threats to fresh water and marine environments. They adversely affect wildlife and their habitats. In addition, the oil itself is toxic and poses a serious threat of harm. Some organisms may be seriously injured or killed immediately after contact with oil, while other organisms suffer slow poisoning caused by long-term exposure.

The OPA was Congress's response to the notorious Exxon Valdez oil spill. It makes owners of vessels discharging oil liable for the costs of clean-up. To help prevent oil spills in the first place, the Act imposed minimum design standards for vessels operating in U.S. waters.

The OPA imposes strict liability on any party that is responsible for an oil spill or the substantial threat of an oil spill. It carries with it liability for a Class D felony for violations, which can carry a prison term of up to five years and/or a $50,000 fine. The statute also creates an Oil Spill Liability Trust Fund to pay for removal costs, claims, and damages not otherwise recoverable from responsible parties.

D. Clean Water Act Enforcement

The EPA can enforce its authority through compliance orders, administrative penalties, and initiation of civil actions. The U.S. Corps of Army Engineers may issue cease and desist orders. Individuals can also file citizen suits. If an individual is denied a permit, there is no administrative process for an adjudicatory hearing; the party must go to court to appeal the decision. A final decision by the agency is subject to judicial review under the Administrative Procedure Act (5 U.S.C. §§ 701–706).

1. Compliance Monitoring

Compliance monitoring is a cornerstone of the EPA's program to achieve clean water. The primary goal of the combined EPA and state compliance monitoring efforts—on-site inspections plus evaluation of self-reported Discharge Monitoring Report (DMR) data—is to ensure that entities possessing NPDES permits are complying with their CWA obligations. EPA and state compliance monitoring programs identify and document compliance and noncompliance, support the enforcement process, monitor compliance with enforcement orders and decrees, establish a presence in the regulated community, support the permitting process, and further the goals of the NPDES program.

Given the competing challenges of reduced budgets and water quality degradation, both the EPA and state NPDES inspection programs have been increasingly innovative and efficient, directing resources toward the most important noncompliance and environmental problems. Regulations found at 40 CFR Part 123.26 set forth requirements for compliance evaluation programs for states seeking to obtain or retain program authorization. Analogous regulations for the pretreatment program are set forth in 40 CFR Part 403.10(f) (2).

2. Penalties

Under section 309 of the CWA, the EPA can issue administrative orders against violators and seek civil or criminal penalties when necessary. For a first offense of criminal negligence, the minimum fine is $2,500, with a maximum of $25,000 fine per day of violation. A violator may also receive up to a year in jail. On a second offense, a maximum fine of $50,000 per day may be issued.

For a knowing endangerment violation, i.e., placing another person in imminent danger of death or serious bodily injury, a fine may be issued up to $250,000 and/or imprisonment up to 15 years for an individual, or up to $1,000,000 for an organization. The EPA, however, has provided an "upset" defense, so that not all discharges above the limit are necessarily violations.

3. Citizen Suits

Citizens or environmental groups may bring a civil action under the CWA. Section 505 of the CWA, the "citizen suit" provision, permits any citizen to initiate on his or her behalf against someone who violates the act. Citizen suits may seek compliance orders or civil penalties. They may not attempt to recover money damages. (A party wishing to challenge the issuance of permit must file a lawsuit in federal district court because there are no direct agency appeal mechanisms for section 404 permits.)

Citizens may also sue federal agencies for failing to conduct nondiscretionary actions under section 404 of the CWA. In fact, citizen suits, rather than actions by the EPA, have often forced state compliance with the CWA. For more on citizen suits, see Chapter 2, "The Authority to Protect the Environment," of this Almanac.

II. THE SAFE DRINKING WATER ACT

The Safe Drinking Water Act (SDWA) is the main federal law that ensures the quality of America's drinking water. It establishes a federal regulatory system designed to protect and ensure the safety of public drinking water supplies. Under the SDWA, the EPA sets standards for drinking water quality and oversees the states, localities, and water suppliers who implement those standards. The SDWA does not regulate private wells which serve fewer than 25 individuals.

The SDWA applies to drinking water regardless of its source. It requires the EPA to set maximum levels for common contaminants in public water supply systems. A public water supply is a system that serves at least twenty-five persons or has 15 service connections on a regular basis not less than 60 days of the year. The law was designed to regulate the quality of water as it flows to and from the tap.

Providing safe water is a comprehensive and coordinated effort by the EPA, state, local, and tribal governments, water suppliers, and the public. In addition, the EPA has established partnerships with other federal agencies, drinking water utilities, and non-profit organizations, to assist in the implementation of EPA standards. The EPA provides grants to implement state drinking water programs and to help states set up "drinking water state revolving funds" to assist public water systems in financing the costs of improvements.

More than half of the nation's drinking water comes from underground wells. The rest of the drinking water comes from surface waters such as rivers, lakes, and reservoirs. Tap water that meets EPA or state standards is considered safe to drink. Thus it is a good idea to check whether the water supplier in any given area meets all of the required standards. The applicable state drinking water agency should be able to provide consumers with this information.

A. Common Drinking Water Contaminants

The EPA prioritizes contaminants for potential regulation based on risk and how often they occur in water supplies. In other words, the decision as to which contaminants to regulate is based on data concerning the adverse health effects of the contaminant, its occurrence in public water systems, and the projected risk reduction. Public health protection is the primary concern on which drinking water standards are based.

To aid in this effort, some water systems monitor for the presence of contaminants even though there are no national standards that would require them to collect such information. Some of the more common water pollutants include:

a. Fecal coliforms (sometimes faecal coliforms) are a type of bacteria usually but not always associated with sewage or animal waste. The presence of fecal coliforms in drinking water is usually caused by a problem in water treatment, or with the pipes that distribute the water. Presence of fecal coliforms in water may not be directly harmful.

b. Lead—This contaminant is particularly dangerous to children. It is almost never found in drinking water when it leaves the water treatment plant. Its presence in water usually comes from interior plumbing in older buildings that have lead pipes or lead joining material. If lead is in the pipes, never consume water from the hot water tap. Boiling only increases the concentration of lead. Home water treatment units designed to remove lead from the water are available for purchase. Alternatively, use bottled water for drinking and cooking.

c. **Green water**—Green water may be an indicator of high copper levels in the water. The adverse health effects of copper include stomach distress, liver and kidney damage, and anemia. To reduce the level of copper in drinking water, the EPA advises consumers to allow the water from the cold water tap to become cold before using it. One should never consume water from the hot water tap if copper is present. Hot water dissolves copper more quickly than cold water. Home water treatment units that are designed to remove copper from drinking water are available for purchase. Alternatively, use bottled water for drinking and cooking.

d. **Radon**—Radon is a soil gas that is present in some areas of the United States. One normally thinks of it as affecting people through exposure in ways other than water, but it can affect underground sources of drinking water. If there is a possibility of radon in drinking water, a state-certified lab should test the water.

e. **Cryptosporidium**—Cryptosporidium is a parasite commonly found in lakes and rivers. It enters water supplies through sewage and animal waste. It causes cryptosporidiosis, a gastrointestinal disease. The most common symptom of cryptosporidiosis is diarrhea, often accompanied by abdominal cramps, nausea, vomiting, fever, headache, and/or loss of appetite. Generally, people recover within one to three weeks, but it can be severe and even fatal for people with seriously weakened immune systems. If there is concern that drinking water is contaminated with cryptosporidium, boil water before using it. It is also possible to purchase a home water treatment unit that is designed to remove cryptosporidium from drinking water.

The SWDA established an advisory committee to assist the EPA in evaluating data and information concerning microbial contaminants. Micro-contaminants have been identified as the highest potential drinking water risk to human health.

B. SDWA Standards

The SDWA authorizes the EPA to set national health-based standards for drinking water. These standards are intended to protect against both naturally occurring and man made contaminants that may be found in drinking water. The standards identify a health goal based on risk (including risks to the most sensitive people, e.g., infants, children, pregnant women, the elderly, and the immune-compromised). The SDWA applies to every public water system in the United States.

The EPA sets legal limits for identified contaminants in drinking water, or it sets a required treatment technique to remove contaminants. This limit or treatment technique is set to be as close to the health goal as feasible. The EPA performs a cost-benefit analysis and obtains input from interested parties when setting standards.

The standards also include requirements for water systems to test for contaminants and to make sure that the standards are achieved. In addition to setting these standards, the EPA provides guidance, assistance, and public information about drinking water, collects drinking water data, and oversees state drinking water programs.

States can apply to the EPA for "primacy," which is the authority to implement the SDWA within their jurisdictions. In order to obtain primacy, the states must show that they will adopt standards at least as stringent as the EPA's and make sure that water systems in the state will meet those standards. States, or the EPA acting as a primacy agent, make sure water systems test for contaminants, review plans for water system improvements, conduct on-site inspections, provide training and technical assistance, and take action against water systems not meeting standards.

Public water systems are responsible for ensuring that contaminants in their tap water do not exceed the standards. Water systems must test their water frequently for specified contaminants and report the results to the state. If a water system is not meeting these standards, the water supplier must notify its customers. Many water suppliers are also required to prepare annual reports for their customers. The public is responsible for helping local water suppliers set priorities, make decisions on funding and system improvements, and establish programs to protect drinking water sources.

The SDWA mandates that states have programs to certify water system operators and make sure that new water systems have the technical, financial, and managerial capacity to provide safe drinking water. The SDWA also sets a framework for the Underground Injection Control program to control the injection of wastes into ground water. These programs help prevent the contamination of drinking water.

National drinking water standards are legally enforceable, which means that both the EPA and states can take enforcement actions against water systems not meeting SDWA standards. The EPA and states may issue administrative orders, take legal actions, or impose fines on utilities. The EPA and states also work to increase the ability of water system operators to understand and comply with SDWA standards.

C. Public Information

All water suppliers must notify consumers quickly when there is a serious problem with water quality. Water systems serving the same people year-round must provide annual consumer confidence reports on the source and quality of their tap water. Both states and the EPA must prepare annual summary reports of water system compliance with drinking water safety standards and make these reports available to the public. The public must have a chance to be involved in developing source water assessment programs, state plans to use drinking water state revolving loan funds, state capacity development plans, and state operator certification programs.

A National Drinking Water Advisory Council (NDWAC) serves as an advisory group. Its role is to support the EPA's drinking water program by providing advice and recommendations to the EPA on drinking water issues. The NDWAC represents the drinking water community, including the public.

CHAPTER 5: WETLANDS

I. WETLANDS REGULATION UNDER THE CLEAN WATER ACT

A. Introduction

The term "wetlands" is applied to many areas, including marshes, swamps, bogs, and similar areas. They can be found in flat vegetated areas, in landscape depressions, and between dry land and water along the edges of streams, rivers, lakes, and other water bodies. Some wetlands contain water for only a short period of time each year. The rest of the year they appear to be dry land, making it sometimes difficult to identify a wetland area.

In 1776, when this nation was founded, 221 million acres of wetlands existed in the territory we now call the United States. At that time, however, wetlands were usually called swamps and were considered nuisances. They inhibited navigation and helped disease-carrying mosquitoes breed. As such, the federal government encouraged the draining and filling of wetlands throughout the 1800s and much of the 1900s through programs like the Swamp Lands Act of 1850, which granted fifteen western states almost 65 million acres for "swamp reclamation." Programs like the Swamp Lands Act established a national policy of draining and filling wetlands which persisted until late in the twentieth century. Throughout the country, conversion of wetlands to urban uses also increased their destruction and degradation.

The U.S. Department of the Interior's Fish and Wildlife Service estimated that over a 200-year period, the United States lost 53% of its original wetlands. Moreover, many activities that adversely impacted the environmental value of wetlands proceeded unregulated. These losses, as well as the degradation, have greatly diminished the nation's wetlands resources. Modern flood damages, drought damages, and declining bird populations have been, in part, the result of wetlands degradation and destruction.

In the 1960s, with rivers catching on fire and lakes being declared dead, people began to notice the benefits of bogs, marshes, swamps, prairie potholes, riparian greenways, tundra, and other wetlands. These ecosystems serve as habitats to numerous species of birds, mammals, reptiles, amphibians, fish, and crustaceans. They are a great source of natural products, including seafood, timber, wild rice, and fur. In fact, two-thirds of major U. S. commercial fisheries depend on estuaries and their associated wetlands as spawning grounds and nurseries for sustainability of the fisheries.

Wetlands filter and purify adjacent lakes, rivers and streams, even when those waterways do not flood directly into the wetland areas. In that manner, wetlands help to control non-point source pollution (see Chapter 4, "Water Quality," of this Almanac) and protect many sources of drinking water. Wetlands also provide flood control by attenuating or storing storm and flood waters, and reducing erosion at the shorelines. They also can function as a source of water reclamation, accumulation of sediment discharge, and groundwater recharge. In addition, wetlands have many economic and recreational functions.

With recognition of the value of wetlands came the push for legal protection. The federal government at first adopted a new interpretation of a law that dated back to 1899. Then, in 1972, Congress enacted legislation designed to prohibit the discharge of pollutants into water and wetlands unless the operators had obtained certain permits.

Today, the stated mission of the EPA's Wetlands Division is to encourage and enable other agencies, private actors, and landowners to act effectively in protecting and restoring the nation's wetlands and associated ecosystems, including shallow open waters and free-flowing streams. It incorporates an integrated wetlands/watershed approach in much of its work with other interested agencies. In carrying out its mission, the Wetlands Division is primarily responsible for establishing national standards and assisting others in complying with those standards.

A number of states also have laws that regulate activities in wetlands, and some counties and towns have adopted local wetlands protection ordinances or have changed the way development is permitted. Most coastal states have significantly reduced losses of coastal wetlands through laws and regulations like this.

B. Identifying Wetlands

As the name implies, wetlands are generally thought of as lands where saturation with water is the dominant factor in determining the nature of soil development in the area and the types of plant and animal life inhabiting the area. Wetlands vary widely because of regional and local differences in such factors as climate, type of soil, topography, and vegetation. They are found on every continent except Antarctica (where they would presumably exist but for the water being frozen).

One way to identify wetlands is to observe them in the growing season, when the upper part of the soil is saturated with water. At this time, soil organisms consume the oxygen in the soil and cause conditions unsuitable for most plants. These conditions cause the development of "hydric soils" which are different in color and texture. Plants that are able to grow in such conditions are called "hydrophytes." The appearance of hydric soils and hydrophytes indicates the presence of wetlands.

By 1987, the EPA organized a National Wetlands Policy Forum ("the Forum") to examine wetlands protection issues and make recommendations. In 1988, the Forum recommended adoption of a national goal of "no net loss" for wetlands and made suggestions for a plan to reach this goal.

In 1989, four federal agencies with jurisdiction over wetlands—the U.S. Army Corps of Engineers (Corps), the EPA, the U.S. Fish and Wildlife Service (FWS), and the Soil Conservation Service (SCS)—developed a common set of guidelines for identifying wetlands, the Federal Manual for Identifying and Delineating Jurisdictional Wetlands (the "Manual"). Prior to this time, each agency had operated with its own identification system. That led to difficult and sometimes conflicting standards. The Manual determined the status of a piece of land based upon hydrology, hydrophytic vegetation, and hydric soil.

The wetlands definition used by both the Corps and EPA under section 404 of the Clean Water Act is as follows:

> The term wetlands means those areas that are inundated or saturated by surface or groundwater at a frequency and duration sufficient to support, and that under normal circumstances do support, a prevalence of vegetation typically adapted for life in saturated soil conditions. Wetlands generally include swamps, marshes, bogs and similar areas.

The most controversial issue revolves around the inclusion of transitional wetlands in the scope of jurisdiction. Transitional wetlands are those which are dry during many parts of the year, and may be identifiable as wetlands only by the presence of water-tolerable vegetation and soils able to absorb significant quantities of waters.

Since some development is inevitable, a system to identify the most valuable wetlands is an important key to ecological balance. The most valuable wetlands must be identified so that they can be preserved. Valuing wetlands, of course, is extremely difficult. The scientific community has not reached a consensus as to whether all the intrinsic values of wetlands have been identified, and uncertainty exists as to how to quantify the values that have been identified. Moreover, controversy exists over which wetland functions are of the greatest significance to long term sustainability of wetland ecosystems.

Experts have some ideas about functions that benefit human interests such as water purification, flood damage reduction, groundwater recharge, wildlife and fish habitat, recreation, and aesthetic enjoyment. As for other values, there is a good deal of debate over their relative importance.

Common examples of wetlands include swamps, bogs, and marshes. Less recognized examples include vernal pools and prairie potholes. A description of several types of wetlands is set forth below.

1. Bogs

A bog is characterized by spongy peat deposits, a growth of evergreen trees and shrubs, and a floor covered by a thick carpet of sphagnum moss. The only water source for bogs is rainwater. Bogs have extremely low nutrient levels that form acidic peat deposits. Much of the acidity in bogs is due to sulfuric acid formed by the oxidation of organic sulfur compounds and from humic acids produced in the water. Bogs serve important ecological functions in preventing downstream flooding by absorbing direct precipitation and runoff, protecting water quality by intercepting and filtering runoff, and providing critical habitat for unique plant and animal life able to survive on the low-nutrient diet. Bogs are usually found in the northern hemisphere.

2. Bottomland Hardwoods

Bottomland hardwood forests are typically found along rivers and streams in the floodplain of the southeast and south central United States. They are deciduous forested wetlands, made up of different species of gum and oak, which have the ability to survive in areas that are seasonally flooded. Bottomland hardwoods serve an important role in the watershed by reducing the risk and severity of flooding to downstream communities. In addition, these wetlands improve water quality by filtering and flushing nutrients, processing organic wastes, and reducing sediment.

3. Estuaries

An estuary is a partially enclosed body of water formed where freshwater from rivers and streams flows into the ocean, mixing with the salty sea water. Estuaries and the lands surrounding them are places of transition from land to sea, and from fresh to salt water. They are also crucial breeding areas and habitat for a great deal of sea life.

The tidal, sheltered waters of estuaries support unique communities of plants and animals, specially adapted for life at the margin of the sea. Estuarine environments are among the most productive on earth, creating more organic matter each year than comparably-sized areas of forest, grassland, or agricultural land. The productivity and variety of estuarine habitats host a diversity of wildlife.

The wetlands that border on many estuaries perform valuable services. For example, water draining from upland carries sediment and other pollutants. As the water flows through fresh and salt marshes, much of the sediment and pollutants are filtered out. Estuarine plants also help prevent erosion and stabilize the shoreline.

The National Estuary Program was established in 1987 by amendments to the CWA to identify, restore, and protect nationally significant estuaries of the United States. The EPA administers the National Estuary Program, but program decisions and activities are carried out by committees of local government officials, private citizens, and representatives from other federal agencies, academic institutions, industry, and estuary user-groups.

4. Fens

Fens are a type of open freshwater marsh. Fens receive nutrients from sources other than precipitation (e.g., upslope sources through drainage from surrounding mineral soils and groundwater movement). Like bogs, fens are found in the northern hemisphere. Unlike bogs, peats associated with fens are not acidic and have higher nutrient mineral levels. They are therefore able to support much more diverse plant and animal life. Fens also provide important benefits to a watershed, including preventing or reducing the risk of floods, improving water quality, and providing habitat for unique plant and animal life.

5. Playas

A playa is a dry or ephemeral lakebed or a remnant of an endorheic lake. Playas are also known as alkali flats, dry lakes, or mud flats. The surface may primarily be salt, in which case they are typically called salt flats. The surface of a playa is typically dry and hard during the dry season, but wet and very soft in the rainy season (when they may actually become small lakes). The largest concentration of playa lakes in the world is in the southern high plains of Texas and eastern New Mexico. While playas are usually devoid of vegetation, they are commonly ringed by salt-tolerant plants that provide critical winter food for herbivores.

6. Prairie Potholes

Prairie potholes are depressional wetlands found primarily in the upper midwest of the United States. Prairie potholes are generally comprised of freshwater marshes. Some are temporary, while others are permanent. They serve to reduce the risk and severity of downstream flooding by absorbing rain, snow melt, and floodwaters.

7. Vernal Pools

Vernal pools are naturally occurring depressional wetlands that are covered by shallow water for variable periods from winter to spring, but may be completely dry for most of the summer and fall. These wetlands range in size from small puddles to shallow lakes and are usually found in a gently sloping plain of grassland. They are found on ancient soils with an impermeable layer such as a hardpan, claypan, or volcanic basalt. The impermeable layer allows the pools to retain water much longer than the surrounding uplands. Nevertheless, the pools are shallow enough to dry up each season. Vernal pools often fill and empty several times during the rainy season. The unique environment of vernal pools provides habitat for numerous rare plants and animals that are able to survive the harsh conditions.

In spring, flowering plants produce brightly-colored concentric rings of flowers for which vernal pools are famous. Native bees nest in vernal pools and pollinate flowers. Insects and crustaceans produce cysts and eggs, and plants produce seeds that are buried in the muddy pool bottom. The mud protects cysts, eggs, and seeds from the hot, dry summer. By late summer, vernal pools have completely dried out and most of the plant and animal species have either disappeared into the soils or set seed and died. In this phase, vernal pools are essentially "banks" full of seeds, cysts, and eggs that can survive through summer and extended droughts until the next rainy season.

II. THE SECTION 404 PERMIT PROGRAM

In 1972, Congress enacted the CWA to restore and maintain the chemical, physical and biological integrity of the nation's waters. It also set forth a national goal to eliminate the discharge of pollutants into the "waters of the United States," including wetlands. The Corps and the EPA administer a permit program under the CWA, with the Corps issuing permits and performing the day-to-day administration of the program, while the EPA maintains a supervisory role, establishing permitting guidelines, identifying exempted activities, and exercising veto authority over Corps permit decisions.

A. The Permitting Process

The primary federal law that regulates wetlands is section 404 of the CWA. As more fully developed in Chapter 4, "Water Quality," of this Almanac, section 404 requires parties who want to discharge dredged or fill material into the navigable waters of the United States to obtain a permit from the Corps. Regulatory agencies and the courts have interpreted "navigable waters" to include wetlands.

There are several ways that these permits are authorized. Typically, permits are issued when the Corps District Engineer determines that the proposed activity is not contrary to the public interest. This begins when an applicant submits a completed permit application. The Corps will post a public notice within 15 days of receiving the application. The notice will describe the proposed activity, its location, and the potential environmental impact of the project. It will also invite comments within a specified time period, typically 15 to 30 days. The public at large, as well as interested federal, state, and local agencies, then have an opportunity to comment on the proposed activity.

The notice must describe the permit application, including the proposed activity, its location, and potential environmental impacts. The notice must also invite comments to be submitted within a specified period of time. The application and comments are then reviewed by the Corps and other interested federal and state agencies, organizations, and individuals. The Corps determines whether an Environmental Impact Statement (EIS) is necessary. The Corps also evaluates the application and the comments received. The permit decision is set forth in a document known as a Statement of Finding, which is also made available to the public.

Permits are issued by the Corps, but the EPA has veto authority. To do so, the EPA (through its Office of Wetlands, Oceans, and Watersheds) must determine that "the discharge of dredged or fill materials will have an unacceptable adverse effect on municipal water supplies, shell fish beds and fishery areas (including spawning and breeding areas), wildlife, or recreational areas." The EPA has rarely used this veto power.

Other federal agencies, including the U.S. Fish and Wildlife Service (FWS), the National Marine Fisheries Service (NMFS), and various state resource agencies have important advisory roles in the permit process. In addition, over 20 states have enacted wetlands protection statutes of their own. State programs provide an additional statutory basis for restriction of private activities. In many cases, the state's regulations are enforced by local boards.

The CWA authorizes issuance of both individual and general permits. An individual permit is usually required for potentially significant impacts. However, for most discharges that will have only minimal adverse effects, general permits are often granted. Section 404(f) exempts some activities from regulation, including many ongoing farming activities. Section 404 permitting requirements apply only to discharges of dredged or fill materials in wetlands, streams, rivers, and "other waters of the United States." In general, farming activities do not occur in wetlands and do not involve dredged or fill material. (See the "Swampbuster" section III, C. below.) In addition, many normal farming, silviculture, and ranching activities that involve discharges of dredged or fill material into waters of the United States are exempted from section 404. In order to be exempt, the farming activity must be part of an ongoing farming operation and cannot be associated with bringing a wetland into agricultural production or converting an agricultural wetland to a non-wetland area.

General permits cover broad categories of activities and require the user to comply with stated conditions. They are issued for fill activities that will result in minimal adverse effects to the environment. Individual permits are used for actions that are not addressed by a general permit or that do not meet the conditions of a general permit. In addition, individual permits typically require more analysis than do the general permits, and they usually require much more time to prepare and to process.

The permitting process under the CWA includes filing of an application and a public notice and comment period, after which the Corps evaluates the application considering conservation; economics; aesthetics; effects on water quality, supply, and navigation; as well as historic and recreational values. The Corps' final analysis involves compliance with the EPA's established guidelines, looking to available alternatives and the risk of significant adverse impacts to the ecosystem. The process takes a comprehensive look at the long term effects of the proposed action. The program's objective is to prevent any discharge of dredged or fill material into wetlands or waters if there is a practicable alternative that is less damaging to the aquatic environment, or if the discharge would cause a significant adverse effect on the nation's waters, regardless of alternatives.

General permits are issued on a state, regional or nationwide basis for projects with small impacts. Wetland projects involving more than three acres may not be permitted under the umbrella of general permits. General permits are often issued for categories of activities that are similar in nature and would have only minimal individual or cumulative adverse environmental effects. A general permit can also be issued on a programmatic basis ("programmatic general permit") to avoid duplication of permits for state, local or other federal agency programs. The mechanized clearing of riparian areas for the control of invasive species may be authorized by a nationwide permit, but the appropriate Corps district office should be contacted to determine if a nationwide permit can be used to authorize a specific activity.

Under CWA section 401, states may veto or condition federally permitted activities which degrade water quality or aquatic habitat. This section requires applicants to be certified by the state that their proposed action is in compliance with state water quality requirements. Under this provision, states can limit impacts on wetlands without actually running their own regulatory programs or assuming the Corps' authority under section 404.

In 1977, Congress amended the CWA to allow delegation of section 404 programs to the states. Under these amendments, states could be given the "authority, responsibility, and capability to exercise the authority." While Congress manifested its intent to facilitate greater involvement by the states, it also expressed concerns for the performance of state programs. The idea is that states are better suited to protect their valuable resources, since they are more responsive than federal agencies to local needs, but states are somewhat more insulated from the influence of local politics than would be a county or municipal board.

Despite the difficulty in precisely evaluating success, the section 404 permitting process appears to have slowed the loss of wetlands. Federal incentives which formerly rewarded the elimination of wetlands have been replaced by incentives to restore wetlands. In the years since 1987 (when the Wetlands Forum took place), the rate of wetlands loss in the United States has slowed dramatically to the point where achieving the goal of "no net loss" may be in sight. Private land owners have made a major contribution, enrolling hundreds of thousands of acres in the national Wetlands Reserve Program, one of the programs recommended by the Forum.

B. Applying for a CWA Section 404 permit

In general, to obtain a section 404 permit, applicants must demonstrate that the discharge of dredged or fill material will not significantly degrade the nation's waters and there are no practicable alternatives less damaging to the aquatic environment. Applicants should also describe steps taken to minimize impacts to water bodies and wetlands and provide appropriate and practicable mitigation, such as restoring or creating wetlands, for any remaining, unavoidable impacts. Permits will not be granted for proposals that are found to be contrary to the public interest. Compliance with the Endangered Species Act and the National Historic Preservation Act may also be required.

In some cases, letters of permission will be issued. This is typical when the Corps District Engineer determines the proposed work will be minor, will not have significant individual or cumulative impact on environmental values, and will not encounter appreciable opposition. Concerned fish and wildlife agencies and adjacent property owners who might be affected by the proposal are typically notified, but the public at large is not. Letters of permission can be issued only in those situations where the Corps District Engineer has previously approved categories of activities for letter of permission procedures. Requesting a letter of permission may be an appropriate and relatively expedient means of complying with the CWA for many relatively localized and non-controversial actions.

On average, individual permit decisions (standard permits and letters of permission) are made within two to six months from receipt of a completed application. For activities authorized by general permits, decisions are usually made in less than 30 days. In emergencies, the Corps may be able to expedite the permitting process. Expedited procedures are authorized only on a case-by-case basis. Permit applications that require the preparation of an Environmental Impact Statement take an average of three years to process.

The CWA authorizes individual states to assume responsibility for administering the dredge and fill permit program. If approved, the state would assume the duties of the Corps and issue permits directly to applicants. The EPA would remain involved in the process and would retain veto power. Few states thus far have assumed this responsibility.

C. Enforcement

The EPA and the Corps share section 404 enforcement authority. A state that has been delegated the authority to run the permitting program may also enforce it. Violations under section 404 generally include failure to comply with the terms or conditions of a permit or the discharge of dredged or fill material to waters of the United States without a permit. Violators are subject to a wide variety of sanctions.

The EPA can issue administrative compliance orders requiring violators to stop any ongoing illegal discharge activity and to remove the illegal discharge and restore the site. The EPA and the Corps can also assess administrative civil penalties of up to $125,000 per illegal action. The EPA and the Corps also have the authority to take civil judicial action, seeking injunctive relief and civil penalties. Finally, the EPA and the Corps have authority to bring criminal judicial enforcement actions for knowingly or negligently violating section 404. For more details on sanctions under the CWA, see Chapter 4, "Water Quality," of this Almanac.

III. OTHER FEDERAL LEGISLATION

While the CWA is the principal federal legislation protecting the nation's wetlands, several other laws also play a role.

A. North American Wetlands Conservation Act

The North American Wetlands Conservation Act (NAWCA) provides funding and administrative direction for implementation of the North American Waterfowl Management Plan ("Management Plan"). The NAWCA specifically references goals of the Management Plan and provides a mechanism to support them and those of other migratory bird recovery programs.

The Management Plan is a blueprint for continental waterfowl and wetlands conservation, other North American migratory bird conservation agreements, and the Tripartite Agreement on wetlands between Canada, United States, and Mexico. Under the NAWCA, funds may be expended, upon approval of the Migratory Bird Conservation Commission, for payment not to exceed 50% of the United States' share of the cost of wetlands conservation projects in Canada, Mexico, or the United States (or 100% of the cost of projects on federal lands). At least 50% and no more than 70% of the funds received are to go to Canada and Mexico each year.

The NAWCA encourages partnerships to conserve North American wetland ecosystems for waterfowl, other migratory birds, fish, and wildlife. It encourages the formation of public-private partnerships to develop and implement wetland conservation projects consistent with the Management Plan. Funds from the NAWCA have been combined with funds from other laws to create the North American Wetlands

Conservation Fund. That fund provides federal matching grants for wetland conservation projects.

The NAWCA also establishes a nine-member North American Wetlands Conservation Council ("Council") to review and recommend grant proposals to be funded under the Act to the Migratory Bird Conservation Commission. The Council is comprised of the Director of the Service, the Secretary of the National Fish and Wildlife Foundation, state fish and game agency directors, and three representatives of different non-profit organizations.

B. The National Coastal Wetlands Conservation Grant Program

Since 1990, when Congress passed the Coastal Wetlands Planning, Protection and Restoration Act, the U.S. Fish and Wildlife Service has been working with coastal states to acquire, restore, manage, and enhance coastal wetlands through a matching grants program. Under the program, the FWS provides matching grants for acquisition, restoration, management, or enhancement of coastal wetlands. Funding for the program comes from excise taxes on fishing equipment and motorboat and small engine fuels.

States which border the Atlantic, Gulf of Mexico, Pacific and Great Lakes are eligible to receive matching grants. Also eligible are the Trust Territories and Commonwealths of the United States. The state of Louisiana has its own coastal plan under the Act.

Projects are selected competitively. The Act calls for projects to be given priority if they are: consistent with the criteria and considerations outlined in the National Wetlands Priority Conservation Plan; located in states with dedicated funding for programs to acquire coastal wetlands, natural areas, and open spaces; and located in maritime forests on coastal barrier islands. Additional ranking factors include giving credit to projects that benefit endangered species, encourage cooperative efforts, and benefit other ongoing projects. Grants awarded under the National Coastal Wetlands Conservation Grant Program generally range between $100,000 and $500,000.

Louisiana's unique wetland resources have been seriously depleted and degraded. It is estimated that 80% of the total loss of coastal wetlands in the United States has taken place in that state. Recognizing the unique problem faced by Louisiana, the Coastal Wetlands Planning, Protection and Restoration Act has special provisions for that state. It calls for the development of both Restoration and Conservation Plans specifically for Louisiana's wetlands. Under this program, Louisiana's cost share for wetland projects is only 15%.

C. Swampbuster

The Wetland Conservation Provision of the 1985 and 1990 farm bills, commonly called "Swampbuster," requires all agricultural producers to protect the wetlands on the farms they own or operate if they want to be eligible for USDA farm program benefits. In other words, Swampbuster is a disincentive program that protects wetlands by making farmers who drain wetlands ineligible for federal farm program benefits.

Producers are not eligible if they plant an agricultural commodity on a converted wetland that was converted by drainage, leveling, or any other means, or if they convert a wetland for the purpose of agricultural development. The Swampbuster program generally allows the continuation of most farming practices so long as wetlands are not converted or wetland drainage increased.

D. Mitigation and Restoration

Federal wetland policies in recent decades have increasingly emphasized restoration of wetland areas and mitigation of harm to wetland areas. It is often required as a condition of a section 404 permit. Without mitigation, effective "no net loss" policies would be virtually impossible.

Mitigation of proposed actions that would adversely affect wetlands has been a cornerstone of the section 404 program in recent years. In 1990, the Corps and EPA signed a memorandum of agreement that set out the type and level of mitigation required to comply with the CWA. A sequencing process was established which requires applicants first to attempt to avoid wetlands destruction, then to minimize the damage, and only after those options have been exhausted is an applicant allowed to use compensatory mitigation to offset the wetlands loss. Mitigated wetland acreage is to be replaced on a one-for-one functional basis.

Mitigation banks are a convenient way to mitigate the loss of wetlands. With a mitigation bank, a regulatory agency will allow the replacement of a small area of isolated wetland with an equivalent area of the same type in a large tract that will be maintained in perpetuity. A small wetland area needed for development can be filled or its function eliminated when an equal area with the same functions in a nearby mitigation bank property is built and operating. The bank can be constructed in advance by an entrepreneur or by a land development agency, and credits may be used or acquired by permit applicants when they are required to mitigate impacts of their activities.

Mitigation and conservation banking is a free market enterprise based on supply and demand of mitigation credits. Credits are supplied by landowners who enter into a Conservation Bank Agreement with the FWS agreeing to protect and manage their lands for one or more species. Other landowners who need to mitigate for adverse impacts to those same species may purchase conservation bank credits to meet their mitigation requirements. This benefits species by reducing the piecemeal approach to mitigation that often results in many small, isolated and unsustainable preserves that lose their habitat functions and values over time.

Wetlands enhancement, restoration, and creation are all technical solutions which are constantly under examination. Wetland mitigation banks are somewhat controversial, because they can be seen as justifying the destruction of natural wetlands. Critics often contend that adverse impacts on wetland values are often not fully mitigated and that mitigation measures are not adequately monitored or maintained.

IV. COASTAL ZONE MANAGEMENT ACT

Although the American coast comprises less than 10% of the land mass of the United States, more than 75% of the population now live within fifty miles of coastal areas, and that percentage is growing. As a natural resource, the coast is richer than the Rocky Mountains and more biologically important than even the wildlife of Alaska. Common law has long recognized coastal waters as corridors for water-borne commerce and as areas where the public is free to fish. The Supreme Court has held that rights in the coast are so important that without their free availability this nation never could have developed. Congress has repeatedly recognized the important ecological, cultural, historic and esthetic values in the coastal zone which are essential to the well-being of all citizens.

In recent decades, a significant percent of the nation's 85,240 shoreline miles has been eroding. Development, water pollution, air pollution, toxins, and other matters all threaten this critical habitat. The federal government took steps to protect the coast by enacting the Coastal Zone Management Act (CZMA). The CZMA is premised on the belief that, with coordination between various levels of government and various agencies within any one level, coastal development can be controlled and environmental damage to the coast can be limited.

Unlike other environmental statutory schemes, the CZMA does not focus on one specific type of pollution (for example, air or water pollution). Instead, it sets forth a plan to protect an entire region from the effects of development and pollution in all their various forms. To do this, the CZMA calls on local, state, and federal governmental units to each play a role. The coastal zone is defined as "the coastal waters (including the lands therein and thereunder) and the adjacent shorelands (including the lands therein and thereunder) strongly influenced by each other and in proximity to the shorelines of the several coastal states . . . inland from the shorelines only to the extent necessary to control shorelands, the uses of which have a direct and significant impact on the coastal waters." 16 U.S.C. § 304(1).

Modern federal coastal protection can be traced back to the Marine Resources and Development Act of 1977 and the establishment of the Commission on Marine Science, Engineering and Resources, commonly known as the Stratton Commission. The Stratton Commission focused national attention on the value of coastal resources and the dangers of unplanned development. The need for a federal coastal protection program was established based on Stratton Commission findings that, by the early 1970s, over 25% of the nation's salt marshes had been destroyed; population was becoming more concentrated in and about coastal waters, estuaries, and marshlands for the growth and development of sea life; increased commercial and recreational use of the coast was endangering aquatic life; and fragmented, uncoordinated state and local regulation was exacerbating pressure caused by economic development. These findings led to passage of the CZMA, which was "aimed at saving the waters of American coasts and the land whose use had a direct, significant, and adverse impact upon that water."

Coastal damage comes not only from physical construction and development but also from water pollution that is carried to the coast, toxins that make their way to the coast, offshore oil exploration (especially accidents), air pollution, greenhouse gases, river channelization and canals, and a wide variety of other activities. As such, the CZMA's integrated watershed-based approach to water and wetlands protection considers the whole system, including other resource management programs that address land, air, and water, to manage problems for a given aquatic resource. This type of integrated approach recognizes that the quality of wetlands and other water resources is directly linked to the quality of the environment surrounding these waters.

The CZMA relies on agreements between coastal states and the federal government, and it offers financial assistance to states that develop a Coastal Management Plan (CMP). As the name implies, a CMP is a comprehensive plan designed to protect coastal resources and prevent environmental degradation within the state. States are not required to develop CMPs, but there are substantial incentives. The CZMA provides grants that pay states up to 80% of the cost of developing a program and 50% of the cost of administering a CMP.

In order to receive federal money, state CMPs must comply with CZMA standards and be approved by the Secretary of Commerce. Those standards permit states to develop plans that differ greatly from one another, but all states are required to consider the national interest as well as local, area wide, and interstate plans affected by the program. The purpose of this consideration is to achieve the Act's spirit of equitable balance between state and national interests.

After the state has promulgated its CMP, the federal government delegates most enforcement authority to the state, though the federal government does review performance and may withhold federal funds and withdraw federal approval if the state fails to meet national standards. Once in place, most CMPs rely on a permit system to control development on the coast.

Once states have an approved CMP, federal programs (and projects that require federal permits) must be "consistent to the maximum extent practicable" with the state CMP. This requirement is designed to achieve better coordination between federal and state agencies. Federal agencies may not approve proposed projects that are inconsistent with a CMP, except on a finding by the Secretary of Commerce that the program is consistent with the purposes of CZMA or necessary in the interest of national security.

V. THE TAKINGS ISSUE

If the government "takes" private property for public uses, the prior owner is entitled to compensation. As early as 1921, the U.S. Supreme Court held that some regulations could be so intrusive as to constitute a taking. The relevant portion of the Fifth Amendment to the U.S. Constitution reads, "nor shall private property be taken for public use, without just compensation." Historically, the courts have interpreted the takings clause as pertaining to cases of condemnation under eminent domain. In other words, the government cannot confiscate private land or other property without paying a fair price for it.

In 1985, while reaffirming broad federal jurisdiction under section 404 of the CWA, the Supreme Court raised, without answering, the question of whether the regulation at issue constituted a taking. In 1987, while again failing to fully address the issue, the Court declared that local governments would be liable in money damages for temporary regulations that are subsequently adjudicated to be takings. In its most recent proclamation, *Nollan v. California Coastal Commission*, the Supreme Court declared that coastal use mitigation requirements, which required landowners to provide public access in return for permission to tear down and rebuild a dilapidated house located on beachfront property, constituted impermissible takings of private property, thus entitling the owners to compensation.

Since wetland legislation applies to privately held property, several landowners have argued that the regulation constitutes a taking and entitles them to compensation. However, only in instances where government regulations have been found to eliminate virtually all economic value of property have the courts supported financial compensation for a "regulatory takings."

The Takings Clause and related issues are discussed in greater detail in Chapter 9, "Restrictions on Development of Private Land," of this Almanac.

CHAPTER 6: TOXIC SUBSTANCES AND HAZARDOUS WASTES

I. FEDERAL INSECTICIDE, FUNGICIDE AND RODENTICIDE ACT (FIFRA)

A. The Pesticides Dilemma

Pesticides are often referred to as "valuable poisons." By definition, pesticides are toxic chemicals; the term "pesticides" literally means "pest killer." Farmers use chemical pesticides to minimize injuries to crops caused by disease and pests, thus increasing crop yields and reducing the costs of foods. Companies and citizens use them to kill disease-carrying or annoying pests in businesses and homes. Similarly, pesticides are used to kill pests and control weed growth on lawns, landscaped grounds, golf courses, ball fields, and rights of way. Insecticides are used to kill insects, fungicides to kill mold and mildews, rodenticides to kill rats and mice, and herbicides to kill plants. These substances are intentionally introduced into the environment in order to make that environment a more pleasant, safe, and economically valuable place for humans.

Widespread application of these substances, however, imposes substantial risks on the health of people, pets, livestock, and wildlife exposed to them. Ecosystems can be polluted by pesticides and they can be found in drinking water, food, air, and soils. In her seminal 1962 book *Silent Spring*, Rachel Carson wrote about the widespread application of pesticides such as DDT and the resulting effects on the environments into which they were introduced. Such pesticides killed many forms of life in addition to the mosquitoes and other pests targeted by them. Their residues moved through the food chain from smaller to larger organisms, causing death to birds and animals and entering into the bloodstreams of humans. *Silent Spring* helped crystallize public concerns about the toxic potency and health risks of pesticides which had been steadily rising since the post World War II boom in the chemical industry.

Following World War II, the scale of farming operations greatly increased and the volume of chemical pesticide production and usage kept pace with this expansion. In the late 1940s, approximately 50 million pounds of pesticides were used in the United States every year. The current annual level of pesticide usage in the United States is now in the billions of pounds, and agricultural pesticide use is around 700 million pounds per year. The volume of pesticide use in this country is staggering, creating substantial risks to public health and the environment and making regulation of the manufacture, use, and disposal of these substances an absolute necessity. However, the dangerous qualities of these substances are precisely what make them so useful and valuable to society. Pesticides are both hazardous and essential. Thus considerable balancing of the risks, costs, and benefits of pesticides must be undertaken in efforts to regulate them.

B. Congressional Enactment of FIFRA

Congress enacted the Federal Insecticide, Fungicide and Rodenticide Act (FIFRA) in 1947. The 1947 Act established labeling requirements for pesticides and provided for seizure of products that did not comply with these requirements. The Act further required pesticides sold or distributed in interstate or foreign commerce to be registered with the U.S. Department of Agriculture (USDA). However, the USDA had no authority to evaluate the environmental effects of pesticides before approving their registration or to reject or cancel a registration request on such grounds. In 1964, however, Congress amended FIFRA to allow the USDA to refuse a registration or cancel an existing registration of a pesticide if necessary to address an imminent hazard to the public. When the EPA was created in 1970, Congress reassigned responsibilities for pesticide matters under FIFRA from the USDA to the EPA.

In 1972, Congress made sweeping amendments to FIFRA through enactment of the Federal Environmental Pesticide Control Act of 1972. The most important change to FIFRA was the mandate that the EPA not register pesticides determined to cause unreasonable adverse effects to the environment. Additional major amendments to FIFRA were made by Congress in 1975, 1978, and 1988.

C. Pesticide Registration under FIFRA

FIFRA requires all pesticides sold or distributed in commerce to be registered with the EPA. FIFRA bars from sale, distribution or use any pesticide which is not so registered. Pesticides are registered under FIFRA either for "general" or "restricted" use. General use pesticides may be sold over the counter. However, restricted use pesticides generally may be applied only by a certified applicator, typically a state licensed exterminator or similar user.

An applicant seeking to register a pesticide with the EPA must demonstrate the following:

- the pesticide's composition is such that it will perform in the manner that the applicant claims it will;
- the pesticide's labeling complies with the labeling requirements of FIFRA;
- the pesticide will perform its intended function without unreasonable adverse effects on the environment; and
- when used in accordance with widespread and commonly recognized practice the pesticide will not generally cause unreasonable adverse effects on the environment.

This requires testing by the applicant that demonstrates the pesticide will be effective (meet the claims made by the applicant as to how it will perform) and not unreasonably dangerous to human health and the environment when used properly. With respect to whether adverse effects are "unreasonable," the EPA will consider the "economic, social, and environmental costs and benefits" of the pesticide.

FIFRA does not prevent states from enacting pesticide registration requirements of their own. States may even prohibit the sale or use of pesticides that have been registered by the EPA under FIFRA, but do not meet state health and safety requirements. However, FIFRA prohibits states from imposing labeling or packaging requirements for pesticides that are different than those imposed by FIFRA. States also are responsible for licensing or certifying applicators of restricted use pesticides. State licensing or certification procedures for this purpose must be approved by the EPA. If no such procedures have been approved for a particular state, the EPA will perform these functions in that state.

D. Cancellation or Suspension of Registrations

FIFRA has several provisions intended to protect the public from dangerous pesticides even after a pesticide has been registered under the statute. A registration of a pesticide under FIFRA is valid for a five-year period, after which the pesticide must be re-registered. FIFRA also allows for the cancellation or suspension of a pesticide's registration if it is subsequently determined that the pesticide violates FIFRA requirements or causes unreasonable adverse environmental effects. In re-registration, cancellation, or suspension proceedings, the burden of showing that the pesticide is not unreasonably dangerous remains on the registrant.

A cancellation bans a pesticide from distribution or use in commerce. FIFRA provides that the EPA may initiate cancellation proceedings whenever it "appears to the [EPA] that a pesticide . . . generally causes unreasonable adverse effects on the environment." Courts have interpreted this to require only that the EPA find a substantial question of safety exists in order to begin proceedings to cancel a pesticide's registration under FIFRA.

Because cancellations proceedings can take considerable time to complete, a suspension proceeding may be used by the EPA to remove a pesticide more swiftly from the market than would occur with a cancellation. The EPA can notify a registrant that it intends to cancel a registration of a pesticide based on a showing that the product constitutes an "imminent hazard" to human health or the environment. Following such notice, the EPA can conduct an expedited hearing on the question of whether such an imminent hazard exists. Additionally, the EPA may impose an emergency suspension without providing notice and a hearing if unreasonable harm would be likely to materialize while ordinary suspension procedures were pending.

E. Labeling Requirements

FIFRA includes detailed requirements regarding labeling, misbranding, and adulteration of pesticides. FIFRA precludes any false or misleading statements on the actual label or any other writings accompanying the pesticide. Directions for the safe use and warnings adequate to protect health and the environment are required to be included on labels and accompanying writings. If pesticides contain ingredients considered toxic to humans, FIFRA requires the word "poison" to be prominently displayed on the label and that the labeling include instructions regarding antidotes or other treatment. Pesticides that do not comply with these requirements are deemed "misbranded" under FIFRA.

II. TOXIC SUBSTANCES CONTROL ACT (TSCA)

A. The Toxic Substances Information Problem

Staggering numbers of chemical substances and mixtures are manufactured and processed in the United States each year. People and the environment are exposed to these substances in countless ways on a daily basis. Chemical substances and mixtures are present in an endless variety of socially useful products. However, countless numbers of these chemical substances are toxic, in the sense that under the proper circumstances, they can cause harm to human health or the environment. The vast quantities of toxic substances in use and the level of potential human and environmental exposure to them are alarming. For the reporting year 2004, the EPA's Toxic Release Inventory (TRI) demonstrated that 4.24 billion pounds of toxic substances considered the most dangerous were released by business and industry to land, water, and air.

Even more alarming, insufficient information exists about the potential hazards of toxic substances. In 1984, the National Research Council of the National Academy of Sciences reported that no information on potential toxicity existed for 80% of the more than 48,000 unregulated chemical substances then in commercial use in the United States. In 1997, an environmental advocacy group, the Environmental Defense Fund, issued the *Toxic Ignorance* report finding that more than 70% of the highest volume industrial chemicals in U.S. commerce lacked sufficient data to conduct basic hazard assessment. High volume chemicals are defined as those produced or imported in amounts of one-million pounds per year and are known as "high production volume" (HPV) chemicals. A study conducted by the EPA following the *Toxic Ignorance* report confirmed that basic toxicity information was inadequate or completely unavailable in the public record for more than 90% of HPV chemicals in use in the United States.

B. Congressional Enactment of TSCA

Recognizing the danger to the public and to the environment from exposure to hazardous chemicals, Congress enacted the Toxic Substances Control Act (TSCA) in 1976. TSCA was primarily intended to close the information gap that existed concerning the health and environmental risk of chemical substances commonly in use in the United States. TSCA seeks to control chemical products prior to their entering the environment by allowing the acquisition of existing information from chemical manufacturers on the chemicals they produce and the creation of new data when necessary. Congress established three national goals in TSCA:

- to gather information on chemical toxicity, use, and exposure;
- to use that information to protect human health and the environment from unreasonable risks of harm; and
- to gather and use this information without creating barriers to technological innovation in excess of those needed to accomplish the goals of TSCA.

C. Chemical Substances and Mixtures

TSCA regulates chemical "substances" and "mixtures." A "substance" is a chemical either occurring in nature or that results from a chemical reaction. A "mixture" is a combination of two or more "substances" that does not occur in nature and is not the result of a chemical reaction. TSCA requires the EPA to maintain a current list of every chemical substance manufactured or processed in the United States. Each new chemical substance reported to the EPA must be added to the list.

TSCA excludes from its coverage pesticides regulated under FIFRA, certain nuclear materials regulated by the Nuclear Regulatory Commission, and food, drug, and cosmetic products regulated by the Food and Drug Administration. However, TSCA has specific provisions addressing the use and disposal of asbestos in schools, radon, lead, and polychlorinated biphenyls (PCBs) (substances formerly used in electrical equipment).

D. TSCA Testing Requirements

TSCA mandates that the EPA issue a rule requiring testing to develop data on the health and environmental effects of chemical substances once the agency makes certain findings. First, the EPA must find either the existence of an "unreasonable risk of injury" to health or the environment, or that a chemical produced in "substantial quantities" may reasonably be expected to enter the environment in such quantities or to result in significant human exposure. Second, the agency must find that insufficient data exist to reasonably determine the effect of a chemical substance on health or the environment. And, third, the EPA must find that testing this substance is necessary to develop sufficient data to make such a determination.

If the EPA issues a test rule, it must establish the standards to be used for the testing of the chemical substance at issue. The testing generally will seek evidence on whether the substance is a possible carcinogen (cancer causing agent), contributes to birth defects or behavior disorders, or causes other unreasonable risks to health or the environment. The EPA is required to give notice to "interested persons" about the proposed test rule and to allow public comment on the proposed testing.

Upon receipt of data from testing, if the EPA concludes a reasonable basis exists to believe a chemical substance presents an unreasonable risk to health or the environment, the agency is required by TSCA, within 180 days, to take appropriate steps to prevent or reduce that risk. Such steps may include prohibiting or limiting the manufacture or use of the chemical substance.

E. Premanufacture Notification

TSCA requires manufacturers to notify the EPA prior to manufacturing a new chemical substance or putting an existing chemical substance to a significant new use. In some cases, the required notice must include submission of test data on the health and environmental effects of the chemical substance in question.

F. Regulation of Chemical Substances

TSCA authorizes the EPA to impose a number of limitations on the use, marketing, labeling, or disposal of chemical substances if the agency has a reasonable basis to conclude the substance "presents or will present an unreasonable risk of injury to health or the environment." Among the limitations the EPA may impose include:

- restricting or prohibiting manufacturing, processing, or distribution of a chemical substance;
- restricting or prohibiting certain commercial uses of that substance;
- requiring labeling or other accompanying written material to include warnings and instructions regarding the use, distribution, or disposal of the chemical; or
- restricting or prohibiting certain disposal practices of the chemical or any product containing the chemical.

Additional restrictions may be imposed by the EPA "to the extent necessary to protect adequately against such risk using the least burdensome requirements." TSCA also grants the EPA emergency powers to seek court orders to seize "imminently hazardous" chemicals or products containing the chemical. The EPA is also authorized to seek injunctions against any manufacturer, processor, distributor, user, or disposer of a chemical requiring a recall of chemicals or products or notifications to purchasers or other public notice of the risks involved.

G. Reporting and Recordkeeping Requirements

TSCA imposes significant reporting and recordkeeping requirements on manufacturers, processors, and distributors of chemical substances. Manufacturers, processors, and distributors must maintain records of significant adverse health or environmental effects allegedly caused by any chemical. Such claims of harm may come from employees, consumers, or other parties. These entities must also maintain lists of health and safety studies for each substance regulated by TSCA. Further, any manufacturer, processor, or distributor obtaining any information "which reasonably supports the conclusion" that a chemical substance poses a substantial risk of harm to health or the environment must immediately notify the EPA.

III. RESOURCE CONSERVATION AND RECOVERY ACT (RCRA)

A. The Solid and Hazardous Waste Problem

The handling and disposal of waste has been a problem for mankind for centuries. Systems of refuse collection and disposal date back to medieval times. Rising population in the United States in the late nineteenth and early twentieth centuries combined with rapid urbanization and industrial growth resulted in ever-increasing volumes of waste that needed to be regularly collected, transported, and disposed of. By 1910, a half-pound of municipal garbage per person per day was produced in the United States. By 1960, the volume of municipal waste in the United States had grown to 2.7 pounds per person per day and a total of 88 million tons per year. By 2005, the United States generated 246 million tons of municipal waste annually or 4.54 pounds per person per day.

Until the 1960s, solid waste management was viewed as primarily a local concern and regulated at the local level. However, concern over the rapidly rising volumes of municipal solid waste induced Congress to pass the Solid Waste Disposal Act of 1965 (SWDA). The SWDA funded federal research and provided financial assistance to states to better control the disposal of trash from all sources.

During the 1960s and 1970s, however, the country began to take stock of a more serious problem associated with waste disposal—the issue of hazardous waste. With the rapid expansion of industry in the United States following World War II, the volume and toxicity of industrial waste streams began to increase dramatically. At the end of World War II, approximately 500,000 tons of industrial hazardous waste was generated per year. Over the next five decades, the annual volume of this waste increased more than 500-fold. The principal industries generating these hazardous wastes were the chemical, petroleum, and metal industries. The manufacturing and other operations associated with these industries often created toxic by-products that needed to be disposed of and such disposal was largely unregulated. Much of this toxic waste was simply dumped on land with no thought to the potential environmental harm it could cause.

Many such wastes were stored or disposed of at sites where water contamination could occur; for example, sites located in floodplains, over aquifers unprotected by impervious rock or soil, and in filled wetlands.

Water filtering through such sites can leach toxic compounds through the soil and into the groundwater, and surface runoff from rain or snowmelt can carry chemicals to nearby lakes, ponds, and streams. The result was the potential impairment or destruction of public water supplies. During the 1970s, hundreds of instances of groundwater contamination were discovered each year and private and public water supply wells were capped in dozens of states. The hazardous waste disposal problem began to be perceived as a looming environmental and public health crisis.

B. Congressional Enactment of RCRA

By the mid-1970s, it had become apparent that the SWDA was not sufficient to address the dangers posed by the increasing volume of solid and hazardous waste in the United States. A congressional report in 1976 stated that millions of tons of hazardous substances that could "blind, cripple, or kill" were being "literally dumped on the ground each year." The report further emphasized that these substances could "defoliate the environment, contaminate drinking water supplies, and enter the food chain under present, largely unregulated disposal practices." To address these threats, in 1976, Congress enacted the Resource Conservation and Recovery Act (RCRA) as an amendment to the SWDA. RCRA established national goals for:

- protecting human health and the environment from the potential hazards of solid and hazardous waste disposal;
- conserving energy and natural resources through waste recycling and recovery;
- reducing or eliminating the amount of waste generated, including hazardous waste; and
- ensuring that wastes are managed in an environmentally sound manner.

Congress expanded RCRA in 1984 with the Hazardous and Solid Wastes Amendments of 1984. These amendments strengthened RCRA by expanding coverage to small quantity generators of hazardous wastes, establishing requirements for hazardous waste incinerators, and mandating the closing of substandard landfills. The amendments also further expanded RCRA to include regulation of underground storage tanks (USTs) that contain petroleum or other hazardous substances. RCRA has separate programs that regulate hazardous wastes, non-hazardous solid wastes, USTs, and used oil.

C. Hazardous Wastes

RCRA mandated that EPA establish a national regulatory program to provide comprehensive protection against mismanagement of hazardous waste "from cradle to grave." The basic idea was to establish a tracking system that would follow such waste from its point of generation to the point of its disposal. RCRA imposes stringent bookkeeping and reporting requirements on generators, transporters and facilities that treat, store or dispose of hazardous waste. Treatment, storage or disposal facilities ("TSD" facility) are stringently regulated to ensure that public health is not threatened by releases of hazardous wastes.

1. Regulated Entities

Three categories of actors fall within RCRA's "cradle to grave" system for hazardous wastes: (1) generators, (2) transporters, and (3) TSD facilities. A generator is the entity that, figuratively speaking, gives birth to the hazardous waste in question. A transporter is any entity that moves a hazardous waste from the site on which it was generated. A TSD facility is the entity that receives hazardous wastes for either treatment, storage, or disposal purposes and which must have a federally issued RCRA permit in order to operate. Examples of TSD facilities are landfills and incinerators. Neither generators nor transporters are required to have permits under RCRA. A TSD hazardous waste permit imposes numerous conditions on the operators of the facility, such as minimum technology requirements for operation, record keeping and reporting requirements, emergency procedures, monitoring programs to detect releases of hazardous substances, and requirements for contingency planning and financing for the closing of the facility in the event it ceases to operate.

2. Manifest Requirement

A cornerstone of RCRA is the manifest system. The manifest is a data sheet that identifies each shipment of hazardous waste. The manifest will accompany the waste from the generating facility to the final disposal site and allows for the "cradle to grave" tracking of the waste. The manifest must be separately signed by the generator, the transporter, and the TSD facility at each point in the waste's journey from the generating facility to its ultimate destination. Upon receipt of the waste, a TSD facility is required to return a signed copy of the manifest to the generator. A generator that does not receive a signed copy of the manifest from the TSD facility within a certain time period is required to notify the government of this omission. The manifest system seeks to ensure that hazardous wastes actually arrive at the TSD facility and are not illegally dumped elsewhere by the transporter.

3. Definition of Hazardous Waste

A two step process applies to determining whether a particular substance is classifiable as a "hazardous waste" for purposes of RCRA. First, it is necessary to determine whether the substance is a "solid waste." If a substance is a "solid waste," then RCRA generally applies. If it is not, then RCRA has no application. Second, once a material has been identified as a "solid waste," then it must be determined if that solid waste should be classified as "hazardous."

a. Solid Waste

Importantly, a waste does not have to be in solid form in order to be considered a "solid waste" for purposes of RCRA. RCRA defines "solid waste" as "any garbage, refuse, sludge from a waste treatment plant, water supply treatment plant, or air pollution control facility and other discarded material, including solid, liquid, semisolid or contained gaseous material resulting from commercial, mining, and agricultural operations, and from community activities." Thus liquid or viscous substances or contained gasses are within RCRA's definition of the term "solid waste." Indeed, the key to the definition of solid waste in RCRA is not the word solid, but the word "discarded." Generally, something that is or can be discarded is a solid waste under RCRA.

Because the definition of "solid waste" is extremely broad, Congress has excluded numerous categories of waste from the definition of solid waste under RCRA. Among the categories of wastes excluded from the statutory definition by Congress are domestic sewage, industrial wastewater discharges subject to regulation under the Clean Water Act, return flows from agricultural irrigation, mining wastes not removed from the ground, and certain nuclear materials regulated by the Atomic Energy Act. The EPA has further excluded certain types of solid waste from classification as a hazardous waste. Among the categories of solid wastes excluded from categorization as "hazardous waste" by way of EPA regulation include household wastes (garbage generated in homes) and fertilizer used in agricultural operations. Thus despite the very broad definition of "solid waste" in RCRA, the high number of exclusions mean that there are potentially millions of tons of hazardous solid waste generated in the United States every year that go unregulated by RCRA.

b. Hazardous Waste

If material is "solid waste" under RCRA, it must then be determined if it should be classified as a "hazardous waste." If it is a "hazardous waste," then the material is subject to the "cradle-to-grave" tracking system for the handling and disposal of hazardous wastes. If the solid waste is deemed not to be "hazardous," then the material is not subject to the manifest requirements and does not have to be disposed of at a TSD facility. However, the material is subject to RCRA's program for non-hazardous solid waste and must be disposed of in a sanitary landfill.

A solid waste is deemed hazardous if it falls within any one of the following four categories:

- *"Listed wastes"*—if a waste is specifically listed on any of several lists of hazardous wastes published by the EPA in the Code of Federal Regulations, it is classified as a hazardous waste;
- "*Characteristic wastes*"—for wastes not specifically listed as a hazardous waste, a waste that exhibits any one of the following four hazardous characteristics is deemed hazardous:
  a. "*ignitability*"—the tendency of a substance to catch on fire;
  b. "*corrosivity*"—the acidity or alkalinity of a substance;
  c. "*reactivity*"—the tendency of a material to explode; or
  d. "*toxicity*"—a substance containing any one of a number of metals or organic constituents above levels established by the EPA.
- "*Mixture rule wastes*"—any mixture of a listed waste with another solid waste is deemed to be itself a hazardous waste (meaning a listed waste cannot be diluted with other solid non-hazardous waste in an effort to avoid its classification as a hazardous waste); and
- "*Derived-from rule wastes*"—any waste derived from the treatment, storage, or disposal of a listed waste (such as the ash residue from burning or incinerating a listed waste) is deemed to be itself a hazardous waste.

The "mixture" and "derived from" rules only apply to listed wastes. These rules do not, on the other hand, apply to characteristic wastes. A characteristic waste is only considered hazardous so long as it continues to exhibit one of the four hazardous characteristics. If a waste derived from a characteristic waste no longer exhibits the hazardous characteristic, it is no longer a hazardous waste. If a waste diluted or mixed with other solid waste no longer exhibits the hazardous characteristic, it is no longer a hazardous waste. In making this distinction, the EPA seeks to reduce incentives for generators to try to evade RCRA regulation of listed wastes by changing the form or content of the waste in a way that does not remove the potential hazard. Thus in this sense the EPA takes a "strict liability" approach to a listed waste in classifying it as hazardous. For a characteristic waste, an actual hazard must be demonstrated for it to be deemed to be hazardous.

EPA regulations require a generator of a solid waste to "determine if that waste is a hazardous waste." If it is a listed waste, it is obviously very easy for the generator to determine the waste is hazardous. All that must be done is for the generator to check to see if the waste is on one of the EPA's published lists. If not listed, then the generator is required to determine whether the waste exhibits a hazardous characteristic. This is done either by (1) testing the waste through specific test methods set forth in the regulations, or (2) by the generator "applying knowledge" of hazard characteristics of the waste in the light of what the generator knows about the materials or the processes used to generate the waste. Thus no testing must be done if the generator "applies knowledge" in this manner. The standards for both testing and applied knowledge are extremely vague. No guidance is given for the "applying knowledge" standard. Further, the regulations do not state what portion of a waste must be tested, or how often testing must occur.

D. Non-hazardous Solid Waste

RCRA establishes a limited regulatory program for the disposal of non-hazardous solid waste. Upon the statute's original enactment in 1976, the non-hazardous waste program under RCRA was almost exclusively a non-regulatory program to encourage states to improve solid waste management planning. However, the Hazardous and Solid Wastes Amendments of 1984 established minimum national standards for municipal landfills at which non-hazardous solid waste may be legally disposed. RCRA establishes a ban on the dumping of non-hazardous solid waste at any location other than a "sanitary" or "municipal" landfill regulated by RCRA.

E. Underground Storage Tanks

RCRA establishes a separate program for the regulation of the storage of materials in underground storage tanks (USTs). USTs containing both a range of unused products (including gasoline) and wastes (other than the hazardous wastes already regulated under RCRA) are included within the program. EPA regulations under the program impose tank design and certain release detection requirements, including spill, overfill, and corrosion protection and regular leak detection monitoring and reporting. The program also imposes requirements relating to standards for the cleanup of contamination from leaking USTs. Owners and operators of USTs covered under RCRA are required to register their tanks, upgrade their tanks to meet certain minimum technology requirements, and ensure that USTs are properly closed when not in use.

F. Used Oil

RCRA separately regulates used oil even if that oil is not a hazardous waste. The statute imposes management requirements affecting the storage, transportation, processing, and recycling of used oil, and on the burning of used oil as a fuel. For generators of used oil, the requirements establish storage standards. For transporters, sellers, and recyclers of used oil, additional tracking and paperwork requirements are imposed.

IV. COMPREHENSIVE ENVIRONMENTAL RESPONSE, COMPENSATION AND LIABILITY ACT (CERCLA)

A. The Problem of Abandoned Hazardous Waste Dump Sites

With the enactment of RCRA in 1976, Congress believed it had passed the last comprehensive environmental regulatory program needed during "the decade of the environment" of the 1970s. This view was shattered by the Love Canal disaster which came to the forefront of the national consciousness less than two years later. In the late 1950s, about 100 homes and a school were built on a 16-acre site that had been transferred to the city of Niagara Falls, New York by the Hooker Chemical Company for the sum of one dollar. Prior to the transfer of this property, the company had used an abandoned canal as a municipal and industrial chemical dumpsite for nearly 30 years. In 1953, the company covered the canal with earth and sold the property to the city. Following unusually heavy rains in 1978, a chemical soup began percolating upward through the soil forming puddles in back yards of homes and seeping into residential basements. Corroding waste-disposal drums began to break up through the ground and into residents' yards. Eventually, eighty-two different chemical compounds were found, including 11 suspected cancer causing substances.

Emergency financial aid was approved by Congress and the President, and 1000 families on and surrounding Love Canal were eventually relocated. The homes along Love Canal were demolished. The environmental disaster became a national media event leading to an emotional public response directed toward the national government. Love Canal forced a national realization of the dangerous consequences of many decades of unregulated waste management in the United States. Concern grew that hundreds of similar abandoned industrial waste dumpsites existed across the country. Moreover, evidence grew that billions of tons of hazardous wastes had been randomly dumped onto the land, and into lakes, ponds, and other water bodies.

Other similar problems capturing public attention were discovered during this same time frame. During the mid-to late 1970s, a leukemia cluster was observed among the children of Woburn, Massachusetts, where municipal drinking water wells were found to be heavily contaminated with industrial toxins. A toxic tort lawsuit against industrial companies alleged to be responsible for the contamination later became the subject of the influential book (and later movie) *A Civil Action* by Jonathan Harr. News reporting on the alarming statistics of leukemia among the children of Woburn in the late 1970s also drew national attention at the time that Love Canal was also viewed by the public as evidence of a looming national environmental crisis.

B. Congressional Enactment of CERCLA

RCRA's enactment in 1976 was intended to establish a system to ensure that wastes coming out of factories and industries going forward would be managed and disposed of in an environmentally sound manner. However, as vividly evidenced by the Love Canal crisis two years later, RCRA did not include a strategy to clean up many decades of past contamination problems. Congress responded to this problem in 1980 when it created the "Superfund" program in the Comprehensive Environmental Response, Compensation and Liability Act (CERCLA). The "Superfund" name derives from the part of CERCLA that established a trust fund to be used by the government to finance cleanups of hazardous substances at abandoned dump sites. In addition to the trust fund, CERCLA imposed a comprehensive liability scheme designed to impose financial responsibility and liability on parties responsible for such contamination.

RCRA and CERCLA are very different types of statutes, but in many ways the two programs compliment each other. Both statutes deal primarily with wastes that are or have been placed on the land and contaminate or could contaminate soil or ground or surface waters. However, CERCLA's focus is on the past; remediation of contamination caused by past waste handling and disposal practices. Further, CERCLA is a liability statute, not a traditional regulatory program that requires anyone to do anything. Instead, CERCLA gives the government the power to compel parties to clean up past contamination or to hold them financially responsible for the costs of that clean up. CERCLA imposes strict liability and financial responsibility for past disposal of waste, even if the disposal in question was completely legal at the time it occurred. Moreover, the liability created by CERCLA is retroactive without limit. This means that it makes no difference to liability under CERCLA how far back in the past the disposal happened.

RCRA, on the other hand, is focused on the present in an attempt to protect the future. That is, RCRA does not deal with abandoned waste sites or past mistakes; RCRA deals with managing what is coming out of the factories now. Unlike CERCLA, RCRA is very much a traditional regulatory program which imposes numerous obligations on the behavior of generators, transporters, and those treating, storing, and disposing of waste. RCRA's primary goal is to prevent the sort of past problems dealt with by CERCLA (the abandoned waste disposal issues exemplified by Love Canal) from happening in the future.

Although in a different manner than RCRA, CERCLA is intended to affect future behavior as well. Financial liability under CERCLA can be absolutely enormous given that clean up of extensive contamination of soil and ground or surface waters can cost millions of dollars. Thus CERCLA's liability provisions have the potential to significantly affect the future behavior of individuals involved in the generation, transportation and disposal of hazardous materials. No one is interested in incurring future CERCLA liability; thus businesses and industry have substantial incentives to avoid carelessness in dealing with these types of substances, and in reconsidering the raw materials used in manufacturing products, or the types of substances utilized during manufacturing processes and operations. There is a significant market-oriented, incentive based deterrent effect inherent in CERCLA that influences individuals to channel future behavior along desirable avenues and away from undesirable ones. This forward looking part of the function of CERCLA can be compared to the similarly forward looking aspect of RCRA.

C. CERCLA Jurisdiction

CERCLA authorizes the EPA to take action whenever (1) "any hazardous substance is released or there is a threat of such a release into the environment," or (2) "there is a release or substantial threat of release into the environment of any pollutant or contaminant which may present an imminent and substantial danger to the public health or welfare." Thus the EPA's authority under CERCLA generally requires only the presence of a "release" or "threatened release" of a "hazardous substance" into the environment. The extreme breadth of these terms gives the EPA a very expansive jurisdiction under CERCLA.

1. Releases and Threatened Releases

Congress defined the term "release" extremely broadly in CERCLA. The statute defines a "release" as "any spilling, leaking, pumping, pouring, emitting, emptying, discharging, injecting, escaping, leaching, dumping, or disposing into the environment (including the abandonment or discarding of barrels, containers, and other closed receptacles containing any hazardous substance or pollutant or contaminant) . . ." In addition, there is no quantitative requirement imposed on the term "release." Thus even a miniscule amount of release of a "hazardous substance" into the environment will fall within the statutory definition of "release."

CERCLA also authorizes response and imposes liability for actions taken in response to a "threatened releases." Thus an actual release may not be required before the EPA is authorized to act under CERCLA. The courts have indicated that a threatened release may be established by evidence that hazardous substances are present at some location together with a lack of willingness by any party to assert present control over those substances.

2. Hazardous Substances

The term "hazardous substance" is defined in CERCLA primarily through a process of references to other federal environmental statutes. CERCLA hazardous substances include:

- any toxic pollutants or hazardous substances designated pursuant to the Clean Water Act;
- any listed or characteristic hazardous wastes under the Resource Conservation and Recovery Act;
- any hazardous air pollutants under the Clean Air Act;
- any imminently hazardous chemical substances or mixtures with respect to which EPA has taken action under the Toxic Substances Control Act; and
- any other substance specifically designated as hazardous by the EPA in lists published in the Code of Federal Regulations pursuant to CERCLA.

Like the term "release," CERCLA imposes no minimum quantitative threshold for a hazardous substance. Thus CERCLA imposes liability when a release of a hazardous substance occurs regardless of the amount of the hazardous substance present. Although the terms used in RCRA and CERCLA seem similar, the concept of a "hazardous substance" under CERCLA is far broader than the concept of a "hazardous waste" under RCRA. As indicated in the above list, every hazardous waste under RCRA will be a hazardous substance under CERCLA. However, the opposite is not true. Not every CERCLA hazardous substance is a hazardous waste under RCRA.

CERCLA contains a number of exemptions of releases of hazardous substances that might otherwise fall under the coverage of the statute. The following are excluded from coverage as "hazardous substances" under CERCLA:

- Applications of pesticides registered under the Federal Insecticide, Fungicide, and Rodenticide Act;
- "Federally permitted releases" which would include releases authorized by permits issued under the Clean Water Act, the Clean Air Act or the Resource Conservation and Recovery Act; and
- Petroleum products (oil, gasoline, etc.), although this exemption only applies to new products not used products. For example, putting new oil into an engine is within the petroleum products exception, but spilling the used oil out of the same engine is outside the exception (that is, it is considered a CERCLA hazardous substance after it is used).

D. EPA Options Under CERCLA

CERCLA provides the EPA with four options for responding to releases of hazardous substances into the environment. First, the EPA has the option of investigating or cleaning up the contaminated property itself and to then seek reimbursement from any party designated as a "potentially responsible party" (PRPs) under CERLCA. Second, instead of investigating or cleaning up itself, the EPA may go to federal district court to obtain an order compelling any PRP or group of PRPs to conduct any necessary investigations or cleanup activities. Third, CERCLA authorizes the EPA to issue one or more PRPs a unilateral order requiring them to conduct such activities. Because the EPA is authorized to issue an order without going to court, the EPA rarely seeks a court order. Finally, prior to obtaining or issuing an order, the EPA may negotiate a settlement with some or all of the PRPs under which they agree to undertake any necessary response actions.

E. CERCLA Liability

1. Potentially Responsible Parties (PRPs)

Persons designated as PRPs under CERCLA may be liable to the government and to other private parties for the cost of cleaning up hazardous substances. Although CERCLA is a liability scheme based on common law tort principles, an important difference between CERCLA and common law liability is the much greater breadth of persons potentially liable and the extent of that liability under CERCLA. CERCLA casts its liability net around numerous persons who would not be held responsible under traditional common law tort principles. There are four categories of PRPs identified in CERCLA.

The first category of PRPs is the current owner or operator of a facility or disposal site at which hazardous substances are located. Either the owner or an operator may be liable; that is, a person may be liable as an "operator" of a disposal site containing hazardous substances even if that person does not also own the site. Moreover, the current owner or operator of a site at which hazardous substances have been released are liable regardless of whether either had any involvement with or responsibility for that release. Subject to the possibility of defenses under CERCLA discussed below, a current owner or operator is liable merely because of the fact that they either own or operate the site in question.

The second category of PRPs under CERCLA is any parties who either owned or operated the facility or site at the time that hazardous substances were disposed there. Past owners or operators of a site at the time disposal of hazardous substances occurred are thus liable even if they no longer own or operate the property.

The third CERCLA category of PRPs include any parties who "arranged for disposal or treatment" of any of their hazardous substances at the facility or site where a disposal occurred. This category typically involves the liability of generators of hazardous substances who send their wastes to another facility or site for disposal. For large disposal sites, literally hundreds of generators whose wastes were sent to that site may be PRPs. This "generator liability" as imposed by CERCLA is considered one of the most substantial expansions of liability from that imposed under common law. The fact that possession and, indeed, ownership of the hazardous substances has passed to another party (generally a waste handler or disposer who agrees to take it off of the generator's hands in exchange for payment) does not also transfer responsibility for those substances under CERCLA. Under CERCLA, the generator of hazardous substances that arranged for disposal at another party's disposal site remains responsible for clean up costs associated with that waste. For CERCLA's purposes, such a generator of waste will be responsible for that waste forever.

The final category of PRPs under CERCLA includes any parties who both chose the site at which the hazardous substances are located and transported the hazardous substances to it. This is known as "transporter" liability under CERCLA. Thus a transporter of hazardous substances is liable only if the transporter, rather than the generator, selected the disposal site to which the substances are transported.

2. Extent of Liability

The standard of liability under CERCLA is known as an "endangerment" standard, rather than a causation standard. Under traditional common law liability principles, a person would be liable if unreasonably careless or negligent in managing hazardous substances and their substances could be demonstrated to have caused specific harm to specific property. CERCLA, however, imposes a much more relaxed standard of liability than imposed under common law liability principles. All that is necessary to establish liability under CERCLA is a "release" or "threat of release" of a hazardous substance into the environment, and the result is that any persons identified as PRPs under the statute are strictly liable for the costs of cleaning up and preventing such releases. This "strict liability" standard means that PRPs are liable without regard to their culpability or fault for the presence of hazardous substances at the disposal site. Thus CERCLA eliminates any need for the government to prove that hazardous substances were released into the environment as a result of a PRP's intentional or unreasonable conduct.

Moreover, the burdens of factual uncertainties in CERCLA actions are generally borne by PRPs rather than the government. In a typical hazardous waste dump site, the waste may be contained in unmarked drums, or even if contained in marked drums, has been released through spillage or leakage with hundreds and thousands of other substances to make a single giant chemical slop. In such circumstances, distinguishing one generator's waste from that of another is virtually impossible. Generator PRPs typically demand in court that the government be required to prove a causal nexus between their specific waste and specific costs incurred by the government to clean up a site. Said another way, generators demand that the government prove its waste is present at the disposal site and was the subject of a specific removal before that generator can be held liable.

The courts have routinely rejected such arguments. Instead, the courts have held that, in order to impose liability on a given generator, the government need only demonstrate that the generator's wastes in fact arrived at the disposal site and that the type of hazardous substances contained in that generator's waste are also found at the site. The government is not required to specifically prove how much of any particular generator's waste was included in the overall costs of cleaning up a particular disposal site. Courts state that such relaxed liability requirements further Congress's remedial purposes in CERCLA, which are to ensure prompt clean up of contaminated hazardous waste disposal sites and to assign responsibility for clean up costs to responsible parties.

The liability of PRPs under CERCLA is also considered to be "joint and several." Joint and several liability means that the government has the option to sue all PRPs jointly in the same action, or, instead, to proceed severally only against any one of them. If the government chooses to proceed severally against only one PRP out of an entire group of jointly liable PRPs, the chosen party can be held liable in the several action for 100% of the cost of a cleanup even if that PRP only contributed a small percentage of the hazardous substances at a disposal site. As with many other aspects of the relaxed liability standards under CERCLA, joint and several liability lessens the burdens on the government and increases the difficulties faced by PRPs.

Congress has included a number of provisions in CERCLA to lessen the harshness and potential unfairness of joint and several liability. First, the EPA is authorized to offer early settlements (known as "de minimis" settlements) to PRPs the agency believes are responsible for only a relatively small portion of the harm. Second, PRPs that have paid costs to clean up hazardous substances at a disposal site have a statutory right to pursue a private cost recovery action against other PRPs. Further, PRPs are granted a statutory cause of action for contribution in CERCLA against other PRPs. Thus even if a PRP is "jointly and severally" liable for 100% of cleanup costs at a disposal site, courts may divide up costs among all the liable PRPs in a contribution action using such equitable factors as the court determines are appropriate.

3. Defenses to CERCLA Liability

CERCLA establishes a limited number of narrow defenses to liability that may be asserted by PRPs. The first defense to liability is if the sole cause of the release of the hazardous substance was an "act of God." This is an extremely difficult defense upon which to win given how narrowly it has been construed by the courts. For example, courts have held that unusually heavy rains causing flooding (which in turn causes a release of hazardous substances) is not an "act of God." Additionally, CERCLA provides a defense when an "act of War" is the sole cause of a release of hazardous substances. To date, no case has successfully asserted such a defense.

A defense providing a greater likelihood of relief under CERCLA is the "third party" defense. Typical situations under which such a defense might arise are the "midnight dumper" scenario (where an unknown person trespasses onto property to dump hazardous substances) or when property is contaminated by the acts of an adjacent landowner.

However, the third party defense is limited. A PRP may not assert the defense if it has a direct or indirect contractual relationship with the third party. Further, a PRP may not assert the defense if it failed to act with reasonable care once the hazardous substances are discovered (such as by notifying authorities promptly). The defense may also be lost if the PRP failed to take reasonable precautions in advance against the possibility of such acts by third parties.

A more specific form of the "third party" defense is the "innocent purchaser" defense which may be asserted by a current owner of property found to be contaminated by hazardous substances. To assert this defense, however, the current owner must establish that, at the time of the purchase of the property, he "did not know and had no reason to know" about the existence of the hazardous substances. This requires that the current owner establish that he undertook "appropriate inquiry" into the status of the property prior to purchasing the property. What will constitute "appropriate inquiry" generally depends upon the specific circumstances. However, for purchases of commercial or business property, "appropriate inquiry" at least will require the purchaser to conduct an environmental audit to assess the environmental conditions of the property.

F. Scope of Cleanup

CERCLA authorizes the EPA to expend Superfund dollars in response to releases and threatened releases of hazardous substances. The primary limitation is that EPA's actions must be consistent with the National Contingency Plan (NCP), which establishes a complex set of both procedural and substantive rules governing EPA's response to actual or threatened contamination.

CERCLA contemplates two different types of cleanup responses that may be undertaken at a particular disposal site. The first, "removal actions," are typically short-term response actions to quickly address releases or threatened releases requiring prompt response. Removal actions are generally classified as either "emergency," "time-critical," or "non-time critical." The second type of response is known as a "remedial action" and is usually a more long-term response action than a removal action. A "remedial action" is intended to permanently and significantly reduce the risks associated with releases or threatened releases of hazardous substances that are serious but are not an emergency or time-critical as is generally the case for a removal action. The NCP forbids the EPA from utilizing the Superfund to undertake the more extensive cleanup measures typical of "remedial actions" unless the relevant disposal site qualifies for listing on the National Priorities List (NPL).

The NPL is a listing of the most contaminated CERCLA sites around the country.

The NCP requires that CERCLA cleanup decisions be made through a prolonged process that includes several different steps and provides opportunities for involvement on behalf of both the affected state and local governments and the general public. The process includes some or all of the following:

- *Preliminary assessment and site investigation* (PA/SI): At this point, a disposal site is evaluated for potential placement on the NPL by use of the Hazard Ranking System, a scoring system to assess such factors as the toxicity of the substances present on the property, the threat to drinking water supplies, and the number of people living near the site. At this point, the decision whether to implement a short-term removal action or investigate the merit of implementing longer-term remedial action will be considered.
- *Remedial investigation and feasibility study* (RI/FS): This is the heart of the CERCLA remedy selection process and is intended to assess site conditions and evaluate alternatives to the extent necessary to select a remedy. The goal is to gather sufficient data to characterize the conditions at the site for the purpose of developing and evaluating effective remedial options.
- Issuance of a proposed plan, providing an opportunity for public comment on the proposal, and the issuance of a record of the EPA's final decision (ROD).

The most controversial and complex questions under CERCLA involve the appropriate scope of cleanup. CERCLA establishes highly detailed (some argue convoluted) cleanup standards and guiding principles. All remedial actions must satisfy the following requirements as to the scope of the cleanup that must be undertaken. First, the response action must attain a degree of cleanup that assures protection of human health and the environment. This is considered a "threshold criteria" by the NCP, meaning if a cleanup plan does not meet this standard it is automatically not approved. Second, with regard to any hazardous substances that will remain after the cleanup is completed, they must, in most circumstances, meet all "applicable" and/or "relevant and appropriate" requirements under federal and state law (ARAs). The cleanup must also utilize permanent solutions and alternative treatment technologies or resource recovery technologies to the maximum extent practicable. It must further provide for a cost-effective response, taking into account the total long and short term costs of the response action. And, finally, the cleanup must be conducted in accordance with the NCP to the extent practicable.

CHAPTER 7: THE NATIONAL ENVIRONMENTAL POLICY ACT

I. NEPA'S HISTORICAL CONTEXT

NEPA was the first major federal environmental law statute in the United States and is often referred to as the "Magna Carta" of this country's national environmental laws. Congress enacted the National Environmental Policy Act (NEPA) in December 1969. On January 1, 1970, President Richard M. Nixon signed NEPA into law on national television, declaring that the 1970s would be the "decade of the environment." This event ushered in the modern environmental regulatory era in the United States.

Congress's enactment of NEPA came at the end of the tumultuous decade of the 1960s in which the risks of a polluted environment came to the forefront of the national public consciousness. The publication in 1962 of Rachel Carson's book *Silent Spring* was a watershed event energizing public concern over health and environmental risks created by polluting activities. Widely publicized environmental disasters during the 1960s were also leading catalysts for growing public environmental alarm. Notable examples include the burning of the Cuyahoga River in Cleveland, Ohio and the massive Santa Barbara oil spill off the coast of California, both of which occurred in 1969 prior to the enactment of NEPA at the end of that year. Creation of the U.S. Environmental Protection Agency (EPA) and enactment of the Clean Air Act of 1970 occurred the following year.

NEPA helped pave the way for the more than a dozen major federal environmental regulatory programs enacted by Congress over the next ten years. From the signing of NEPA on New Year's Day 1970 through the end of 1980, virtually all of the major legislation constituting the modern federal environmental regulatory system was enacted by Congress. This includes such notable statutes as the Clean Water Act of 1972, the Coastal Zone Management Act of 1972, the Federal Environmental Pesticide Control Act of 1972, the Endangered Species Act of 1973, the Safe Drinking Water Act of 1974, the Resource Conservation and Recovery Act of 1976 (RCRA), the Toxic Substances Control Act of 1976, and the Comprehensive Environmental Response, Compensation and Liability Act of 1980 (CERCLA or "Superfund").

II. NEPA'S DECLARATION OF ENVIRONMENTAL POLICY

The preamble to NEPA states that among its purposes are:

> To declare national policy which will encourage productive and enjoyable harmony between man and his environment; to promote efforts which will prevent or eliminate damage to the environment and biosphere and stimulate the health and welfare of man; [and] to enrich the understanding of the ecological systems and natural resources important to the Nation . . .

In this regard, NEPA directs the federal government to use all "practicable means and measures" to create conditions under which the policy objectives of the statute may be realized while at the same time fulfilling "the social, economic, and other requirements of present and future generations of Americans." NEPA further directs the federal government "to improve and coordinate Federal plans, functions, programs, and resources" in order to carry out the policies set forth in the statute.

The congressional declaration of policy in NEPA includes the following aspirational goals:

- fulfill the responsibilities of each generation as trustee of the environment for succeeding generations;
- assure for all Americans safe, healthful, productive, and aesthetically and culturally pleasing surroundings;
- attain the widest range of beneficial uses of the environment without the degradation, risk to health or safety, or other undesirable and unintended consequences;
- preserve important historic, cultural, and natural aspects of our national heritage, and maintain, wherever possible, an environment which supports diversity, and variety of individual choice;

- achieve a balance between population and resource use which will permit high standards of living and a wide sharing of life's amenities; and
- enhance the quality of renewable resources and approach the maximum attainable recycling of depletable resources.

NEPA also emphasizes that, to the fullest extent possible, the policies, regulations, and public laws of the United States should be interpreted and administered in accordance with the policies set forth in the statute.

III. NEPA'S PURPOSES

NEPA is an unusual statute in comparison to most federal environmental regulatory programs. Unlike many of the statutes enacted by Congress in the decade following NEPA's enactment, NEPA does not directly regulate the polluting or other environmental risk causing behavior of business and industry. Instead, NEPA focuses on the manner in which decision-making is conducted within the federal government, specifically by federal agencies.

In NEPA, Congress recognized that actions of the federal government may cause significant environmental effects. Thus NEPA requires federal government agencies to utilize a specific process to assess the environmental effects of proposed actions prior to making decisions to undertake them. The process that NEPA establishes to evaluate the potential environmental effects of proposed actions applies to all agencies in the executive branch of the federal government. NEPA does not apply, however, to the President, Congress, or the federal courts, nor does it apply to individuals, businesses, or corporations. NEPA also does not apply to state governments, although many, but certainly not all, states have statutes quite similar to NEPA that operate with respect to state agencies. These state environmental policy acts are often referred to as SEPAs.

To ensure that federal agencies meet their responsibilities under NEPA, Congress established the Council on Environmental Quality (CEQ) in NEPA. Congress placed CEQ in the Executive Office of the President and gave it the authority to issue regulations that implement the procedural requirements of NEPA that federal agencies must follow. CEQ also reviews and approves NEPA procedures that federal agencies create for purposes of complying with their responsibilities under the statute. NEPA also requires an annual national Environmental Quality Report from the President to Congress which is the responsibility of CEQ to prepare and transmit.

IV. ENVIRONMENTAL IMPACT STATEMENTS

The most important aspect of NEPA is the requirement that federal agencies take environmental factors into consideration when making significant decisions. Specifically, federal agencies must prepare detailed statements assessing the environmental impact of any "major federal actions significantly affecting the quality of the human environment." These detailed statements are commonly referred to as environmental impact statements (EIS). NEPA expressly requires that these statements analyze:

- the environmental impact of the proposed action;
- any adverse environmental effects which cannot be avoided should the proposal be implemented;
- alternatives to the proposed action;
- the relationship between local short-term uses of man's environment and the maintenance and enhancement of long-term productivity; and
- any irreversible and irretrievable commitments of resources which would be involved in the proposed action should it be implemented.

Importantly, NEPA does not require an EIS every single time a federal agency proposes or undertakes to do something. A proposed undertaking must both qualify as "major federal action" and have the potential to "significantly affect" the environment before the requirement that a federal agency prepare an EIS is triggered.

A. "Major Federal Action"

The key statutory phrase "major federal action" has been interpreted broadly by the courts. Thus the range of actions to which NEPA potentially applies is extremely broad. Certainly, "major federal action" includes direct involvement by a federal agency in an action, such as an agency decision to construct a publicly owned building or road or to create a plan to manage and develop federally owned land. More generally, a proposed action is "major federal action" if some federal agency has the power to regulate, prohibit, or otherwise control the action. Thus federal agency approvals of projects or programs, or approval of grants, licenses and permits for private activities, may also be subject to NEPA. Further, any project which includes federal funding from any source or some other commitment of federal resources will be enough to qualify that project as "major federal action." As a practical matter, the federal government takes hundreds of actions every day that are, in some way, covered by NEPA.

B. "Significant Affect"

In addition to qualifying as "major federal action," a proposal also must have the potential to "significantly affect the quality of the human environment" in order to trigger NEPA's EIS requirement. The statutory phrase "significantly affecting the quality of the human environment" has also been broadly interpreted by the courts. Certainly, a federal agency decision to undertake some action that would lead to air pollution or water pollution or threats to endangered species or their habitats would constitute a "significant environmental impact." However, the concept of a "significant environmental impact" is not limited only to the impacts of federal agency actions on the natural environment. NEPA's emphasis on "the *human* environment" indicates that the statute addresses broader concerns. Thus courts have found that the affects of federal actions on interests such as public health, housing, unemployment, crime, or other matters affecting the quality of human life may also fall within the scope of the statute's coverage.

In assessing the "significant environmental impact" of a project, it is not only the incremental change that this project will have on the environment that is important. The cumulative effect of many related projects must also be taken into consideration. Thus an individual subdevelopment on a large island may not have a significant impact; however, by the 15th subdevelopment the cumulative impact may be quite significant. In order to assure that the island will not gradually be covered without the environmental impact ever being studied, at some point, a developer may be required to do an EIS, not just to the incremental impact of his or her project, but to look at the cumulative impact from all of the development that has already taken place.

Additionally, if cumulative impact can be thought of as development that occurred in the past, reasonably foreseeable future impacts caused by a given development must also be considered under NEPA's "indirect effects" analysis. For instance, when an interchange is built so that two roads now converge where they did not in the past, the direct impact may be thought of as the clearing of vegetation, leveling of the land, and the laying of the asphalt. This may not constitute a significant impact. Under the indirect effects analysis, however, NEPA requires consideration of reasonably foreseeable additional development caused by this new interchange. Even unrelated, private development (such as new hotels, gas stations, restaurants, and living units) may be considered part of the impact from the project.

C. The Purpose of the EIS

The purpose of preparation of an EIS is to allow federal agency decision makers to make informed decisions. NEPA contemplates an evaluation of the environmental effects of a federal undertaking including consideration of potential alternatives to the proposed course of action. This evaluation is intended to occur prior to any final decision by the agency as to what course of action it will undertake regarding the proposal, if any. Thus the NEPA process—including preparation of an EIS if required and consideration of the information contained in that analysis —must be completed before an agency makes a final decision on the proposed action. Importantly, NEPA does not require the decision makers to select the most environmentally preferably alternative action or prohibit potentially adverse environmental effects. Concerns and policy considerations in addition to significant environmental impacts of the action (such as, for example, economic, social, or national security) may be given greater weight in the decision making process by federal agencies. However, NEPA requires that the decision makers be informed of the potential environmental consequences of their decisions prior to making a final decision.

V. THE NEPA PROCESS

The NEPA process begins when a federal agency develops a proposal to address a need to take some action. The need to take an action may be something the agency identifies itself, or it may be a need to make a decision brought to it by someone outside of the agency, such as an application by a private party for a federally required license or permit. With respect to the proposed action, the agency must decide if the "major federal action significantly affecting the quality of the human environment" test is met. If it is, the agency is required to prepare an EIS. Two different levels of analysis are undertaken by the agency to make the "significant environmental impact" determination. The first level is known as a "categorical" analysis. The other level is known as an "environmental assessment" (EA).

A. Categorical Analysis

CEQ regulations direct federal agencies to determine whether proposals for agency action fall within either of two categories: (1) actions that normally require preparation of an EIS, or (2) actions that normally do *not* require a detailed environmental analysis. The reason that an action would or would not normally require preparation of an EIS is because the agency has determined in advance that actions falling within these categories have (or do not have) a significant effect on the quality of the human environment. Thus if an action falls within the first category, the agency *presumes* an EIS should be prepared prior to a decision to undertake that action and proceeds to do so. If an action falls within the second category, the agency *presumes* an EIS should not be prepared (known as a "categorical exclusion" or CE) and therefore does not do so.

Agencies develop lists of proposed actions that will fall into either of these presumptive categories. Such lists are developed based on the agency's prior experience with certain types of actions. Such prior experience usually comes by way of previous environmental analyses conducted by the agency under NEPA. Through these past analyses, the agency learns that particular types of action normally do or do not have significant environmental effects. Thus because similar actions likely will need to be undertaken in the future, the agency will continually update its lists of actions for which an EIS is categorically presumed to be either necessary or unnecessary. Thus when a decision must be made in the future as to whether to undertake an action included on either of these lists, the agency has determined in advance whether that action has the potential to cause significant environmental effects and thus requires preparation of an EIS.

B. Environmental Assessment

Many proposed "major federal actions," however, will not clearly fall within either of the two presumptive categories. Thus for these proposed actions, an EIS will be neither categorically excluded nor categorically presumed to be necessary. In such cases, a federal agency must prepare a written "environmental assessment" (EA) to determine whether the proposed action would significantly affect the environment (thus requiring preparation of an EIS). An EA is a "mini-EIS" designed to provide sufficient information to allow the agency to decide whether preparation of a full-blown EIS is necessary. The EA will include brief discussions of the following:

- the need for the proposed action;
- alternatives to the proposal (if there are unresolved conflicts concerning alternative uses of available resources);
- the environmental impacts of the proposed action and alternatives; and
- a listing of agencies and persons consulted.

If the EA determines that the environmental affects of a proposed federal action may be significant, an EIS will be prepared. If, instead, the EA determines the opposite, the agency issues a "finding of no significant impact" (FONSI), and no EIS is done. A FONSI is a document that sets out the reasons why the agency has determined that no significant environmental impacts are expected to occur if the proposed action is undertaken.

C. Notice of Intent and Scoping

If it is determined that an EIS is required for a particular proposal, the federal agency will publish a Notice of Intent (NOI) stating its intent to prepare the EIS. This notice is published in the *Federal Register*, a daily publication that provides notice to the public of federal agency actions. The NOI will provide a description of the proposed action and describe the "scoping process" that will be conducted by the agency in preparation to draft the EIS. The purpose of the "scoping process" is to define the scope of issues to be addressed in the analysis that will be included in the EIS. In particular, the "scoping process" will:

- identify people or organizations who are interested in the proposed action;
- identify the significant issues to be analyzed in the EIS;
- identify and eliminate from detailed review issues that are insignificant or that have been adequately covered in prior environmental reviews;
- determine the roles and responsibilities of lead and cooperating federal agencies;
- identify any related EAs or EISs;
- identify gaps in data and informational needs;
- set the time limits for the process and page limits for the EIS;
- identify other environmental review and consultation requirements so they can be integrated with the EIS; and
- indicate the relationship between the development of the environmental analysis and the agency's tentative decision making schedule.

As part of the scoping process, federal agencies are required to identify and invite the participation of interested persons, including the public. As such, the public has an important role to play in the scoping process by providing input on what issues should be addressed in the EIS. There are a number of ways the agency may involve the public in the process, including scheduling public meetings, conference calls, formal hearings or informal workshops seeking input from interested persons and communities on the proposed action. This involvement in the scoping process provides opportunities for the public to present views and information on potential environmental impacts of the proposed action. Similarly, the public can assist the agency by identifying or developing alternatives to the proposed action that can be evaluated in the EIS.

D. Notice of Draft EIS and Public Comment Period

The next step in the NEPA process is preparation of a draft EIS that must be submitted for public review and comment. The comment period is typically 45 days long, but can be longer in individual cases. The Environmental Protection Agency publishes public notices in the Federal Register that draft EISs are available for comment. The federal agency in question may also communicate notice to the public that a draft EIS is available for public comment on websites or through local news sources. During the public comment period, the agency also may conduct public meetings or hearings as a way to solicit comments. As during the scoping process, submitting comments is another way for the public to provide input on potential environmental impacts of the proposed action and possible alternatives.

CEQ regulations require agencies to include a "Purpose and Need" statement in the draft EIS describing what it is trying to achieve by proposing the action in question. This identifies why the agency believes the action is necessary and serves as a basis for identifying reasonable alternatives that substantially meet the agency's purpose and need. Evaluation of alternative means of achieving the agency's purpose and need is the primary objective of the analysis conducted in an EIS. CEQ regulations require agencies to "objectively evaluate all reasonable alternatives, and for alternatives which were eliminated from detailed study, briefly discuss the reasons for their having been eliminated." Even for proposed actions as simple as considering an application for a permit or some other federal approval, all reasonable alternatives must be considered by the agency. Among the required alternatives that must be considered is the "no action alternative," which is what would happen if the agency took no action on the proposal. In the draft EIS, the agency is required to evaluate all reasonable alternatives in sufficient detail so that the environmental effects of the various alternatives can be compared and contrasted by the reader.

E. Final EIS

Following the close of the public comment period, the agency must analyze the comments and conduct whatever further analysis that may be necessary. All substantive comments received from other governmental agencies and the public and interested persons must be considered by the agency. After this process, the final EIS is prepared. The agency then publishes the final EIS and the Environmental Protection Agency publishes a public notice in the Federal Register that the document is available. Publication of this notice begins a waiting period of a minimum of 30 days that must pass before the agency can make a decision on the proposed action. The waiting period allows the agency sufficient time for the decision makers to consider the purpose and need for the action and the reasonable alternatives and to make a decision. Again, it bears repeating that the agency decision maker is not required by NEPA to select the most environmentally preferably alternative action or prohibit potentially adverse environmental effects that may result from the decision. Instead, NEPA only requires that the decision makers be informed of the potential environmental consequences of their decision prior to making the final decision.

F. Record of Decision

The final step in the EIS process is the Record of Decision (ROD). The ROD is a public record of the agency's decision addressing how the findings of the EIS, including consideration of alternatives, were incorporated into the agency's decision making process. The ROD will also identify all factors, including non environmentally related factors, that were contemplated when the agency reached its decision on whether to proceed with the proposed action. CEQ regulations also require the ROD to discuss whether all practical means to avoid or minimize environmental harm were adopted, and if not, why they were not. The ROD is a publicly available document that can be obtained directly from the federal agency in question and is sometimes published in the Federal Register or on the agency's website.

CHAPTER 8: ENDANGERED SPECIES

I. THE ENDANGERED SPECIES ACT

Species and habitat endangerment are among the most urgent environmental problems facing the nation. Without protection, many species and the benefits they provide could be lost forever. Endangered species and their habitats are protected under the Endangered Species Act (ESA).

The purpose of the ESA is to protect and recover imperiled species and their habitats. It is administered by the Department of the Interior's U.S. Fish and Wildlife Service (FWS) and the Department of Commerce's National Marine Fisheries Service (NMFS). The FWS has primary responsibility for terrestrial and freshwater organisms, while the responsibilities of the NMFS are mainly marine wildlife. Anything living or a part thereof is covered.

The ESA requires the Secretaries of Commerce and Interior to determine whether any species is endangered and to designate critical habitat, based on the best scientific data available. The ESA also requires consultation among various agencies to ensure that their actions do not jeopardize any endangered species. Section 9 of the ESA forbids "taking" any endangered species.

Under the ESA, species may be listed as either endangered or threatened. All species of plants and animals, except pest insects, are eligible for listing as endangered or threatened. A "species" under the act can be a true taxonomic species, a subspecies, or in the case of vertebrates, a "distinct population segment." In other words, very specialized, distinct branches of animals and plants are recognized for protection. A species is "endangered" only if it is in danger of extinction throughout all or a significant portion of its range.

"Threatened" species are likely to become endangered in the foreseeable future. Even though a species may have a healthy viable population in one area, it could be threatened with extinction in another locale. The category of threatened species would also include species that have been "successfully restored" and removed from the endangered list, but are still in need of protection.

The ESA encourages states to develop and maintain conservation programs for threatened and endangered species. Federal funding is available to promote the development of programs for management of threatened and endangered species. Pursuant to these provisions, each state prepares a list of endangered and threatened species within its boundaries. These state lists often include species which are considered endangered or threatened within a specific state but not within all states, and which therefore are not included on the national list of endangered or threatened species. Some state laws and regulations are more protective of species and their habitats than is the ESA.

Within the statute, the term "Secretary" refers to the agency head who has authority for the implementation of respective sections of the ESA. The power vests according to the type of species. The Secretary of the Interior is responsible for land animals and freshwater fish, while the Secretary of Commerce takes the lead for marine mammals and saltwater fish; and the Secretary of Agriculture is in charge when it comes to the import and export of animals and plants.

A. Identifying Endangered Species

The ESA's primary goals are to prevent the extinction of imperiled plant and animal life and to recover and maintain those populations by removing or reducing threats to their survival. The ESA requires species to be listed as endangered or threatened on the basis of their biological status and threats to their existence.

1. Listing

No species receives full ESA protection until it is listed. The listing process is done solely in accordance with the best scientific and commercial data available. Congress intended for the Secretary to use only biological criteria to determine which species are listed. Economic factors are not considered when listing a species. Species with similar characteristics may be listed jointly or generically to increase protection for the truly endangered subspecies. Public notice is not necessary, but actual notice must also be given to the affected state agencies.

To be considered for listing, the species must meet five criteria that are set forth in the ESA: 1) damage to, or destruction of, a species' habitat;

2) overutilization of the species for commercial, recreational, scientific, or educational purposes; 3) disease or predation; 4) adequacy of existing protection; and 5) other natural or manmade factors that affect the continued existence of the species. When one or more of these factors imperils the survival of a species, the FWS takes action to protect it.

During the listing process, economic factors cannot be considered. The status of the candidate species must be based solely on the best scientific and commercial data available. The ESA provides a process for exempting development projects from the restrictions of the law if a cabinet-level "Endangered Species Committee" decides the benefits of the project clearly outweigh the benefits of conserving a species.

A species can be listed in two ways. The FWS or NMFS can directly list a species through their candidate assessment programs, or anyone may petition the FWS or the NMFS to initiate the listing process. The listing procedures are the same for both types except that the petition process has a 90-day screening period.

After receiving a petition to list a species, the two federal agencies take the following steps, with each step being published in the Federal Register:

1. If a petition indicates that the species is imperiled, a 90-day screening period begins. If the petition does not present substantial information to support listing, it is denied.
2. If the information is substantial, a status review is started. This is a comprehensive assessment of the species' biological status and threats, and it results in a finding of the listing being warranted, not warranted, or warranted but precluded.

A finding of "not warranted" ends the listing process.

A finding of "warranted" means that the agencies will publish a proposed rule within one year of the date of the petition, proposing to list the species as threatened or endangered. Comments are solicited from the public, and one or more public hearings may be held. A public hearing is mandatory if any person has requested one within 45 days of the published notice. Within another year, a final determination (a final rule) must be made on whether to list the species. The final rule time limit may be extended for 6 months and listings may be grouped together according to similar geography, threats, habitat, or taxonomy.

A "warranted but precluded" finding means that other, higher-priority actions will take precedence over this species. This finding results in a deferral under which the species is automatically recycled back through the 12-month process indefinitely until a result of either "not warranted" or "warranted" is determined.

Species that are potential candidates for listing are prioritized, with "emergency listing" given the highest priority. To be put in this category, species must face a "significant risk to their well being." For example, an emergency listing of a rare plant growing in a wetland that is scheduled to be filled in for development purposes would be higher-priority than most other candidates.

The FWS maintains a list of "candidate" species. These are species for which the FWS has enough information to warrant proposing them for listing but is precluded from doing so by higher listing priorities. While listing actions of higher priority go forward, the FWS works with states, tribes, private landowners, and various agencies to protect these species to prevent further decline.

2. Delisting

To delist species, several factors are considered: whether the threats are eliminated or controlled, the population size and growth, and the stability of the habitat quality and quantity. When some of the threats have been controlled and the population has met recovery objectives, the species can be reclassified from "endangered" to "threatened."

As this Almanac was being written, there were just under 2,000 foreign and domestic species on the threatened and endangered lists. About 50 species have been delisted, including the American Bald Eagle, the Gray Wolf, the Red Wolf, the Gray Whale, and the Grizzly Bear. Of the delisted species, about 22 were delisted due to recovery, nine due to extinction (several of which apparently were extinct prior to being listed), seven due to changes in taxonomic classification, five due to discovery of new populations, one due to an error in the listing rule, and one due to an amendment to the ESA. Twenty-three others have been downlisted from "endangered" to "threatened" status.

Some have argued that the recovery of the bald eagle and certain other bird species (notably the brown pelican and the peregrine falcon) is more attributable to the 1973 congressional ban on the pesticide DDT than to the ESA. (DDT impaired the release of calcium from adult birds to their eggs, which caused the eggshells to be thin and subject to breakage. As a result, reproductive failures were widespread until the pesticide was banned. Afterward, the species steadily recovered.) The listing of these species as endangered, however, was a major reason why Congress instituted the DDT ban. In addition, due to the ESA, many actions were undertaken, including captive breeding, habitat protection, and protection from disturbance.

B. "Taking"

The ESA protects endangered and threatened species and their habitats by prohibiting the "taking" of listed animals. "Take" is defined as "to harass, harm, pursue, hunt, shoot, wound, kill, trap, capture, or collect or attempt to engage in any such conduct." Regulations define "harass" as "an intentional or negligent act or omission which creates the likelihood of injury to wildlife by annoying it to such an extent as to significantly disrupt normal behavioral patterns which include, but are not limited to, breeding, feeding, or sheltering." The Supreme Court upheld this broad definition in *Babbitt v. Sweet Home Chapter of Communities for a Great Oregon*, (1995).

Harm is defined in the same regulation as: "an act which actually kills or injures wildlife. Such an act may include significant habitat modification or degradation where it actually kills or injures wildlife by significantly impairing essential behavioral patterns, including breeding, feeding, or sheltering."

Any commercial activity involving a protected species is prohibited. Transport of a protected species is prohibited. Malicious destruction of a species or a habitat under federal jurisdiction is prohibited. The term "take" does not apply to plants, but the interstate or international trade in listed plants and animals, including their parts and products, is restricted. States may also have their own laws restricting activity involving listed species.

Some commentators believe that the ESA may actually encourage habitat destruction by landowners who fear losing the use of their land because of the presence of an endangered species. This has been called "Shoot, Shovel and Shut-Up." Thus a farmer who notes the presence of a listed animal on his property might first kill the animals that are already there and then make the property a less hospitable habitat for other endangered animals. That, of course, would be illegal.

1. Tennessee Valley Authority v. Hill

The 1978 Supreme Court case of *Tennessee Valley Authority v. Hill*, also known as the Snail Darter case, brought national attention to the ESA, the concept of habitat, and a previously unknown endangered fish. The Tennessee Valley Authority (TVA) began building the Tellico Dam on the Little Tennessee River in 1967. The ESA was enacted in 1973. That same year, a distinct species of fish, the Snail Darter (a small perch), was found upstream of the planned dam. In 1975, the Snail Darter was put on the list of endangered species.

By this time, construction of the dam was about 90% complete. Operation of the dam, however, would destroy the Snail Darter's habitat. A group of plaintiffs brought this suit to prevent the TVA from completing or operating the dam (though their real motivation seems to have been a desire to protect their homesteads, not the Snail Darter).

To stop the project would be an enormous waste of federal funds, but on its face the ESA prohibited operation of the dam because it would destroy the habitat of an endangered species, and the ESA makes the value of every endangered species "incalculable."

The federal trial court said that the dam was too far along and refused to enjoin further construction or operation. The court of appeals reversed that holding, saying that the lower court had abused its discretion by ignoring the ESA. The U.S. Supreme Court agreed with the appellate court and said that the ESA required that completion and operation of the dam be enjoined. Congress later went back and permitted the dam to be completed, but only after taking precautions to move a significant population of snail darters to a new habitat. Ironically, it was later found that the Snail Darter was present not only on the affected river, but also on several other rivers in Tennessee. Its status was down-listed from "endangered" to "threatened."

In response to *TVA v. Hill*, Congress amended the ESA to provide an escape hatch in the form of a special committee, the Endangered Species Committee (sometimes called the "God Squad"). This is really an *ad hoc* panel composed of members from the executive branch and at least one appointee from the state where the project is to occur. It can override the normal provisions if there are no reasonable alternatives to the agency action, the benefits clearly outweigh those of compliance with the statute, and the action is in the public interest and has at least regional significance. Five of the seven committee members must vote for the exemption to allow taking of a listed species.

2. Exemptions

The ESA requires federal agencies to consult with the NWS or the NMFS if any project occurs in the habitat of a listed species. If the project might impact a listed species, a biological assessment is prepared by the applying agency, and it is reviewed by the NWS, the NMFS, or both.

The question to be answered is whether a listed species will be harmed by the action and, if so, how the harm can be minimized. If harm cannot be avoided, the project agency can seek an exemption from the Endangered Species Committee. Before that takes place, however, the project agency and either the NWS or the NMFS must consult on the biological implications of the project. The questions in such consultations are whether the species will be harmed, whether the habitat will be harmed, and whether the action will aid or hinder the recovery of the listed species.

If harm is likely to occur, the consultation evaluates whether "reasonable and prudent alternatives" exist to minimize the harm. If an alternative does not exist, the NWS or NMFS will issue an opinion that the action constitutes "jeopardy" to the listed species either directly or indirectly. The project is then stopped unless an exemption is granted by the Endangered Species Committee.

C. Critical Habitats

Degradation of habitat is a critical part of the problem facing endangered species, because species cannot live without their supporting environment. In fact, the leading cause of species endangerment and extinction is loss of habitat, which is often caused by human activity.

The ESA instructs the FWS and the NMFS to designate specific areas as protected "critical habitat" zones on the basis of the best scientific data available, taking into consideration the economic impact and other results of designating the area as a critical habitat. The ESA requires that critical habitat be designated within one year of a species being placed on the endangered list. In general, the agencies try to designate critical habitat at or near the time of listing. The Secretary uses the same listing criteria for both species and habitat.

Critical habitats must include all areas essential to the conservation of the target species. Such lands may be private or public. It all depends upon the physical and biological features of the land that are essential to the conservation of the species. Critical habitat may include areas that are not occupied by the species at the time of listing but that are essential to its conservation. Despite the language of the ESA, most species do not have a critical habitat listed for them.

Critical habitat designations affect federal agency actions and federally funded or permitted activities. Federal agencies are required to avoid "destruction" or "adverse modification" of designated critical habitat. While the regulatory aspect of critical habitat designation does not directly apply to private landowners, approximately two-thirds of all federally listed species have at least some habitat on private land. Large-scale development, construction, logging, mining, and other projects on private land typically require a federal permit and thus become subject to critical habitat regulations.

A habitat may be excluded from protection if, after weighing the best scientific data available along with any other relevant impacts, the Secretary determines that the benefits of exclusion outweigh the benefits of inclusion. Unlike the listing of a species, the economic impact on a particular area may be considered in designating a habitat. An area can be excluded from critical habitat designation if an economic analysis determines that the benefits of excluding it outweigh the benefits of including it, unless failure to designate the area as critical habitat may lead to extinction of the listed species. This exclusion factor is widely used.

Developers have complained bitterly about federal restrictions on private lands. Besides raising Commerce Clause issues and taking claims (discussed in greater detail in Chapter 9, "Restrictions on Development of Private Land," of this Almanac), which so far have been unsuccessful, they have also exerted considerable political pressure on state, local, and federal regulators. Section 9 of the ESA has been particularly controversial with private landowners, because they may be deprived of the right not only to remove animals causing them economic harm, but also to modify areas of their own land that are needed by the endangered species. Not surprisingly, the concept of "property rights" is frequently invoked in support of these claims.

1. Habitat Conservation Plans

The ESA provides relief to landowners who want to develop property inhabited by listed species. Landowners can receive a permit to take such species incidental to otherwise legal activities, provided they have developed an approved Habitat Conservation Plan (HCP). HCPs must include an assessment of the likely impacts on the species from the proposed action, the steps that the permit holder will take to minimize and mitigate the impacts, and the funding available to carry out the steps.

HCPs often permit a degree of development of some tracts of land in return for mitigation measures and development restrictions on other tracts. Many of these HCPs involve small parcels, but several are over 100,000 acres, and some are over a million acres in size.

The applicant seeking a permit to take an endangered species submits a HCP, a notice of the application action is published in the *Federal Register*, and a public comment period of 30 to 90 days begins. If the HCP is approved by the FWS or the NMFS, that agency will issue an

Incidental Take Permit (ITP) which allows a certain number of "takes" of the listed species. The permit can allow incidental takes for varying amounts of time. Part of the thought is that the HCPs may benefit not only landowners but also species by giving incentives to private landowners to help protect listed and unlisted species, while allowing economic development even though it may harm the species. If problems develop, the permit may be revoked at any time.

The goal of the section is to balance development interests with conservation interests. Permits are available to private parties for incidental takes as long as the "taking is incidental to and not the purpose of, the carrying out of an otherwise lawful activity." The permit process requires a lengthy and potentially expensive notice and comment hearing. The permit will issue after adequate assurances are made to the Secretary that the applicant will minimize and mitigate the effects of the taking and that the required habitat conservation plan will be implemented. A conservation plan must accompany the request for an incidental take permit. If an incidental take permit is issued, it is valid for one year.

A "No Surprises Rule" is meant to protect the landowner if unforeseen circumstances occur which make the landowner's efforts to prevent or mitigate harm to the species fall short. This policy means that once an ITP is granted, the FWS has less authority to impose new conditions if initial mitigation measures by a landowner prove less satisfactory than had been anticipated. If that happens, the landowner would not be required to set aside additional land or pay more in conservation money. The federal government would have to pay for any additional protection measures.

2. Safe Harbor Agreements

A Safe Harbor Agreement (SHA) is a voluntary agreement between private landowners and the FWS. The landowner agrees to alter the property to benefit or even attract a listed or proposed species in exchange for assurances that the FWS will permit future takes up to a predetermined level. A landowner can have either a SHA or an Incidental Take Permit, or both.

The Safe Harbor Policy encourages voluntary management for listed species to promote recovery on private lands by providing assurances to property owners that no additional management activities will be required for the species.

In exchange for actions that contribute to the recovery of listed species, participating property owners receive formal assurances from the FWS that if they fulfill the conditions of the SHA, the FWS will not require any additional or different management activities without their consent. In addition, at the end of the agreement period, participants may return the enrolled property to the baseline conditions that existed at the beginning of the SHA.

Central to this approach is that the actions taken under the SHA will provide a net conservation benefit that contributes to the recovery of the covered species. The contribution toward recovery will vary from case to case, and the SHA does not have to provide permanent conservation for the enrolled property. The benefit to the species depends on the nature of the activities to be undertaken, where they are undertaken, and their duration.

By entering into a SHA, property owners receive assurances that land use restrictions will not be required even if the voluntary actions taken under the agreement attract particular listed species onto enrolled properties or increase the numbers of distribution of those listed species already present on those properties. The assurances are provided by the FWS through an Enhancement of Survival Permit issued to the property owner under section 10(a)(1)(A) of the ESA. This permit authorizes incidental take of species that may result from actions undertaken by the landowner under the SHA. The permit also specifies that the FWS will not require any additional or different management activities by participants without their consent.

A SHA may be initiated by a property owner, or the FWS—in concert with state agencies or other federal agencies—may approach a property owner with a proposal to enter into an agreement. Although many SHAs and permits involve only a single property owner, the FWS encourages the development of "programmatic" SHAs and permits with state, local, or tribal governments that, over time, will include multiple property owners.

The FWS works with interested property owners in applying for an SHA. The FWS also assists property owners in identifying actions that they can voluntarily undertake or forego to benefit listed species covered by the SHA.

3. Candidate Conservation Agreements

The Candidate Conservation Agreement (CCA) is closely related to the SHA, the main difference being that a CCA is meant to protect *unlisted* species by providing incentives to private landowners to restore, enhance, or maintain habitat of unlisted species. In return, the

FWS promises that if in the future the unlisted species becomes listed, the landowner will not be required to do more than already agreed upon in the CCA.

The idea behind CCAs, of course, is that it is easier to conserve species before they need to be listed as endangered or threatened than to try to recover them when they are in danger of extinction. Parties to the CCA work with the FWS to design conservation measures and monitor the effectiveness of plan implementation.

4. Conservation Banks

Conservation banks are lands that are permanently protected and managed as mitigation for the loss elsewhere of listed and other at-risk species and their habitat. Conservation banking is a free market enterprise based on supply and demand of mitigation credits. Credits are supplied by landowners who enter into a Conservation Bank Agreement (CBA) with the FWS agreeing to protect and manage their lands for one or more species. Other landowners who need to mitigate for adverse impacts to those same species may purchase conservation bank credits to meet their mitigation requirements. Conservation banking is sometimes controversial, but it benefits species by reducing the piecemeal approach to mitigation that often results in many small, isolated, and unsustainable preserves that lose their habitat functions and values over time.

5. International Trade

One leading cause of species endangerment and extinction is over-exploitation or over-hunting. Another major cause of species endangerment and extinction involves the accidental or intentional introduction of a species into a new setting, thereby disrupting the delicate ecological balance of the existing habitat.

In order to limit the adverse impact on species from over-exploitation, the ESA implements U.S. participation in the Convention on International Trade in Endangered Species of Wild Fauna and Flora (CITES), a 175-nation agreement designed to prevent species from becoming endangered or extinct due to international trade. Except as allowed by permit, CITES prohibits importing or exporting certain endangered species listed on its three appendices. A species may require a permit under the ESA, CITES, or both.

D. Recovery Plans

The ESA's ultimate goal is to "recover" species so that they no longer need protection. Recovery plans describe the steps needed to restore a species to ecological health. As such, the Secretary must establish recovery plans for each listed species. The Secretary may allocate resources according to those species most likely to benefit from recovery efforts. The decision is based on the Secretary's reasonable belief of what promotes conservation, and the plans are therefore discretionary.

Recovery plans outline the goals, tasks, likely costs, and estimated timeline to recover endangered species (increase their numbers and improve their management to the point where they can be removed from the endangered list). Agency biologists write and implement these plans with the assistance of various experts as well as federal, state, and local agencies.

Three types of information must be included in all recovery plans: 1) a description of "site-specific" management actions to make the plan as explicit as possible; 2) the "objective, measurable criteria" to serve as a baseline for judging when and how well a species is recovering; 3) an estimate of money and resources needed to achieve the goal of recovery and delisting.

There is also a ranking order for recovery plans, similar to the listing procedures, with the highest priority being for species most likely to benefit from recovery plans, especially when the threat is from construction or other commercial activity.

E. Enforcement and Penalties

The FWS plays the predominant role in enforcing the ESA. There are different degrees of violation of the law. The most serious offenses are related to trafficking and any act of knowingly "taking" an endangered species. The penalties for these violations can be a maximum fine of up to $50,000, imprisonment for one year, or both. Civil penalties of up to $25,000 per violation may be assessed. Lists of violations and exact fines are available on the webpage of the National Oceanic and Atmospheric Administration.

In addition to fines or imprisonment, a license, permit, or other agreement issued by a federal agency that authorized an individual to import or export fish, wildlife, or plants may be revoked, suspended, or modified. Any federal hunting or fishing permits that were issued to a person who violates the ESA can be canceled or suspended.

A citizen may enjoin any person, including the United States, "who is alleged to be in violation of any provision of the ESA." A reward will be paid to any person (other than a local, state, or federal employee in the performance of official duties) who furnishes information which leads to an arrest, conviction, or revocation of a license. The Secretary may also provide reasonable and necessary costs incurred for the care of fish, wildlife, or plants pending resolution of the charges.

II. MARINE MAMMALS PROTECTION ACT

The Marine Mammal Protection Act (MMPA) was the first article of federal legislation to call specifically for an ecosystem approach to natural resource management and conservation. The MMPA prohibits the taking of marine mammals, and it enacts a moratorium on the import, export, and sale of marine mammals, along with any marine mammal part or product within the United States.

A. Overview

In passing the MMPA in 1972, Congress found that:

1. Certain species and population stocks of marine mammals are, or may be, in danger of extinction or depletion as a result of man's activities;

2. Such species and population stocks should not be permitted to diminish beyond the point at which they cease to be a significant functioning element in the ecosystem of which they are a part, and, consistent with this major objective, they should not be permitted to diminish below their optimum sustainable population level;

3. Measures should be taken immediately to replenish any species or population stock which has diminished below its optimum sustainable level;

4. There is inadequate knowledge of the ecology and population dynamics of such marine mammals and of the factors which bear upon their ability to reproduce themselves successfully; and

5. Marine mammals have proven themselves to be resources of great international significance, aesthetic and recreational as well as economic.

The NMFS Office of Protected Resources (OPR) is charged with the implementation of the MMPA, ESA, and the Fur Seal Act. The marine mammals at issue include whales, dolphins, porpoises, seals, and sea lions. The FWS implements programs and regulations for the remaining marine mammal species, including walruses, polar bears, sea otters, and manatees. The MMPA provides for enforcement of its prohibitions, and for the issuance of regulations to implement its legislative goals.

B. "Taking" of Marine Mammals

The term "take" as it pertains to marine mammals is similar to the same term under the ESA. It means the act of hunting, killing, capturing, and/or harassing any marine mammal; or the attempt to do these things. The term "harassment" means any act of pursuit, torment, or annoyance which either: 1) has the potential to injure a marine mammal or marine mammal stock in the wild (Level A Harassment); or 2) has the potential to disturb a marine mammal or marine mammal stock in the wild by causing disruption of behavioral patterns, including, but not limited to, migration, breathing, nursing, breeding, feeding, or sheltering (Level B Harassment).

The MMPA established a moratorium, with certain exceptions, on the taking of marine mammals in U.S. waters and by U.S. citizens on the high seas, and on the importing of marine mammals and marine mammal products into the United States. The MMPA provides that the moratorium on the taking of marine mammals can be waived for specific purposes if the taking will not disadvantage an affected species or stock. It also provides that permits may be issued to take or import any marine mammal species, including depleted species, to conduct scientific research or to enhance the survival or recovery of a species or stock.

Permits may also be issued to allow for the taking of a marine mammal from the wild or the importation of a non-depleted species for purposes of public display. These permits are very specific and designate the number and species of animals that can be taken and the time, date, location, and method of takings.

C. Exceptions

Despite the MMPA's moratorium on the "taking" of marine mammals and the ban on importing marine mammals and marine mammal products, certain activities are exempted from that moratorium. The moratorium, for instance, does not apply to taking by any Indian, Aleut, or Eskimo who resides in Alaska and who dwells on the coast of the North Pacific Ocean or the Arctic Ocean if such taking is for subsistence purposes or for creating and selling authentic Native articles of handicrafts and clothing, and is not done in a wasteful manner.

Additionally, these activities are exempted from the moratorium:

1. Scientific research;
2. Enhancing the survival or recovery of a marine mammal species or stock;

3. Commercial and educational photography;
4. First-time import for public display;
5. Capture of wild marine mammals for public display;
6. Incidental take during commercial fisheries; and
7. Incidental takings during non-fishery activities.

Permits and/or authorizations are required for any marine mammal takes within U.S. waters and for marine mammal takes by U.S. citizens on international waters.

CHAPTER 9: RESTRICTIONS ON DEVELOPMENT OF PRIVATE LAND

I. THE TAKINGS CLAUSE

The "Takings Clause" of the U.S. Constitution states that private property shall not be taken for public use without just compensation. Implicit in that statement is the idea that private property can be taken if just compensation is provided. In the last quarter century, this clause has taken on a prominent role in constitutional jurisprudence, particularly with respect to environmental regulation.

The federal government and the various state governments have the power to take private property for public use. The just compensation provision of the Fifth Amendment did not originally apply directly to the states, but the federal courts now hold that the Fourteenth Amendment extends that provision to the states.

Only certain types of takings present serious constitutional questions. Certainly, when the government physically seizes property for a highway or a park, it will have to pay just compensation. It is also clear that serious, sustained physical invasions of property (as in the case of runoff from an artificial water body) require compensation. The difficult cases are those where government regulations, enacted to secure some sort of public benefit, fall disproportionately on some property owners and cause a significant diminution of property value.

As has already been seen, at times the owners of private property can be foreclosed from building on it or using it in ways that might impact the habitat of an endangered species, harm a wetland, or in some other way affect a critical environmental ecosystem. More than two-thirds of the nation's threatened and endangered species use habitat found on private land. The question that often arises is whether regulations like these are "takings" for which compensation is required.

The Supreme Court has had a difficult time articulating a test to determine when a regulation becomes a taking. There is no set formula, and courts look to the particular circumstances of individual cases. The Court has identified some relevant factors to consider: the economic impact of the regulation, the degree to which the regulation interferes with investor-backed expectations, and the character of the government action. Still, there is a lot of room to argue about how these factors should be weighed.

A. Regulatory Takings

While every regulation of property diminishes the owner's freedom in some respect, not every regulation can be deemed a taking. A regulation that restricts the use of property in order to further legitimate public ends is not a taking merely because it impairs the value of that land. The Supreme Court has repeatedly upheld land-use regulations even though they adversely affected recognized real property interests. Zoning laws are the classic example.

The so-called "police power" is the inherent governmental power to do what is reasonably necessary to promote and protect public health, safety, welfare, and morals. This is commonly said to be the basis for the power to protect the environment. Governmental land-use regulation under the police power does not normally amount to a "taking." Such regulation is a taking only if the ordinance does not substantially advance legitimate state interests or it denies an owner economically viable use of his land. When a government regulation does affect a taking of private property, the owner may initiate proceedings to recover the value of the taken property, but such challenges have been found to be without merit in a wide variety of cases.

In 1922, the Supreme Court's decision in *Pennsylvania Coal v. Mahon* ruled that a use regulation constituted a compensable taking of private property. The case provided a rather vague and ambiguous standard, but it established the general framework under which the relationship between private property and the state's authority to regulate could be understood: if regulation *goes too far* it will be recognized as a taking. Any regulation that deprives an owner of all economically viable uses of the property is a *per se* taking and must be compensated.

The Court's first attempt to establish such a workable standard for when regulation goes too far was in the 1978 case *Penn Central*

Transportation Co. v. New York City. In that case, the U.S. Supreme Court denied a takings claim brought by the owner of Grand Central Terminal after the New York City Landmarks Preservation Committee denied plans for construction of a 50-story office building over Grand Central Terminal. Denial of the application was predicated upon designation of the facility as "landmark." The terminal owner charged that application of landmarks preservation law constituted a "taking" of the property without just compensation.

The Supreme Court held that the owners could not establish a "taking" merely by showing that they had been denied the right to exploit the airspace above the building, irrespective of the remainder of the parcel. That the law affected some property owners more than others did not make the regulation a "taking," and the law did not interfere with owners' present use or prevent it from realizing a reasonable rate of return on its investment.

The *Penn Central* case essentially said that taking questions are *ad hoc* determinations made on a case by case basis. While the Court has recognized that the Fifth Amendment's guarantee is designed to bar the government from forcing some people alone to bear public burdens which, in all fairness and justice, should be borne by the public as a whole, the Court has been unable to develop any set formula for determining when economic injuries caused by public action need to be compensated by the government, rather than remain disproportionately concentrated on a few persons. The Court has frequently observed that whether a particular restriction will be rendered invalid by the government's failure to pay for any losses proximately caused by it depends largely upon the particular circumstances of the case.

In engaging in these essentially *ad hoc*, factual inquiries, the Court's decisions have identified several factors that have particular significance. They are: (1) the economic impact of the regulation on the claimant; (2) the extent to which the regulation has interfered with distinct investment-backed expectations; and (3) the character of the governmental action.

The idea that the present regulatory background in which an owner acquires property limits the reasonable expectations he or she has for that property is sometimes called the consent rule. On the other hand, the preexisting presence of a regulation does not automatically preclude a claim of a regulatory taking.

In recent years, property rights groups have initiated several ballot initiatives to extend the takings concept to include regulations that reduce property values. The impact of legislation like this has not been fully evaluated by the courts.

B. Public Benefit

The government's police power authorizes it to take private property for "public use," provided that displaced property owners receive fair market value in compensation. Courts have generally been willing to defer to the determinations of Congress and state legislatures as to whether a particular project constitutes a "public use." The property need not actually be used by the public; rather, it must be used (or disposed of) in a manner that benefits the public welfare or public interest. In other words, "public use" should be defined broadly to include public ownership, use by the public, public benefit, or public advantage.

The most controversial case discussing this issue was the 2005 Supreme Court case, *Kelo v. City of New London*. In this case, there was no doubt that the land owners were entitled to compensation. The issue was whether the use of eminent domain solely for economic development purposes was a valid public use.

The City of New London, Connecticut had created an economic development corporation to redevelop a former military facility and the surrounding area, turning much of the site into a research facility and associated uses owned by private parties. The City adopted a plan with the objectives of providing 1000 new jobs, increasing tax and other revenues, and transforming the city's economically depressed area. Nine landowners, however, declined voluntary to sell their property. When the development corporation sought to use the power of eminent domain to implement the plan, the landowners filed suit contending that their lands were not blighted and the purpose of the acquisitions was solely for economic development. They challenged the condemnation action as a violation of the Public Use clauses of the state and federal constitutions and of state statutory law.

In a 5–4 opinion upholding the Connecticut Supreme Court, the U.S. Supreme Court found the actions to be both constitutional and consistent with state law. The Court found that it was appropriate to defer to the city's decision that the development plan had a public purpose, saying: "the city has carefully formulated a development plan that it believes will provide appreciable benefits to the community, including, but not limited to, new jobs and increased tax revenue." The comprehensive character of the city's plan and the thorough deliberation that preceded the plan's adoption were the determinative factors in finding that the taking was for the public benefit.

In response to *Kelo*, a number of states passed laws and/or state constitutional amendments which make it more difficult for state governments to seize private land. As a result, the growing trend under various state constitution taking clauses is to compensate those whose property was destroyed or "taken" as a result of police action. Some courts have moved away from their earlier tendency to defer to other branches of government when it comes to determining the proper restraints on private property to protect a public interest.

C. Just Compensation

The owner of property that is taken by the government must be justly compensated. When determining the amount that must be paid, the government does not need to take into account any speculative schemes that the owner claims he had planned for the property. Normally, the fair market value of the property determines the "just compensation." If the property is taken before the payment is made, interest accrues on the amount due (though many courts have refrained from using the term "interest").

When a court is asked to assess the economic impact of a regulation, the court must determine the fractional diminution in value of the property. The determination of such diminution in value is done by calculating to what degree a regulation removes an ownership or use value from the owner. Short of stating that actual takings of property have occurred, courts have stated that the imposition of a regulation that restricts a property's use, even if the regulation is later ruled invalid, can still be challenged as having temporarily taken property, and compensation can be sought for that period of time.

D. Ripeness

There is a ripeness requirement that a plaintiff must meet before a court becomes involved in balancing private property rights and police power. The traditional rule is that a dispute must proceed to the point of receiving a final administrative decision before the court becomes involved. Such a requirement serves to protect justice by preventing premature adjudications; it stops courts from becoming entangled in abstract disagreements over administrative policies. It also protects the agencies from judicial interference until an administrative decision has been formalized. Courts have also recently required claimants to receive a final decision from the state courts before their claim can be determined to be ripe for review in federal court.

There is a significant exception to the ripeness requirement. Courts usually do not require landowners to pursue measures that obviously will be fruitless. Thus a challenge to an agency's policy, which would certainly be rejected in an administrative hearing, might be permitted to proceed directly to court.

II. THE PUBLIC TRUST DOCTRINE

With rare exception, private landowners do not own beachfront land from the high-tide line down. Nor do private citizens normally own the land under running waterways. These lands are held by the state in trust for the benefit of the people of the state. This public trust exists so that the citizens of the state may navigate the waters, carry on commerce, and have the ability to fish and recreate free from interference from private parties. In other words, the public trust is an affirmation of the duty of the state to protect the people's common heritage of tide and submerged lands for their common use.

The public trust doctrine is based upon principles that trace back to Roman law and English common law. A body of Roman civil law, the Institutes of Justinian, supported the notion that waterways and shores should not be privately owned, because they were "common to mankind by the law of nature." The Romans designated the air, waterways, and shores as "common property" which was entitled to public protection from total private acquisition. The free availability of these natural resources was vital to societal development. Similarly, English common law recognized that the community's interests must be balanced with private ownership rights. This principle evolved into the public trust doctrine pursuant to which the sovereign held the navigable waterways and submerged lands, not in a proprietary capacity, but rather "as trustee of a public trust for the benefit of the people" for uses such as commerce, navigation, and fishing.

After the American Revolution, the colonial governments took over trust lands previously held by the Crown. Upon uniting, the states retained their shores, and accordingly, the shores were held in public trust for the people. As new states entered the Union, they entered under the equal footing doctrine, meaning they entered "on an equal footing with the original states" and kept title to their tidelands and navigable waterways in trust.

A. Purpose of the Trust

The state holds lands in the public trust for the benefit of the public; therefore the state's authority regarding such lands is generally restricted in three ways. First, the property subject to the trust must be used for a public purpose, and it must be held available for use by the general public; second, the property may not be sold, even for a fair market price; and third, the property must be maintained for particular types of uses.

The purpose of the public trust is said to include navigation and transportation, commerce, fishing, bathing, swimming, and other recreational activities; development of mineral resources and environmental protection and preservation; the enhancement of aquatic, avian, and marine life; sea agriculture, and more. Uses that do not accommodate, promote, foster, or enhance the statewide public need for essential commercial services or the enjoyment of tidelands are not appropriate uses for public trust lands.

Traditionally, public trust uses were limited to water-related commerce, navigation, and fishing. In more recent years, however, courts have said that the public trust embraces the right of the public to use the navigable waters of the state for bathing, swimming, boating, and general recreational purposes. It is sufficiently flexible to encompass changing public needs, such as the preservation of the lands in their natural state for scientific study, as open space, and as wildlife habitat. The administrator of the public trust is not burdened with an outmoded classification favoring one mode of use over another.

The legislature, acting within the confines of the public trust doctrine, is the ultimate administrator of the tidelands trust and often serves as the ultimate arbiter of permissible uses of trust lands. All uses, including those specifically authorized by the legislature, must take into account the overarching principle of the public trust doctrine that trust lands belong to the public and are to be used to promote public rather than exclusively private purposes. The legislature cannot commit trust lands irretrievably to private development because it would be abdicating the public trust. Within these confines, however, the legislature has considerable discretion.

All structures built on tide and submerged lands should have as their main purpose the furtherance of a public trust use. Any structure designed or used primarily for a non-trust purpose is suspect. Mixed-use development proposals, however, frequently justify non-trust uses as "incidental" to the entire project.

Historic public trust uses may be replaced by new technologies. Thus piers, wharves and warehouses that once served commercial navigation but no longer can serve modern container shipping may have to be removed or converted to a more productive trust use. Antiquated structures on the waterfront may be an impediment rather than a magnet for public access and use of the waters. Public trust uses may and often do conflict with one another. The state and local tidelands grantees, as administrators of their respective public trust lands, are charged with choosing among these conflicting uses, with the legislature as the ultimate arbiter of their choices.

B. Extent of the Trust

In 1953, Congress granted the submerged lands to the states, in accordance with the Submerged Lands Act, thus vesting states with ownership of tidelands and submerged lands. The Supreme Court concluded "that the normally applicable rule puts the inland boundary line to the trust property at the line of mean high tide."

The right to the waterways is also interpreted to include tidelands, those lands that are sometimes under water, and at other times are not. Due to the variable nature of tidelands and the uncertainty of the boundaries of the new states, the U.S. Supreme Court had to determine the boundaries. The Court faced additional challenges because of the great rivers and inland seas in the United States.

Tidelands boundaries are constantly changing, through accretion, reliction, or erosion. At common law, accretions to the shores of the sea vested in the owner of the land bordering the sea. On the other hand, landowners could lose title to lands in the event of the reliction. Therefore, those lands that were not tidelands in 1817, but are now subject to the ebb and flow of the tide due to natural accretion or a gradual imperceptible increase in the tidal level, have been added to the public trust and their title is held by the state.

C. Limits on Disposal of Trust Property

Although the state may not dispose of trust lands completely, the state may convey some interest in trust lands to a private party. That private party's title, the *jus privatum* interest, is subservient to the state's title, the *jus publicum* interest. While a private landowner can own the *jus privatum* interest, a private landowner cannot own the public's *jus publicum* interest.

Conveyances of public trust lands are narrowly construed and great judicial skepticism follows them. When a state conveys trust property, courts have a strong presumption against limiting or terminating public trust uses of such property. By the same token, courts do not infer a conveyance of public trust lands unless specific granting language is present.

The foundational public trust case is *Illinois Central Railroad Co. v. Illinois*. In 1869, the Illinois legislature granted the Illinois Central Railroad over one thousand acres of land that included all submerged lands under Lake Michigan. Five years later, the legislature repealed the grant, and the state sought to have it declared invalid. In a four to three split, the U.S. Supreme Court affirmed the circuit court's decision that declared the grant invalid. The Court reasoned that the state could not abdicate its trust by disposing of property, just as it could not abdicate its police powers by failing to preserve peace. The state, however, can convey some trust property for improving the public interest, or if the conveyance does not substantially impair the remaining public interest in trust property.

Courts have established a few principles related to the leasing of public trust lands for particular uses. For example, tidelands granted in trust to local entities may be leased and improved if the leases and improvements promote uses authorized by the public trust. Leases for the construction of structures that directly promote port development have been approved since early in the 20th century. Leases for structures incidental to the promotion of port commerce are also valid because although they do not directly support port business, they encourage trade, shipping, and commercial associations to become familiar with the port and its assets. Visitor-serving facilities such as restaurants, hotels, shops, and parking areas are also appropriate uses because as places of public accommodation they allow broad public access to the tidelands and, therefore, enhance the public's enjoyment of these lands.

Tidelands may be leased to private entities, but only for purposes consistent with the trust upon which those lands are held. When leasing tidelands for construction of permanent structures to serve a lessee's development project, the structure must directly promote uses authorized by the trust, it must be incidental to the promotion of such uses, or it must accommodate or enhance the public's enjoyment of the trust lands.

The state is prohibited from disposing of public trust property unless it is done pursuant to a higher public purpose that is not detrimental to the public, and it is approved by appropriate state authorities (usually the legislature, but in some states it could be the Secretary of State, the Attorney General, or some other official). Similarly, the state must not enter a long-term lease for less than fair market prices, because doing so would violate the state's duty as trustee. Furthermore, even if the legislature approves disposition of trust property, that transaction may later be revoked.

Many state laws provide that trust property may be exchanged for lands of equal value, as long as it is in the best interests of the people of the state. Appropriate "swaps" might be for the improvement of navigation, to aid in reclamation, for flood control protection, or to enhance the configuration of the shoreline. The swap must not substantially interfere with the right of navigation and fishing in the waters involved. The grantee may thereafter improve, fill, or reclaim the lands, free of trust restrictions.

III. THE NAVIGATIONAL SERVITUDE

The navigation servitude is a term used to describe the paramount interest of the United States in navigation and the navigable waters of the nation. The servitude derives from the Commerce Clause of the U.S. Constitution and is a concept of power, not of property. The power to regulate commerce necessarily includes power over navigation. To make its control effective, Congress may keep the navigable waters of the United States open and free and impose sanctions against any interference with the country's water assets. It may also prohibit or license dams in the waters. Its power over improvements for navigation in rivers is absolute.

Under the servitude, when the United States, in the exercise of its powers over navigation, affects the interests of owners of private property, it is not generally required to compensate them. The Commerce Clause gives Congress the power to regulate commerce among the several states. That power to regulate commerce includes the authority to control, to the extent necessary, the navigable waters of the United States.

The phrase "navigable servitude" may wrongly imply that the Commerce Clause power over navigable waters is limited to governmental activities that have a navigation purpose. In fact, the power is as broad as the needs of commerce. This power to regulate navigation confers upon the United States control over all navigable waterways, extending to the entire stream and the stream bed below the ordinary high-water mark.

Someone whose land abuts upon a stream or waterway is called the riparian owner or riparian possessor. Governmental action designed to assist commerce can impact the rights of the riparian owner, and their rights are often at issue in these cases. For these purposes, a renter or tenant has the same rights as the riparian owner.

A. Not a Taking

When the federal government condemns land on or near a navigable waterway, it is not constitutionally obligated to pay compensation to the landowner, because this is not a taking of property from riparian owners within the meaning of the Fifth Amendment. Rather, this is the lawful exercise of a governmental power to which the interests of riparian owners have always been subject. Thus without being constitutionally obligated to pay compensation, the United States may change the course of a navigable stream or otherwise impair or destroy a riparian owner's access to navigable waters, even though the market value of the riparian owner's land is substantially diminished.

If the United States changes the course or current of a navigable water, or changes the access, or prevents its use for generating power, no compensation is due, unless specific legislation calls for compensation.

The U.S. Supreme Court case, *Scranton v. Wheeler* (1900), dealt with a situation where the government had constructed a long dike on submerged lands in a river to aid navigation. The dike, however, cut the riparian owner off from direct access to deep water, and he claimed that his rights had been invaded and his property had been taken without compensation. The Supreme Court disagreed.

The Court explained that the primary use of the waters and the lands under them was for purposes of navigation. The erection of piers in them to improve navigation for the public was consistent with such uses, and it did not infringe on the rights of riparian owners. Whatever the nature of the interest of riparian owners in submerged lands adjacent to their property and bordering on a public navigable river, their title is not as full and complete as their title to fast land which has no direct connection to navigable water. It is a qualified title, a bare technical title, not at the owner's absolute disposal, but to be held at all times subordinate to such use of the submerged lands and of the waters flowing over them as may be consistent with or demanded by the public right of navigation.

The navigational servitude does not extend beyond the high-water mark. Consequently, when fast lands are taken by the government, just compensation must be paid. Fast lands are the lands located above the high water mark.

Just as the navigational privilege permits the government to reduce the value of riparian lands by denying the riparian owner access to the waterway without compensation, it also permits the government to disregard the value arising from this riparian location in compensating the owner when fast lands are appropriated.

B. The Rivers and Harbors Act

The Rivers and Harbors Act (RHA) makes it a misdemeanor to discharge refuse matter of any kind into the navigable waters of the United States without a permit. The RHA also makes it a misdemeanor to excavate, fill, or alter the course, condition, or capacity of any port, harbor, channel, or other areas without a permit. Although many activities covered by the RHA are regulated under the Clean Water Act, the RHA retains independent vitality.

Although the navigational servitude permits the government to affect streams and waterways without paying compensation to riparian owners, Congress may limit the power of the United States to exercise the navigational servitude, and Congress has decided to exercise that authority.

Section 111 of the RHA provides a right to compensation which the Supreme Court has declared is not constitutionally required. The amount of compensation paid to any landowner for land appropriated by the government must include any value attributable to the land's proximity to a navigable waterway. The practical effect of Section 111 is that compensation is paid in accordance with the usual constitutional rules regarding just compensation. When real property is taken for public use in connection with any improvement of rivers, harbors, canals, or waterways, or in any condemnation proceedings to acquire lands or easements for such improvements, the compensation to be paid for real property above the normal high water mark of navigable waters shall be the fair market value of such real property based upon all uses to which such real property may be reasonably put.

CHAPTER 10: THE GREENHOUSE EFFECT AND CLIMATE CHANGE

I. THE GREENHOUSE EFFECT AND CLIMATE SCIENCE

A. The Greenhouse Effect

The greenhouse effect and the global warming resulting from it are necessary to support life on our planet. The greenhouse effect itself can be explained simply enough. The Sun is, essentially, a nuclear fusion reactor. Nuclear reactions inside the Sun cause its surface to become intensely hot. The Sun's surface radiates energy (in the form of light) uniformly away in all directions. A relative fraction of that solar radiation reaches the Earth approximately 93 million miles away. Some of that solar radiation is reflected back into space by the Earth's atmosphere. About 70% of the radiant energy reaching our planet from the Sun passes through the atmosphere and is absorbed by the Earth.

The radiation from the Sun absorbed by the Earth warms its surface. Eventually, the Earth's surface warms up to the point where it sends away this radiant energy at the same rate it receives it. This radiation is called infrared radiation and is not visible to our eyes. Generally, the Earth's surface radiates infrared energy (heat) away at the same rate it receives it at an average surface temperature of 0 degrees Fahrenheit. Absent some process to prevent it, that energy would be radiated back into space and leave the Earth cold and lifeless.

Fortunately, the Earth has a gaseous atmosphere that traps a part of the energy (heat) radiating away from the Earth's surface and re-radiates it back to the surface. The Earth's atmosphere is comprised mostly of nitrogen and oxygen, but also contains traces of other gases that cause the effect of trapping infrared radiation and directing it back toward the Earth. These trace gases are the "greenhouse gases" (GHGs). Water vapor is the most abundant GHG, but other atmospheric GHGs include carbon dioxide, methane, ozone, nitrous oxides, and chlorofluorocarbons. The energy (heat) radiating back from the atmosphere warms the Earth's surface. This is the "greenhouse effect." The action of GHGs in letting in sunlight but preventing heat from escaping into space is somewhat similar to the manner in which the glass panels of a greenhouse operate. The greenhouse effect causes the Earth's surface temperature to be an average of about 60 degrees warmer than it would be otherwise (a relatively constant surface temperature of around 0 degrees Fahrenheit). Such frigid temperatures, of course, would not support life on our planet as we know it.

B. Increasing Greenhouse Gas Emissions

Many GHGs, like water vapor and carbon dioxide, occur naturally. Levels of GHGs in the atmosphere have fluctuated over the entirety of the Earth's history, but complex natural cycles have kept these levels fairly constant for the past few thousand years. One important example of such a natural process is the "carbon cycle." Carbon dioxide is produced naturally during respiration by plants and by all animals (including humans), fungi, and microorganisms that depend either directly or indirectly on plants for food. Carbon dioxide is also released to the atmosphere when plants and animals die and decompose. Carbon dioxide is removed from the atmosphere through absorption by growing plants (through the process of photosynthesis). Oceans also absorb vast quantities of carbon dioxide. The carbon dioxide absorbed by plants and oceans is eventually released back into the atmosphere and then reabsorbed again and then released again in an endless cycle. When in balance, total carbon dioxide emissions and removals from the natural carbon cycle are roughly equal and thus the level of carbon dioxide in the atmosphere is kept relatively stable.

However, since the beginning of the Industrial Revolution in the 1700s, human activities have caused significant increases of carbon dioxide and other GHGs in the atmosphere. Because of the burning of fossil fuels, such as coal and oil, and the phenomenon of deforestation, by the year 2005, atmospheric concentrations of carbon dioxide had increased by 35% since the year 1750. Concentrations of methane in the atmosphere, mainly from natural gas production, landfills, and farm animals, have increased 148% since 1750. Nitrous oxide levels, produced primarily by fossil fuel combustion, have increased 18% over that time period. The activities responsible for these emissions have overwhelmed the natural cycles that absorb and remove GHGs from the atmosphere. Moreover, concentrations of GHGs in the atmosphere due to human activities are continuing to rise. If current trends in fossil fuel consumption continue, estimates are that by the end of this century atmospheric concentrations of carbon dioxide will have well more than doubled since the beginning of the Industrial Revolution.

C. Global Warming and Climate Change

These increases in atmospheric concentrations of GHGs are enhancing the greenhouse effect. Generally, greater concentrations of GHGs increase the amount of infrared radiation trapped by the atmosphere and redirected back to the Earth. Thus the Earth's average surface temperature is climbing above past levels. According to data from the National Oceanic and Atmospheric Administration (NOAA) and the National Aeronautics and Space Administration (NASA), the Earth's average surface temperature has increased by about 1.2 to 1.4 degrees Fahrenheit since 1880. Also according to the NOAA, the eight warmest years on record (since 1850) have all occurred since 1998. Most of that warming is very likely the result of human activities. The scientists of the United Nation's Intergovernmental Panel on Climate Change (IPCC) issued a report in 2007 finding a greater than 90% chance that most of the increase in global average temperatures since the 1950s is due to the increase in GHG emissions from human activities.

Should increases in atmospheric concentrations of GHGs continue to occur at or above the current pace, predictions are that global temperatures will continue to rise throughout the twenty-first century. The IPCC's 2007 report estimates that that the average global surface temperature may increase from 2.5 to 5.6 degrees Fahrenheit above 1990 levels by 2100. More recent scientific studies predict even higher temperature increases during that time period. Even if worldwide GHG emissions from human activities were suddenly and dramatically reduced, some global warming would continue to occur over the next 100 years. This is due to the lengthy period of time that GHGs persist in the atmosphere, the slow cycling of heat from the ocean to the atmosphere, and the gradual rates of natural absorption of GHGs within natural cycles.

For many years, scientists have asserted that global warming resulting from human caused increases in GHG emissions has caused and will continue to cause changes to the Earth's climate. In addition to changes in temperature, the term "climate change" refers to significant changes in rainfall, snowfall, ice cover, or wind patterns lasting for decades or longer. The Earth's climate is extremely complex. Climate science is by no means exact and how interactions between the air, land and oceans influence climate on a global, regional or local basis are only partly understood. Nonetheless, many scientists believe that increases in global temperatures will very likely change the Earth's climate in ways that will have significant long term effects on people and the environment.

Scientists assert that the Earth is already showing many signs of worldwide climate change. Such changes include melting polar ice in the Artic and Antarctica, shrinking glaciers and permafrost, modest sea level rise over the last century, increases in ocean temperature, salinity, and acidity, and alteration of currents, impacts on other ecosystems such as forests, freshwater, and deserts, and changes in growing seasons and in the range and distribution of plants and animals. Whether and the extent to which such climate change impacts will continue in the future is of critical concern to scientists and policymakers worldwide.

Significant uncertainty exists concerning the ultimate future impacts of climate change. Scientists are certain that human activities are increasing the concentrations of GHGs in the atmosphere and that this will result in additional changes to the planet's climate. However, scientists are not certain how much climate change will occur, at what rate it might change, or what the exact effects will be. Notwithstanding the difficulty in making predictions about the consequences of increasing global warming, the projections from some scientists are dire. The IPCC's 2007 report suggests the potential for sea level rise between 7 and 23 inches by the end of the century due to melting polar ice caps and glaciers. A rise of only 4 inches could flood South Sea islands, swamp large parts of Southeast Asia, threaten major coastal cities worldwide, and completely reshape the world's coastal areas. Numerous species might face extinction from disappearing habitat, changing ecosystems, and acidifying oceans.

Many scientists also believe that a warming climate may affect the frequency and severity of extreme weather events such as hurricanes, droughts, heat waves, floods, and other natural disasters. Human health and safety would be at considerable risk if dramatic climate change occurs, including increases in heat-related deaths, infectious diseases and other illnesses, and the negative impacts from food and water shortages. The economic costs of seeking to reduce GHG emissions, probably by imposing significant limits on industry and transportation, to avoid the potential that these threats may come to fruition would be extraordinary. Similarly, the economic costs necessary for society to adapt to the actual occurrence of dramatic climate change impacts could be astronomical.

The debates over what the potential magnitude and impacts of climate change might be and how the world should respond to the threats of increased global warming are impassioned and controversial. The climate change debate involves science, economics, and politics. Each of these areas has its own complexities and uncertainties, and there are many difficult issues and sub-issues. Moreover, exaggerations, misleading hyperbole, and political posturing by special interests on both sides of the debate—environmental activists on one side and "climate skeptics" on the other—make the issues more difficult to understand rather than easier. Nonetheless, the debates are of critical importance. Decisions on whether and how to respond to the threats represented by increasing atmospheric concentrations of GHGs and evidence of resulting global temperature increases have occupied vast amounts of worldwide attention and effort over the past few decades. Here at the end of the first decade of the twenty-first century, the international community is placing ever increasing importance on determining how to address these issues.

II. INTERNATIONAL PROTOCOLS ON CLIMATE CHANGE

A. Intergovernmental Panel on Climate Change (IPCC)

The genesis of international efforts to respond to issues associated with climate change is the Intergovernmental Panel on Climate Change (IPCC). The IPCC is a multinational scientific body formed in 1988 by the World Meteorological Organization and the United Nations Environment Programme. The mission of the IPCC is to convene scientists and other experts to publish reports assessing the state of the science on climate change and to evaluate economic and technical issues on the subject. The IPCC brings together the world's top scientists, economists, and other experts and synthesizes peer-reviewed scientific literature on climate change studies. Thousands of scientists from all over the world contribute to the work of the IPCC on a voluntary basis. Review is an essential part of the IPCC process in an effort to provide an objective and complete assessment of current information. Differing viewpoints existing within the scientific community are reflected within the scope of the IPCC's "Assessment Reports."

The IPCC has issued four comprehensive Assessment Reports since its establishment, in 1990, 1995, 2001, and 2007, which have greatly influenced the evolution of the international climate change regime.

The IPCC is currently working on its Fifth Assessment Report on the state of climate change science.

B. United Nations Framework Convention on Climate Change (UNFCCC)

The IPCC's First Assessment Report in 1990 concluded that GHG emissions from human activities were substantially increasing atmospheric concentrations which would enhance the greenhouse effect and result in additional global warming. In response to this report, the United Nations General Assembly initiated negotiations in 1990 on what would eventually become the United Nations Framework Convention on Climate Change (UNFCCC). The UNFCCC is a nonbinding treaty among signatory nations to reduce atmospheric concentrations of GHGs for the purpose of preventing interference with the Earth's climate system by human activities.

Negotiations on the UNFCCC were conducted between February 1991 and May 1992. The UNFCCC was opened for signature at the 1992 United Nations Conference on Environment and Development in Rio de Janeiro (the "Earth Summit"). The United States was an active participant in the negotiations that led to creation of the treaty. President George H.W. Bush attended the Earth Summit and signed the UNFCCC on June 12, 1992. The U.S. Senate subsequently unanimously ratified the treaty on October 7, 1992, and President Bush signed the instrument of ratification on October 13, 1992. The UNFCCC obtained a sufficient number of ratifications from signatory countries to enter into force in 1994. The total number of countries that are signatories to the treaty now stands at 191.

The UNFCCC does not establish binding GHG emission limitations for any country, instead forming a framework for further action and cooperation by signatory countries on climate change. The UNFCCC established a Conference of the Parties (COP), a legislative-like body that meets annually and is charged with devising ways to implement the UNFCCC's goals. The UNFCCC divides the parties into two groups: Annex I countries (primarily developed countries), and non-Annex I countries (primarily developing countries). The treaty commits both Annex I and non-Annex I countries to develop and submit national inventories of GHG emissions by sources, promote and cooperate in technology transfer, and promote and cooperate in scientific research on climate change.

The UNFCCC reflects the view that developed countries bear greater responsibility for GHG emissions and a greater capacity to take action. Thus Annex I countries made (nonbinding) commitments to adopt national policies to mitigate climate change by reducing GHG emissions to 1990 levels by the year 2000. No such restrictions were imposed on developing countries, such as China and India, which could choose to become Annex I countries when sufficiently developed.

C. The Kyoto Protocol

The IPCC's Second Assessment Report in 1995 concluded that "the balance of evidence suggests that there is a discernible human influence on the global climate." At the first COP meeting in Berlin in 1995, the parties to the UNFCCC collectively determined that a more forceful international response to the threat of climate change was needed. This led to the "Berlin Mandate," a commitment to develop a protocol with binding GHG emission limits which should apply only to developed-country (Annex I) parties.

Negotiations subsequent to the "Berlin Mandate" resulted in the Kyoto Protocol which was adopted by the parties at the third COP meeting in Kyoto, Japan in 1997. Mandatory targets for industrialized nations to reduce GHG emissions were assigned. The United States actively participated in these negotiations and Vice President Al Gore played a central role. However, because emission targets did not apply to developing and heavily polluting nations such as China and India, in July 1997, the U.S. Senate passed a unanimous resolution (95–0) directing the government not to enter into the Protocol. Accordingly, President Clinton did not submit the Kyoto Protocol to the Senate for ratification.

At the Kyoto COP meeting, the parties agreed that many key details of the Kyoto Protocol had yet to be resolved. Thus negotiations on development of the Kyoto Protocol continued during the next few years, and the United States was actively involved in these negotiations. However, at the sixth COP in The Hague in 2000, these negotiations collapsed over a disagreement between the United States and the European Union regarding credit for GHG emission removals resulting from forestry.

The subsequent election of President George W. Bush in 2000 was followed by the March 2001 repudiation of the Kyoto Protocol by the Bush Administration, creating a crisis for future negotiations on the treaty and the possibility of it eventually entering into force. Reasons given for United States' repudiation of the Kyoto Protocol were "because it exempts 80% of the world, including major population centers such as China and India, from compliance, and would cause serious harm to the United States economy." The 1997 unanimous Senate resolution of disapproval of the treaty was also cited in support of the Bush Administration's repudiation of the Kyoto Protocol.

Negotiations at the seventh COP in Marrakesh in 2001 produced the "Marrakesh Accords," a detailed rulebook elaborating procedures and rules for trading mechanisms, compliance systems, and other key elements of the Kyoto Protocol. In February 2005, Russia ratified the Kyoto Protocol. This event provided the necessary number of Annex I country ratifications to allow the treaty to enter into force. At present, the only major developed countries that are not parties to the Kyoto Protocol are the United States and Australia.

Instead of a single fixed-year limit, the Kyoto Protocol's GHG emissions commitments for Annex I countries apply as an annual average to be achieved over a five-year period. This point was in response to concerns that any particular country's GHG emissions could rise or fall in any particular year because of difficult-to-control factors. Thus the Kyoto Protocol sets forth binding GHG emission limits for developed-country parties of at least a collective net 5.2% reduction from 1990 levels by 2008–2012. The period 2008–2012 is referred to in the treaty as the "first commitment period." The treaty contemplated that subsequent commitment periods would be entered into following this initial round of commitments. The Kyoto Protocol gave developed country parties full discretion in developing combinations of national policies and measures to meet their respective assigned reduction amounts (calculated individually for each party with reference to their 1990 emissions levels). No particular policies or measures were proscribed, although "preferred policies" were encouraged, such as energy efficiency, sinks and reservoirs of GHGs, and increased use of renewable energy.

Perhaps the most important international environmental law innovation of the Kyoto Protocol was the establishment of "flexible mechanisms" (market based approaches) as a means of meeting emissions reduction targets. Thus Annex I countries were allowed to meet their reduction targets by investing in emission reduction or sequestration opportunities in other countries. The Kyoto Protocol states that market based approaches should be "supplemental" to direct GHG reduction efforts by countries, but no quantitative limit on the extent to which parties would be able to rely on trading was established.

To facilitate the use of "flexible mechanisms," the Kyoto Protocol established an international emissions trading system in which permits covering GHG emissions are allocated to Annex I countries which may trade them freely with one another. For example, if country "A" can reduce its GHG emissions by 100 tons at a lower cost than country "B" which can achieve the same reduction, the two countries can agree on the sale of the permits for this amount from country "A" to country "B."

Country "B" then gets the credit for the emissions reduction toward its individually assigned amount under the Kyoto Protocol. Kyoto Protocol rules limit the amounts of credits that most countries can sell to no more than 10% of their assigned reduction amounts.

The Kyoto Protocol also established a form of emissions trading among Annex I countries that revolves around projects that reduce or remove GHG emissions, referred to as "Joint Implementation" projects. Thus an Annex I country may invest in a GHG emissions abatement project in the country of another Annex I party. The country hosting the project transfers a portion of its assigned amount of reductions under the Kyoto Protocol to the purchasing country. The purchasing country adds these reductions to its assigned amount of reductions under the treaty. The Kyoto Protocol further establishes a "Clean Development Mechanism" program by which Annex I countries can purchase reductions generated by emission reduction projects in non-Annex I countries. These reductions would be added to the assigned reduction amounts under the Kyoto Protocol for the purchasing Annex I country. This mechanism was perceived as a method for involving developing countries in GHG emissions reduction efforts.

The Kyoto Protocol established a compliance system that includes mechanisms to generate information about performance, to facilitate compliance, and to deter noncompliance through penalties. An Annex I country that fails to meet its reduction targets during the first commitment period is subject to a penalty of having its assigned reduction amounts for the second commitment period (post-2012) increased by the number necessary to make up the difference in noncompliance during the first period plus a penalty interest rate of 30%.

D. Weaknesses of the Kyoto Protocol

The Kyoto Protocol has been subjected to considerable criticism from its earliest beginnings. This is exemplified by the U.S. Senate's unanimous resolution of disapproval of the treaty in 1997 and the Bush Administration's subsequent refusal to continue to participate in the Kyoto negotiating process in 2001. Critics note that the emission limits included in the treaty cover only a relative fraction of the world's GHG emissions. This greatly reduces the likelihood that the treaty could lead to significant progress in decreasing worldwide GHG emissions at a level sufficient to affect current global warming trends. Of course, the refusal of the United States to participate in the Kyoto Protocol's first commitment period is a large part of this problem. The United States contributes roughly 20% of worldwide GHG emissions and its absence created a gaping hole in the overall Kyoto regime.

The Kyoto Protocol also failed to extend commitments for GHG reductions to developing countries, including major emitters such as China and India. As of 2000, the combined total of GHG emissions for both of those countries was roughly equal to that of the United States. Towards the end of the current decade, China had passed the United States as the largest worldwide emitter of GHGs. Moreover, the Kyoto Protocol has been further criticized for its blanket exclusion of developing countries from emissions reductions commitments given that overall emissions from those countries are expected to surpass those of developed countries within the next couple of decades. Exacerbating problems with insufficient coverage, critics also assert that few of the roughly 40 Annex I countries are on track to meet their reduction targets under the treaty for the first commitment period. Indeed, many countries have indicated that they absolutely will not meet their compliance targets.

There is also considerable debate whether the Kyoto Protocol's system of absolute emissions caps can be feasibly extended to developing countries in future commitment periods. Developing countries such as China and India have shown considerable reluctance to accept fixed caps on emissions because they represent restrictions on their country's economic growth. Many developing country governments also lack the capacity to develop economy-wide regulatory programs that could achieve precise numerical limits on GHG emissions. Many critics argue that such problems are the reason the emissions targets approach of the Kyoto Protocol is fundamentally flawed as a method to address the global problem of GHG emissions. Instead, such critics assert that a technology-based approach should be pursued instead. In this view, resources and efforts would be better directed toward development of a new generation of clean energy technologies and to programs to transfer such technologies to fast-growing developing countries.

E. Negotiations on Post-Kyoto Protocol Commitments

The Kyoto Protocol established an independent governing body for implementation of the treaty separate from the UNFCCC's COP. The Kyoto Protocol's governing body is known as the "Conference of the Parties serving as the Meeting of Parties to the Protocol" (or COP/MOP). The COP still operates within the structure of the UNFCCC. The COP/MOP has been in place since the Kyoto Protocol entered into force in February 2005. The Kyoto Protocol directed that, by no later than 2005, the COP/MOP was to initiate consideration of subsequent GHG reduction commitment periods following expiration of the treaty's first commitment period in 2012.

At the 11th meeting of the COP and the first of the COP/MOP in 2005, the parties to the Kyoto Protocol agreed to create an ad hoc working group to consider post-2012 commitments for Annex I countries. At the Poznan, Poland COP/MOP in 2008, the parties issued a mandate that a document to replace the Kyoto Protocol once its emissions-reduction provisions expire at the end of 2012 be completed by December 2009 at the Copenhagen COP/MOP. Following his election in 2008, President Barack Obama pledged to re-engage the United States in the negotiations to draft and finalize this agreement for post-2012 emissions reductions at the December 2009 Copenhagen conference.

However, many observers believe that insufficient progress has been made on post-Kyoto commitments since 2005 for a fully developed agreement to be ready by the time the Kyoto Protocol expires in 2012. It is widely believed that such an agreement will not be possible if the United States does not commit to full participation in the post-2012 commitment period. President Obama attended the Copenhagen conference in December 2009 and announced that the United States would offer a GHG emissions reduction target of 17% below its 2005 levels by the year 2020. Such a proposal was in line with legislation on climate change that had passed earlier in the U.S. House of Representatives in June 2009 (discussed in section III of this chapter), although similar legislation was still pending and had not yet passed in the U.S. Senate at the time of the Copenhagen conference. The United States emphasized at Copenhagen that any final commitment to reduction targets in a second Kyoto Protocol commitment period would depend upon final passage of domestic climate change legislation by Congress.

Moreover, it is further widely believed that agreement on a post-2012 commitment period will not be possible unless all 191 parties to the UNFCCC are obligated to reduce GHG emissions, rather than just the 40 industrialized countries with emissions targets under the first Kyoto commitment period. Commitments from particularly large emitters of GHGs such as China and India not obligated during the first commitment period are considered especially critical to the ability of the countries that are parties to the UNFCCC to reach any final agreement on post-2012 reduction targets.

These difficulties make it unlikely that any final agreement on post-2012 commitments will result from the Copenhagen COP/MOP conference in December 2009. Instead, the expectation is that a "political" commitment with broad outlines will emerge from the Copenhagen conference and that the parties will pledge to negotiate a final deal in mid-to late 2010. Thus the Copenhagen meetings are most likely to reach a result similar to that of the Kyoto meetings in 1997; an overall framework with an agreement to decide the details later. However, reaching final accord on a new legally binding treaty in time for it to be in place by the end of 2012 (three years after Copenhagen) will be a difficult challenge. The new agreement will be far more complex than the Kyoto Protocol itself, and it took the parties to the framework agreement reached in Kyoto four years to eventually finalize the details of the Kyoto Protocol (in Marrakesh in 2001).

III. UNITED STATES CLIMATE CHANGE POLICY

At the present time, no permanent body of law in the United States directly governs this country's response to the threats associated with increasing concentrations of atmospheric GHGs and the potential impacts of climate change. Following the November 2008 Presidential elections, momentum appeared to shift dramatically towards the United States moving to direct regulation of greenhouse gas (GHG) emissions in some form or fashion. However, predicting the precise form such regulation may eventually take is substantially hindered by the considerable uncertainty surrounding the legal landscape on the climate change issue in the United States.

A. Voluntary Programs

Since the 1990s, the primary policy approach of the federal government to the issue of GHG emissions and climate change has been to create and encourage voluntary environmental programs to reduce emissions and support research in climate technology and science. Such voluntary programs are a popular choice when policymakers lack the political will to impose strict requirements through mandatory regulation. Because legislative authority to directly regulate GHG emissions has been at best difficult and controversial to obtain, voluntary programs have become especially prevalent in this area.

The United States has been relying on voluntary environmental programs as the primary component of its federal climate change policy since the announcement of President Clinton's Climate Change Action Plan in 1993. European Union countries began adopting voluntary approaches as their national policy on climate change in the 1990s, and countries that signed on to the Kyoto Protocol relied heavily on voluntary programs to encourage reductions in GHG emissions prior to binding restrictions coming on line under the protocol in 2008. Voluntary programs have also become a preferred policy instrument in many countries for other global problems such as ozone depletion, and for more localized concerns such as non-point source water pollution or solid waste.

President Clinton's 1993 Climate Change Action Plan spawned numerous well known EPA public voluntary programs, including Climate Wise, Green Lights, Energy Star, and Motor Challenge, the majority of which focus on encouraging increased investment in energy efficiency. Other EPA initiatives such as Climate Leaders and Methane Voluntary Programs encourage GHG emissions reductions from large corporations, consumers, industrial and commercial buildings, and many major industrial sectors. Notwithstanding their popularity at the EPA, the agency's focus on such voluntary initiatives is marginal when compared to the agency's activities under its statutory and regulatory programs. Voluntary environmental programs comprise only a fraction of the EPA's total operating budget (less than 2%), and budgets for individual programs are also relatively small. Further, voluntary programs at the EPA are strongly criticized for extremely low rates of participation by firms eligible to participate. Thus the potential for voluntary environmental programs to result in meaningful reductions of GHGs in the United States is extremely limited.

B. Climate Change Legislation

There has been considerable activity since 2007 designed to move Congress towards addressing the issue of GHG emissions through comprehensive federal legislation. In December 2007, the Senate Environment and Public Works Committee reported out the Lieberman-Warner Climate Security Act ("Lieberman-Warner"), which advocated a "cap-and-trade" approach to reducing nationwide GHG emissions. Lieberman-Warner was the first bill addressing GHG emissions and climate change to ever pass out of a congressional committee. The bill was withdrawn in June 2008 before the Senate had the opportunity to vote on it. This occurred primarily due to Senate Democrats' inability to obtain the 60 votes needed to avoid a Republican filibuster of a vote to continue debate on the bill.

During the subsequent 2008 Presidential campaign, both Senators John McCain and Barack Obama agreed that a comprehensive legislative approach to the problem of climate change was desirable. Both candidates also agreed that a cap-and-trade approach was their preferred solution, although they disagreed on the exact details of what such legislation should include. Under the basic concept of a "cap-and-trade" system, each regulated company would have a limit on the amount of GHGs it could emit. Each company would be required to have an "emissions permit" for every ton of GHG emissions it releases into the atmosphere. These permits establish an enforceable limit, or cap, on the amount of GHGs that each company is allowed to emit. Over time, the limits become stricter, allowing fewer and fewer emissions, until the overall reduction goal under the legislation is met. This is similar to the cap and trade program enacted by the Clean Air Act (see Chapter 3, "Air Pollution," of this Almanac) for the purpose of reducing sulfur dioxide and nitrogen oxides emissions that had created an interstate and international acid rain problem.

Under the basic concept of a cap-and-trade system, some companies would be able to reduce their emissions below their required limit more easily or cheaply than others. These more efficient companies, who emit less than their allowance, would be allowed to sell their extra permits to companies unable to make reductions as easily. This creates a system that seeks to achieve a set level of overall reductions, while rewarding the most efficient companies and seeking to meet the cap at the lowest possible cost to the economy.

Following his election in the fall of 2008, President Obama again expressed preference for a national cap-and-trade program to reduce GHG emissions to 1990 levels by 2020 and by 80% below 1990 levels by 2050. These were the reductions proposed in the Lieberman-Warner bill earlier that year. On June 26, 2009, the House of Representatives passed the American Clean Energy and Security Act, known as "Waxman-Markey" for its two principal sponsors Representatives Henry Waxman (D-Cal.) and Ed Markey (D-Mass.). The bill proposed reductions of GHG emissions to 17% below 2005 levels by 2020 and to 83% below those levels by 2050. The emissions reductions requirements would begin in 2012 when the bill mandates a 3% reduction in national GHG emissions below 2005 levels. Waxman-Markey was the first bill ever passed by either house of Congress to reduce GHG emissions.

Following the House of Representatives passage of Waxman-Markey, various Senate committees began work on companion climate change legislation. Efforts to bring a Senate climate change bill to a floor vote prior to the December 2009 United Nation's Copenhagen conference proved unsuccessful. Supporters of the United States' re-engagement in international climate change treaty negotiations believed that prior enactment of domestic climate change legislation by the United States would help the international community reach final agreement at the Copenhagen meetings on a framework to replace the expiring Kyoto Protocol. Numerous factors affected the ability of a climate bill to be passed by the Senate prior to Copenhagen, including significant attention given to other national priorities such as health care reform and financial regulatory reform.

Final passage of climate change legislation by the Senate is by no means a certainty. Numerous obstacles to final passage of climate change legislation by Congress exist, including concerns over the economic costs of such legislation during a time of national economic turmoil. The country's struggles with the effects of a prolonged recession are expected to continue. Thus the political climate may not be favorable for legislative enactment of a comprehensive national GHG emissions reduction program. Among the concerns raised in opposition include the potential for increases in energy prices at a time that energy prices are already volatile, imposition of tens of billions of dollars in new compliance costs on industry at a time that many companies are struggling for economic survival, and the specter of job losses that might result if companies fail at a time of already high unemployment in many parts of the country. Adding to the uncertain prospects for passage of final legislation by the Senate is the politically controversial nature of the climate change issue itself. It remains unclear whether the 60 votes in the Senate necessary to avoid a filibuster of the sort that derailed the Lieberman-Warner bill in 2008 can be obtained.

C. Clean Air Act

During the 2008 Presidential campaign, Senator Obama proposed that one alternative for addressing the climate change issue would be to amend the Clean Air Act (CAA) (see Chapter 3, "Air Pollution," of this Almanac) to give the EPA authority to directly regulate GHG emissions. However, both candidate and later President Obama expressed a preference for a comprehensive legislative program for GHG reductions from Congress rather than utilization of the existing CAA for this purpose. Nonetheless, while the merits of comprehensive GHG emission legislation continue to be debated in Congress, the recent U.S. Supreme Court case of *Massachusetts v. EPA,* (2007) has the EPA moving down the road towards eventual regulation of GHGs under the CAA.

In *Massachusetts v. EPA*, the Supreme Court held that the CAA's sweeping definition of "air pollutant" includes any physical or chemical substance which can be emitted into the ambient air. Thus GHGs qualify as "air pollutants" under this definition. The Court further held that the EPA was required by the Act to determine whether or not emissions of GHGs cause or contribute to air pollution which may reasonably be anticipated to endanger public health or welfare, or whether the science is too uncertain to make a reasoned decision.

In response to the Court's ruling, in April 2009, the EPA issued a proposed finding that six GHGs—carbon dioxide, methane, nitrous oxide, hydrofluorocarbons, perfluorocarbons and sulfur hexafluoride—contribute to air pollution that may endanger public health or welfare through the threat of climate change. This is known as an "endangerment finding" under the Clean Air Act. Following issuance of the proposed finding, the EPA initiated a 60-day public comment period and eventually received and considered more than 380,000 comments on the issue. On December 7, 2009, the EPA announced its final "endangerment finding" that GHGs threaten the public health and welfare of the American people. This finding does not, however, impose any requirements or obligations on industry or other entities under the CAA to reduce GHGs. Instead, this final endangerment finding creates the authority under the CAA for the EPA to move forward with creating regulations designed to reduce emissions of GHGs. This regulatory process will take anywhere from a few to several years before regulation of GHGs under the Act can begin.

Further, Congress may eventually decide to preempt any coverage by the CAA to GHGs in favor of comprehensive legislation directly addressing issues relating to climate change. Indeed, both President Obama and EPA Administrator Lisa Jackson emphasized their preference for comprehensive legislation to address this issue at the time both the proposed and final endangerment findings were issued by the EPA. Thus it will be some time before it is known whether the CAA will be actually utilized to address emissions of GHGs.

D. National Environmental Policy Act

The National Environmental Policy Act (NEPA) (see Chapter 7, "The National Environmental Policy Act," of this Almanac) requires federal agencies to consider significant environmental impacts during the agency's decision making process when considering whether to undertake proposed "major federal actions." In addition to considering significant environmental impacts of the proposed action, the agency must consider reasonable alternatives to the proposed plan and discuss why it selected the proposal rather than the alternatives.

Court decisions have found that NEPA requires consideration of GHG emissions or climate change issues as potential "significant environmental impacts" of proposed agency actions. NEPA is, however, a weak statute for purposes of regulating activity that might contribute to climate change. NEPA imposes only procedural requirements on federal agencies. Judicial review is limited to determining whether an agency adequately evaluated a proposal's environmental impacts. A court may not reject an agency decision because it believes the proposal is unwise or does not select the most environmentally appropriate alternative, including alternatives that would avoid increasing atmospheric concentrations of GHG emissions.

E. Endangered Species Act

The Endangered Species Act (ESA) (see Chapter 8, "Endangered Species," of this Almanac) requires federal agencies to ensure that any projects they fund, authorize, or permit will not jeopardize endangered species or their critical habitats. Federal courts have ruled that agencies must consider the effects of climate change when assessing risks to endangered species. In a vigorously litigated example, in May 2008, the Department of the Interior listed the polar bear as a species threatened with extinction under the ESA because of shrinking sea ice attributed to climate change.

On December 16, 2008, the Secretary of the Interior issued a new rule under the ESA in direct response to the polar bear listing decision. The rule found that GHGs and global warming impacts of specific projects need not be considered in ESA reviews because of the difficulty in linking such emissions to specific impacts on specific listed species. A number of environmental groups challenged the new rule in court and members of Congress sought to invoke legislative authority to review and overturn administrative agency rules.

On March 3, 2009, President Obama issued a memorandum instructing the Secretaries of the Interior and Commerce to review the December 16 rule and determine whether new rules were needed. In the interim, Obama requested that agency heads "exercise discretion" and follow the previous regulations (which courts had found require consideration of the effects of climate change when assessing risks to endangered species). On March 11, 2009, Congress passed legislation giving the Obama Administration authority to rescind the December 16 Department of Interior rule immediately, without undertaking a formal rulemaking process.

F. Common Law Litigation

Both private and public (state government) plaintiffs have attempted to sue emitters of GHGs under common law tort theories. Such suits contend that large producers of GHG emissions are contributing to the alleged public nuisance (see Chapter 2, "The Authority to Protect the Environment," of this Almanac) of global warming and climate change. The two most significant cases have been *Connecticut v. American Electric Power*, (S.D. N.Y. 2005) (suit by eight states and New York City against electric power companies emitting 650 million tons of carbon dioxide annually) and *California v. General Motors*, (N.D. Cal. 2007) (suit by the state of California against six automakers producing vehicles emitting over 289 million metric tons of carbon dioxide).

Until recently, such common law tort suits against emitters of GHGs had been uniformly unsuccessful and were dismissed primarily under the "political question doctrine." Under this doctrine, the plaintiffs' tort claims were deemed to present "political" questions that should not be resolved by the judicial branch. This doctrine assumes that "political" questions involve policy determinations more properly reserved for the political branches (legislative and executive) of government. The district court's dismissals of the public nuisance suits in *American Electric Power* and *General Motors* found that numerous policy determinations on the subject of global warming must first be made by the political branches of government before the courts could properly resolve the plaintiffs' tort claims. The *General Motors* court cited *Massachusetts v. EPA* as evidence that policy decisions concerning the authority and standards for GHG emissions lie with the political branches of government, and not with the courts.

However, recent court decisions have reversed the earlier trend of dismissal of global warming based public nuisance suits on political question doctrine grounds. In September 2009, the U.S. Second Circuit Court of Appeals reversed the district court decision in *Connecticut v. American Electric Power*, holding that the public nuisance suit against the electric power companies could go forward notwithstanding the political question doctrine challenge. Similarly, in October 2009, the U.S. Fifth Circuit Court of Appeals reversed a similar decision of a Mississippi federal district court in the case of *Comer v. Murphy Oil Company*. In *Comer*, the district court had dismissed on political question doctrine grounds a suit by Mississippi coastal property owners alleging the GHG emissions of 31 oil, gas, and coal companies had contributed to the public nuisance of global warming. The property owners' suit argued that their properties would not have been damaged as severely by Hurricane Katrina in 2005 if the defendant's GHG emissions had not contributed to climate change that intensified the storm's ferocity.

Although the rulings by the Second and Fifth Circuits allow the *American Electric Power* and *Comer* cases to continue, this does not necessarily mean the plaintiffs will be ultimately successful in these suits. A number of difficult issues remain to be resolved in these cases. This includes the particularly challenging burden for the plaintiffs to establish that the specific GHG emissions of the defendants were the factual and legal cause of the plaintiffs' specific damages. In this regard, the physical characteristics of GHGs are of particular importance. When GHGs are released into the atmosphere, they disperse evenly around the globe and intermingle with other existing atmospheric concentrations of GHGs. A ton of a GHGs emitted in Mississippi has the same effect on global warming, if any, as a ton emitted anywhere else in the world (such as in New York City, or Moscow, or Bejing). In addition, atmospheric GHGs circling the globe remain in the atmosphere for many decades. Thus whatever impact GHGs may have on global warming and climate change, such an impact is cumulative together with all other GHG emissions from all other sources. This makes it quite problematic to demonstrate in a tort based law suit that specific GHG emissions have localized effects or that specific emissions are the cause of specific localized impacts.

CHAPTER 11: PUBLIC ENVIRONMENTAL INFORMATION AND ENVIRONMENTAL ATTORNEYS

I. THE IMPORTANCE OF ENVIRONMENTAL INFORMATION

Information is of critical importance in environmental law. A strong system of environmental protection depends upon federal and state regulators having access to necessary information. This is especially true in such areas as pollution control, natural resources management, and regulation of toxic substances and hazardous wastes. Thus environmental regulators must have access to information about the activities of businesses and individuals that might have an adverse affect on human health and environmental conditions. Information allows identification of the causes of environmental problems. It allows environmental regulators to design appropriate solutions and programs to deal with those problems. Information must be gathered on whether businesses and other environmental actors are complying with their obligations under environmental regulatory programs. Similarly, information is necessary to tell whether solutions are working and environmental conditions are improving.

Information is also of great importance to the general public. The ability of citizens to participate in important governmental activities such as environmental regulation depends upon access to information about the environmental activities of businesses and industry. Access to public environmental information also greatly enhances the ability of citizens to know what environmental risks they may face in their communities. Public environmental information empowers citizens with knowledge about environmental conditions in the places where they live, work, go to school, or recreate. Such knowledge helps citizens to evaluate the environmental hazards and risks posed by the activities of businesses and industry that they encounter in their daily lives.

During the last few decades, federal and state "right-to-know" laws have sought to make more data on environmental risks and hazards available to the public. The basic purpose of such laws is to allow individuals to make informed decisions about the presence of pollution, hazardous substances, or other similar concerns in their environments. Access to information about the presence of pollution or hazardous substances in communities allows individuals to take appropriate actions in response. Such actions might include avoiding areas where such pollution is occurring or toxic substances are located. Informed citizens can take other precautions against exposure to pollution or other hazards, or can make decisions about where to live or work or play. Informed citizens can also raise concerns with local businesses or employers, seek to publicize such concerns in the media, or create political pressures for government to address specific problems in the community.

II. THE EMERGENCY PLANNING AND COMMUNITY RIGHT-TO-KNOW ACT (EPCRA)

A. Congressional Enactment of EPCRA

Congress enacted the Emergency Planning and Community Right-to-Know Act of 1986 (EPCRA) as a national legislative program for toxic chemical risk and community safety. EPCRA establishes requirements for federal, state, and local governments and industry regarding emergency planning and "community right-to-know" reporting on hazardous and toxic chemicals and substances. EPCRA is designed to increase the public's knowledge and access to information on chemical hazards at individual facilities, the uses made of such chemicals, and the manner in which they are released into the environment. States and local communities work with industry under EPCRA to utilize the information generated to improve safety and protect public health and the environment.

EPCRA was enacted in response to public concerns over the environmental and safety hazards inherent in the storage and handling of toxic chemicals. Such public concern exploded following notorious accidental chemical releases in the mid-1980s by Union Carbide plants in Bhopal, India and Institute, West Virginia. The December 1984 Bhopal tragedy was by far the more serious of the two incidents, as an accidental release of methyl isocynate killed over 3,000 persons and severely injured scores of others. In contrast, no deaths were attributed to an

August 1985 accidental release of aldicarb oxime at Union Carbide's West Virginia plant, and the scores of residents adversely affected were only briefly hospitalized. However, coming on the heels of the already impassioned controversy over Bhopal, and following industry assurances that a similar accident could not happen in the United States, the West Virginia incident, at the very least, strengthened the resolve of Congress to affirmatively respond to Bhopal. That response came in the form of EPCRA's provisions requiring comprehensive emergency planning for the potential risks of chemical storage and handling and the reporting of chemical releases.

B. Emergency Planning

1. State Emergency Response Commissions

EPCRA contains emergency planning requirements intended to assist communities in preparing for and responding to emergencies involving toxic chemicals and hazardous substances. EPCRA required each state to establish a State Emergency Response Commission (SERC). Each SERC was required to designate local emergency planning districts and for each such district to appoint a Local Emergency Planning Committee (LEPC). The SERC is responsible for supervising and coordinating the activities of each LEPC in the state.

2. Local Emergency Planning Committees

Each LEPC is required to develop an emergency response plan for its district and review it at least annually. Emergency response plans are developed through a process involving participation by local stakeholders. The membership of the LEPC must include: (1) police, fire, civil defense, and public health professionals; (2) environment, transportation, and hospital officials; (3) a representative from every facility in the district subject to EPCRA emergency planning requirements; (4) elected state and local officials; and (5) representatives from community groups and the media. The emergency response plan developed by the LEPC is required to contain the following elements:

- identification of facilities and transportation routes of extremely hazardous substances;
- description of emergency response procedures both on and off the site of a chemical accident or release;
- designation of a community coordinator and facility emergency coordinators to implement the plan;
- outline of emergency notification procedures;

- description of how to determine the area and populations that will probably be affected by chemical accidents or releases;
- description of local emergency equipment and facilities and the persons responsible for them;
- outline of evacuation plans;
- training programs for emergency responders; and
- methods and schedules for practicing emergency response plans.

3. Facilities Subject to Emergency Planning Requirements

Determining whether a facility storing or handling toxic chemicals or hazardous substances is subject to emergency planning requirements is relatively straightforward. The Environmental Protection Agency (EPA) publishes a list of "extremely hazardous substances" (EHS) subject to EPCRA requirements. For each chemical or substance on the EHS list, the EPA designates a number, expressed in pounds, known as a threshold planning quantity (TPQ). If a facility has on its property an amount of an extremely hazardous substance that is equal to or larger than its threshold planning quantity number, that facility is subject to emergency planning requirements under EPCRA. The facility is required to notify both their SERC and LEPC within 60 days of producing or receiving a substance on the EHS list in an amount that equals or exceeds the TPQ. The facility is also required to cooperate in emergency plan preparation and designate an emergency response coordinator who will work with the LEPC on developing and implementing the local emergency plan at the facility.

C. Emergency Notification

EPCRA requires facilities to immediately report to their SERC and LEPC accidental releases of a "reportable quantity" (RQ) of either of two types of "hazardous chemicals:" (1) substances on the EPA's EHS list, and (2) substances appearing on the EPA's list of "hazardous substances" under the Comprehensive Environmental Response, Compensation, and Liability Act (discussed in Chapter 6, "Toxic Substances and Hazardous Wastes," of this Almanac). On both of these lists, the EPA designates a number, expressed in pounds, that constitutes the "reportable quantity" for that substance. The following information is required to be included in the emergency notification:

- the name of the substance;
- an indication of whether the substance is extremely hazardous;
- an estimate of the quantity released into the environment;

- the time and duration of the release;
- whether the release occurred into air, water, and/or land;
- any known or anticipated severe or chronic health risks associated with the release in question and, where necessary, advice regarding medical attention for exposed individuals;
- proper precautions that should be undertaken; and
- the name and telephone number of the appropriate contact person at the facility.

EPCRA requires a written follow-up notice to be submitted to the SERC and LEPC as soon as practicable after the release. The follow-up notice must update the information included in the emergency notification. It must further provide information on actual response actions taken and advice regarding medical attention necessary for citizens exposed to the release.

D. Community Right-to-Know Reporting Requirements

In order to increase community awareness of chemical hazards and to facilitate emergency planning, EPCRA imposes certain continuous reporting requirements on facilities under two categories: (1) MSDS reporting, and (2) inventory reporting.

1. Material Safety Data Sheet (MSDS) Reporting

Facilities that manufacture, process, or store any hazardous chemical for which that facility is required to maintain a Material Safety Data Sheet (MSDS) must submit that MSDS to their SERC, LEPC, and local fire department. MSDSs are required under Occupational Safety and Health Administration (OSHA) regulations for hazardous chemicals stored or used in the work place. MSDSs are detailed information sheets that provide data on health and physical hazards of chemicals together with related protective measures. Over 500,000 products have a MSDS which is normally created by and obtained from the manufacturer of the chemical substance in question. This reporting requirement is subject to the following threshold limits established by the EPA: (1) for "extremely hazardous substances" (EHSs), either the lower of 500 pounds or the threshold planning quantity (TPQ), and (2) 10,000 pounds for all other hazardous chemicals.

2. Inventory Reporting

Facilities must also report to their SERC, LEPC, and local fire department their inventories of all on site chemicals for which a MSDS exists. This level of reporting is intended to provide information on the amounts, location and storage conditions of hazardous chemicals and mixtures containing hazardous chemicals present at facilities. The inventory report must include the following information:

- the chemical name or the common name indicated on the MSDS;
- an estimate of the maximum amount of the chemical present at any time during the preceding calendar year and the average daily amount;
- a brief description of the manner of storage of the chemical;
- the location of the chemical at the facility; and
- an indication of whether the owner of the facility elects to withhold location information from disclosure to the public.

E. Toxics Release Inventory (TRI) Reporting Requirements

Perhaps the most significant impact of EPCRA was its requirement that the EPA create the Toxics Release Inventory (TRI). EPCRA requires certain companies to submit annual data to the EPA on amounts of certain toxic chemicals released into the air, water, land, or transferred off-site. The EPA maintains this data in a national computer database—the TRI—accessible by the public, primarily through the Internet. The TRI database contains detailed information on nearly 650 chemicals and chemical categories that about 22,000 industrial and other facilities release annually through disposal or other waste management and recycling practices.

EPCRA requires facilities to submit a Toxic Chemical Release Inventory Form (Form R) to the EPA and designated state officials by July 1 of each year reflecting releases during the preceding calendar year. A facility will be subject to the TRI reporting requirements if it:

- has ten or more full time employees; and
- falls within a specified "Standard Industrial Classification Code" (which include various manufacturing sectors, metal and coal mining, electric utilities, commercial hazardous waste treatment, and other industrial sectors); and
- manufactures more than 25,000 pounds per year of a toxic chemical included on the EPA's TRI list; or
- processes more than 25,000 pounds per year of a toxic chemical included on the EPA's TRI list; or
- otherwise uses more than 10,000 pounds per year of a toxic chemical included on the EPA's TRI list; or

- manufactures, processes, or otherwise uses a listed "persistent bioaccumulative toxic chemical" (such as dioxin compounds or lead) above the respective reporting thresholds designed for that chemical.

The TRI reports are required to include estimates of the "annual quantity of the toxic chemicals entering each environmental medium"—primarily air, water, and land. EPCRA authorizes individuals to bring citizen suits against companies that fail to comply with TRI reporting requirements.

The EPA's national TRI database provides the public with access to a wealth of information about toxic chemical releases and other waste management activities at a local, state, regional, and national level. Citizens are able to utilize the TRI data for a variety of purposes, including informing themselves of risks and concerns in their own communities and environments. For example, TRI data can inform citizens of whether they live near businesses that use toxic chemicals or whether toxic chemicals are being released near local schools or public sources of drinking water. TRI information can also be utilized by federal, state and local governments to identify and gain a better understanding of potential concerns, to prioritize among those concerns, and to assess ongoing pollution prevention activities. Researchers, public interest groups, the media, as well as others are able to access the information for various purposes as well.

The EPA provides public access to TRI data over the Internet through the *TRI Explorer*, located at www.epa.gov/triexplorer. The *TRI Explorer* is a search engine capable of generating reports of TRI data summarized for individual states or the entire country, or reports on releases, waste transfers, or waste quantities grouped by state, by industry classification, by specific facility name, or by zip code. Another option provided by the EPA for public utilization of TRI information is the TRI.NET data engine, accessible at www.epa.gov/triinter/tridotnet/index.html. TRI.NET is an application that can be downloaded on a personal computer to allow for more interactive and user friendly analyses of TRI data. For example, TRI.NET utilizes mapping technologies (such as Google Maps, Google Earth, or Virtual Earth) allowing users to visualize where TRI releases are occurring. TRI.NET also includes the "My TRI Neighborhood" feature allowing searches to limit results to facilities releasing TRI chemicals located within a specified distance of a specific street address. This allows the public to visualize facilities releasing TRI chemicals in small communities and neighborhoods.

Public access to TRI information has been credited with influencing companies to make voluntary reductions in releases of chemicals subject to the reporting requirement. Manufacturing facilities have been required to report to the TRI program since 1987. The EPA asserts that public dissemination of information from the TRI database, especially through media reporting and such well-known outlets as the non-profit group Green Media Toolshed's "Scorecard" Internet website, has induced companies to sharply reduce overall levels of releases of TRI chemicals since the program's beginning. Based on 2007 information, the EPA asserts that overall releases of TRI chemicals that have been consistently reported since 1988 have been reduced by 61%. These reductions in reported releases have occurred notwithstanding the fact that the releases themselves may be completely lawful under existing environmental regulatory programs, such as the Clean Air Act (see Chapter 3, "Air Pollution," of this Almanac), the Clean Water Act (see Chapter 4, "Water Quality," of this Almanac), and the Resource Conservation and Recovery Act (see Chapter 6, "Toxic Substances and Hazardous Wastes," of this Almanac). Importantly, EPCRA's TRI reporting requirement does not itself make the releases of toxic chemicals to air, water or land unlawful. The requirement is simply for the releases to be annually reported and the information to be made available to the public.

Nonetheless, since the beginning of the program, TRI disclosures have indeed led to significant voluntary reductions in releases of reported chemicals. However, uncertainty exists as to the specific reasons the annual TRI reporting requirements have had such an effect. Some limited studies by economists have shown that public disclosure of negative environmental information by companies can motivate them to improve their future environmental performance. Companies may be concerned about negative reaction to disclosure of information that is perceived by the public as evidence that the company is acting in ways that are environmentally harmful. Thus the TRI's ability to identify companies with high levels of releases of toxic chemicals into the environment can create strong incentives for companies to reduce such pollution in the future. Reports by the media or public interest groups that a particular company is the largest releaser of TRI chemicals in a particular community can lead to considerable undesirable attention for that company. This may in turn motivate the company to change its operations or performance in order to reduce the amount of TRI releases that will be disclosed in future TRI reports.

III. ADDITIONAL SOURCES OF PUBLICLY ACCESSIBLE ENVIRONMENTAL INFORMATION

The perceived success of the TRI in demonstrating that public distribution of information may improve the environmental performance of business and industry has encouraged even greater public demands for access to environmental information. Further, the belief that the public has a fundamental right to know about pollution problems and other environmental hazards in their communities has also strongly contributed to increased demands for publicly available environmental information.

Thus over the last several years, the amount and types of environmental information made available to the public has grown considerably. Similarly, much greater use is being made of that information by federal and state governments, environmental groups, communities, and concerned citizens. More environmental information is currently produced and made publicly available by the EPA and many other private information providers than at any time in the past. Moreover, tremendous advances in Internet based information sharing technologies have made it far easier for these information providers to produce this information and make it publicly available. The following are several examples of sources of publicly accessible environmental information.

A. Envirofacts Data Warehouse

The Envirofacts Data Warehouse is a public environmental information database created and operated by the EPA and which can be accessed over the Internet at www.epa.gov/enviro/. Envirofacts is designed to provide a single point of public access to information collected by the EPA under its many national environmental regulatory programs. Envirofacts integrates information from several different EPA databases that collect information from facilities required to report about such activities as hazardous waste disposal, air pollution emissions, toxic chemical releases, Superfund sites, or water discharge permits. Individual users of the Envirofacts program may conduct broad searches for information within all of these integrated databases simultaneously. The program's "Quick Start" feature allows users to retrieve all information in the entire Envirofacts database about environmental regulatory activities in their area by simply entering either a specific zip code or the name of a city or county. Users may also conduct more narrowly focused searches for information within specific databases in the system. For example, users may retrieve information about specific facilities or groups of facilities within specific subject areas included in the database under such discrete topics as Water, Air, Waste, Land, Toxics, and Radiation.

The Envirofacts Data Warehouse includes the following specific environmental information databases and data retrieval options.

1. Water

Envirofacts integrates water information from such EPA databases as the Safe Drinking Water Information System (SDWIS), the Permit Compliance System (PCS), and the National Drinking Water Contaminant Occurrence Database (NCOD). The SDWIS contains information about violations of EPA's drinking water regulations by public water systems. The PCS includes information on companies which have been issued permits to discharge waste water into rivers. Information can be retrieved on when permits were issued and expire, how much waste a company is permitted to discharge, and monitoring data showing what the company has actually discharged. The NCOD was created pursuant to the Safe Drinking Water Act (see Chapter 4, "Water Quality," of this Almanac) and contains data from public water systems and other sources regarding the occurrence of physical, chemical, microbial, and radiological contaminants.

2. Air

Databases related to air include the Aerometric Information Retrieval System (AIRS), a computer based repository for information about air pollution in the United States. AIRS is operated by the EPA and state and local air pollution control agencies. The information included in the AIRS database comes from reporting by various stationary sources of air pollution, such as electric power plants, factories, and other industrial sources, regarding the air pollutants they produce. Additionally, Envirofacts contains a UV Index database which provides information on amounts of harmful ultraviolet (UV) radiation likely to reach the Earth at any given time as a result of stratospheric ozone layer depletion combined with variations in seasons and weather. The UV Index predicts ultraviolet radiation levels on a 0–10+ scale to assist in making decisions on appropriate sun-protective behaviors.

3. Waste

Envirofacts contains Biennial Reporting system information on the generation of hazardous waste from large quantity generators and data on waste management practices from treatment, storage and disposal facilities. The Resource Conservation and Recovery Act (RCRA) (see Chapter 6, "Toxic Substances and Hazardous Wastes," of this Almanac) requires the EPA to compile such information twice a year into a Hazardous Waste Report (Biennial Report) to provide a basis for analysis of trends regarding hazardous waste disposal. Similarly, the EPA has created the Resource Conservation and Recovery Act Information System (RCRIS) to compile information on activities reported to state environmental agencies by hazardous waste generators, transporters, and facilities that treat, store, and dispose of hazardous waste. RCRIS database information is also searchable within the Envirofacts database.

Pursuant to its obligations under the Comprehensive Environmental Response, Compensation, and Liability Act (CERCLA) (see Chapter 6, "Toxic Substances and Hazardous Wastes," of this Almanac), the EPA has created the Comprehensive Environmental Response, Compensation, and Liability Information System (CERCLIS) database for the purpose of compiling information on Superfund sites around the country. Envirofacts includes the CERCLIS database allowing users to search for any combination of facility name and geographic location in order to retrieve Superfund data.

4. Land

In addition to the RCRIS and CERCLIS databases, other databases are included in Envirofacts that provide searchable information relating to activities that may affect land. The Assessment, Cleanup and Redevelopment Exchange System (ACRES) contains information on assessment, cleanup and redevelopment activities at Superfund sites known as "brownfields" (primarily urban properties contaminated by CERCLA hazardous substances). Similarly, Envirofacts contains an interactive tool known as Cleanups in My Community (CIMC) which allows users to map, list, and find cleanup progress profiles for facilities or properties contaminated by hazardous substances and that are being, or have been, cleaned up under CERCLA or RCRA programs.

5. Toxics

The Envirofacts database integrates information from the EPA's publicly accessible computerized TRI database described earlier in this chapter.

6. Radiation

Envirofacts contains information from two databases relating to radiation, the Radiation Information Database (RADINFO) and RadNet. The RADINFO database collects information about facilities subject to EPA regulations on radiation and radioactivity. The RadNet is a national network of monitoring stations that regularly collect air, precipitation, drinking water, and milk samples for analysis of radioactivity. The RadNet network has been used to track environmental releases resulting from nuclear emergencies and to provide baseline data during routine conditions.

7. Facilities Information

The Envirofacts database integrates information from the Facility Registry System (FRS), a database managed by the EPA to identify facilities, sites, and places subject to environmental regulations or which are otherwise of environmental interest. Facilities information is also included from the EPA's Enforcement and Compliance History Online (ECHO) database. The ECHO database relates to facilities regulated as Clean Air Act stationary sources of air pollutants, as permitted dischargers under the Clean Water Act, or which have permits or are otherwise regulated under the Resource Conservation and Recovery Act. Four components of the enforcement process for these regulatory programs are documented in the ECHO database: (1) the occurrence of a monitoring event such as an inspection or a self-report; (2) the determination of a violation; (3) the occurrence of an enforcement action to address a violation; and (4) penalties associated with enforcement actions.

8. Mapping Capabilities

The Envirofacts database includes search tools allowing the public to select a specified geographic location and map a cross-section of environmental data pertaining to that location. All of the integrated environmental information regarding facilities or locations of environmental concern contained in the Envirofacts database can be accessed through the mapping features. Two primary mapping tools—EnviroMapper, located at www.epa.gov/emefdata/em4ef.home, and MyEnvironment, located at www.epa.gov/myenvironment/—are accessible through the Envirofacts database.

Users can enter a geographic area (such as a street address, zip code, city, county, water body, national park name, etc.) into either of these mapping tools and generate a map image showing the different EPA regulated facilities or other environmental concerns present within that area. Users may also use the mapping tools to conduct narrower searches targeting specific industries or regulatory programs (such as water, air, or land based). For example, users can search by neighborhood and generate maps that show regulated facilities and present community environmental statistics on air quality (including daily ozone and particulate matter forecasts). Another search can generate a map specific to cancer risk levels or water quality or any other factors that might affect the overall environmental quality and livability of a community. A map generated to show facilities releasing toxic chemicals in a specific geographical location would allow users to zoom into a specific facility shown on the map to learn about statistics specific to that facility. This might include such information as how much of those chemicals the facility can lawfully release, the facility's compliance record under applicable statutes, or any records of current violations. The options for conducting such searches and generating information of interest are virtually endless.

B. Scorecard

Perhaps the most well known source of public environmental information over the last decade has been Scorecard, an Internet website managed by the environmental organization Green Media Toolshed, and located at www.scorecard.org. The application was originally launched in 1998 by the non-profit organization the Environmental Defense Fund. Scorecard integrates over 400 scientific and governmental environmental information databases to allow users to generate customized profiles of local environmental problems and the health effects of toxic substances. Virtually all publicly available data on polluters and other regulated environmental actors collected by federal regulatory agencies is captured by Scorecard making it a powerful tool for assessing environmental risks nationwide. The environmental information contained in the Scorecard database can be revised as the data sources upon which it draws are updated.

Scorecard was an immediate sensation upon its initial launch. The website received more than a million hits over its first two days of operation in April 1998. It was the first web-based application to seek to centralize and integrate the vast amounts of obscure and, at the time, largely inaccessible data contained in numerous EPA regulatory databases. The goal of the Environmental Defense Fund was to make that information relevant and applicable to the daily lives of any and every citizen in the United States. Users can simply type in their zip code and immediately access lists of the top polluters in their area or information on the presence of specific toxic chemicals or other pollutants. In addition to learning about environmental concerns in their communities, such data can be compared between counties or states. The website also provides explanations, in understandable language, about each type of pollutant tracked by Scorecard and their associated health effects.

The success of Scorecard is credited with pushing the EPA to eventually develop its own online interface for its many environmental informational databases, the Envirofacts Data Warehouse. In November 2005, the Environmental Defense Fund transferred ownership of Scorecard to Green Media Toolshed.

C. Right-to-Know Network

The Right-to-Know Network (RTK Net), located at www.rtknet.org, is a project of OMB Watch, a nonprofit advocacy organization originally created to monitor and make transparent the activities of the White House Office of Management and Budget. OMB Watch later expanded its focus to address issues of federal regulatory policy, including environmental. The organization created the RTK Net to provide public access to environmental and public health information such as pollution releases, chemical spills, and hazardous waste generation. The RTK Net is an Internet search engine that integrates data from a number of EPA databases. These databases include the TRI, the RCRIS, the Biennial Reporting system, toxic chemical spill and other accident data reported to the National Response Center, and "Risk Management Plans" required by the Clean Air Act for companies that use certain flammable and toxic substances.

D. ChemicalRight2Know.org

The ChemicalRight2Know.org forum, located at www.ChemicalRight2Know.org, was created through a partnership between the EPA and the Environmental Council of States (ECOS), a non-profit, non-partisan association of state and territorial environmental agency leaders. The ChemicalRight2Know.org website is, in part, a one-stop point of Internet access to a wide variety of information about the TRI and other related environmental data. In addition to making TRI data publicly available, the website further allows the EPA and other knowledgeable individuals from government, public interest groups, industry, and academia to collaborate in supporting efforts by the concerned public to find, understand, and use environmental information. These entities and individuals use the forum to post discussion items, position papers, and original research on various TRI-related topics as well as to provide commentary and feedback on these items. The online discussion aspect of the ChemicalRight2Know.org forum seeks to build public understanding of the TRI program and the different ways in which TRI data is used.

E. ToxicRisk.com

In April 2009, Mapcruzin.com, an independent firm specializing in Geographic Information Systems (GIS) projects, launched ToxicRisk.com, accessible at www.ToxicRisk.com. ToxicRisk.com is an Internet mapping application utilizing TRI data. The website utilizes Google Maps and Google Earth to allow users to map and visualize facilities releasing TRI chemicals, using searches by city, state, zip code, or place name. Once a facility is located, links are provided to the Right-to-Know Network for detailed chemical pollution release data for that facility and to Scorecard for chemical information and associated health affects.

IV. ENVIRONMENTAL ATTORNEYS

Citizens armed with information and knowledge about polluting activities or other conduct causing environmental risk or harm may want to take some legal action in response. Initially, this might involve bringing that information or knowledge to the attention of federal, state, or local environmental regulators in the hope that appropriate legal action will follow. Citizens might also consider pursuing a "citizen suit" authorized by a federal or state environmental statute. A citizen suit is a legal proceeding in court that seeks to enforce environmental laws against violators or to compel government to take some regulatory action required by the laws. Further, such information or knowledge may form the basis for private legal actions to compensate people for contamination of property or personal injury they may have suffered as a result of harmful environmental activities.

Individuals wanting to navigate the often extremely complicated world of environmental law will likely need to consult or otherwise interact with environmental attorneys. As the various chapters of this Almanac would suggest, the world of environmental law can be quite intimidating. Environmental law is often unflatteringly compared to tax law because of its similar maze of complex federal and state statutes and regulations. In many ways, environmental law is like another language, with a multitude of mystifying acronyms and endless technical terms each with its own very specific definition. Experienced environmental attorneys speak this language and understand the regulatory landscape from which it originates. Further, environmental attorneys can communicate in this language with the federal and state environmental agency regulators who are responsible for enforcing the laws. Indeed, these agencies generally have attorneys working in them to assist the regulators in navigating this often extremely complex world. Thus communicating with an environmental attorney may help in understanding the legal ramifications of the problems at hand and what options might be available in response to those problems.

Environmental attorneys can work for federal and state environmental agencies, for public environmental interest groups, for companies or businesses with environmental problems or obligations under federal or state law, or may be private attorneys who specialize in environmental law. A discussion of the various types of environmental attorneys and the variety of tasks they may perform follows.

A. Federal and State Environmental Agencies

Federal and state environmental agencies employ many attorneys. The types of responsibilities undertaken by environmental attorneys who work for governmental agencies are extremely varied. Agency attorneys may work directly on development of environmental laws. This would include drafting legislation and regulations and working within the legislative or administrative process by which these laws and rules are created. Environmental attorneys for government agencies may also act as legal advisors to agency administrators or federal and state legislators on the working of environmental regulatory programs.

Agency environmental attorneys can also work with or as the regulators who are responsible for enforcing environmental laws and regulations. Thus government attorneys may be responsible for monitoring compliance with environmental statutes and regulations and in bringing legal actions to enforce non-compliance with those laws. And, certainly, agency environmental attorneys will represent the agency in litigation in court or in administrative hearings before administrative law judges.

B. Non-Governmental Environmental Organizations

Environmental attorneys work for public interest groups and other nonprofit organizations that specialize in environmental advocacy, research, or litigation. Such groups seek to influence federal, state, and local environmental policies. Thus attorneys who work for such organizations may draft proposed legislation or regulations, specialize in research on issues of environmental concern, or lobby on behalf of the organization and the public in behalf of environmental causes. Examples of "cause-based" public environmental interest groups include the National Wildlife Federation, the Sierra Club, Greenpeace, and the National Audubon Society.

Attorneys for public environmental interest groups may also participate in litigation activities intended to pursue environmental objectives or causes of importance to the group. Thus some environmental interest groups specialize in "citizen suit" litigation that seeks to enforce environmental laws of particular importance or interest to the organization. Similarly, such organizations may bring "citizen suits" against government agencies seeking to compel them to take some regulatory action required by the laws. Examples of "litigation-based" public environmental interest groups include the National Resources Defense Council and the EarthJustice Legal Defense Fund.

C. Business and Industry

Companies and businesses that are subject to environmental statutes and regulations often employ attorneys who specialize in environmental law. Attorneys who work as employees of companies, rather than for private law firms who represent such companies, are referred to as "corporate in-house counsel." "In-house" environmental attorneys for companies and businesses may undertake a wide variety of responsibilities for their employer. These attorneys may be responsible for obtaining permits or licenses the company is required to have under various environmental regulatory programs, such as discharge permits under the Clean Water Act or emissions permits under the Clean Air Act. In-house corporate counsel may also assist the company in identifying the environmental statutes and regulations it is obligated to comply with and in monitoring the company's compliance with those laws.

In-house environmental attorneys may represent the company, or assist private law firms in such representation, in investigations or enforcement proceedings against the company for violations of environmental law. Similarly, these attorneys may participate in representing the company in litigation against the company brought by individuals because of personal injury or property damage as a result of environmentally harmful activities.

Corporate environmental attorneys may also advise the company on establishing its corporate environmental policies and in deciding on how to manage its environmental operations and activities. Also in an advisory role, corporate in-house attorneys may analyze proposed new environmental legislation and regulations and assess the potential impact on the company and its operations.

D. Private Attorneys

Environmental attorneys may also work for law firms with clients who have environmental interests, or may be individual attorneys who specialize in environmental law or litigation. All of the various activities described above for in-house corporate counsel may also be performed for corporate clients by private environmental attorneys. Thus these private attorneys may advise companies as to their obligations under environmental laws, assist them in meeting their compliance obligations, and represent them in enforcement proceedings or litigation.

Importantly, private attorneys who specialize in environmental law may also advise individual clients affected by environmental issues. Such advice may involve potential responses to actions in neighborhoods or communities that violate the environmental laws or create risks of environmental harm. Additionally, private environmental attorneys may represent individuals in "citizen suit" proceedings against environmental law violators or government agencies, or in individual litigation seeking some legal redress for harm or injury caused by environmental actions.

GLOSSARY

Accretion. The increase of the actual land on a stream.

Adjacent wetland. Wetlands that border or are contiguous to navigable waterways.

Affirmative defense. Once the plaintiff (or the prosecution in a criminal case) establishes the elements of its case, the defendant can still win the case by proving the elements of an affirmative defense. Self defense in a criminal case is one example.

Ambient air. Outdoor air; does not include air inside a building or structure.

Aquifer. A geologic formation, group of formations, or part of a formation that is capable of yielding a significant amount of water to a well or spring.

Coastal zone. Waters and affected adjacent land subject to the public trust and interest, as defined by the Coastal Zone Management Act.

Commercial Activity. Any activities of industry and trade, not limited simply to buying and selling.

Contributory negligence. A doctrine of common law that if a person was injured in part due to his or her own negligence, the injured party is not entitled to collect any damages (money) from the party who supposedly caused the accident.

Critical habitat. An area necessary for a species' survival. Unique food needs, shelter requirements, or breeding sites all delineate a critical habitat.

Discovery. The efforts of a party to a lawsuit to obtain information before trial through demands for production of documents, depositions, written interrogatories (questions and answers written under oath), written requests for admissions of fact, and the pretrial motions.

Dredged material. Material that is excavated or dredged from the waters of the United States. Dredged spoils are considered pollutants under the Clean Water Act.

Ecosystem. The relationships between living things and their nonliving support environment in a given location.

Effluent. A waste liquid discharge from a manufacturing or treatment process—whether in its natural state, or partially or completely treated—that discharges into the environment.

Endangered species. Any species threatened with extinction in all or a significant part of its range.

Epidemiology. This is the study of factors affecting the health of populations. It serves as the foundation for interventions made in the interest of public health, preventative medicine, and environmental regulation. Because is is focused directly on people (as opposed to animal testing), it is highly regarded in courtroom settings.

Epidemiological evidence. Evidence derived from the science of epidemiology.

Erosion. The process by which the surface of the earth is worn away by the action of water, glaciers, winds, waves, etc.

General permits. Under the Clean Water Act, general permits allow for activities that are similar in nature, that have minimal adverse environmental effects if performed separately, and that have minimal cumulative adverse effects on the environment.

Groundwater. Water beneath the land surface in the saturated zone that is under atmospheric or artesian pressure. The water that enters wells and issues from springs.

Habitat modification. Any activity that would significantly impair essential behavior patterns of species, such as breeding, feeding, or sheltering behavior patterns.

Injunction. An order from a court ordering someone to do something or prohibiting some act.

Isolated wetlands. Wetlands that are not hydraulically connected to waters of the United States.

Joint and several liability. When more than one party is responsible for damage, joint and several liability says that each defendant is responsible for the entire amount of the damage. The plaintiff may not recover more than the actual damage, but if only one of ten potentially responsible defendants is located—and hence only one is found to be responsible—that one defendant can be required to pay the full amount of the damages to the plaintiff, even though that defendant was actually responsible for only a small part of the damage. The idea is that the plaintiff is entitled to fully recover for the extent of his or her damages, even if not all of the responsible parties can be located.

Jus privatum. A right of private ownership

Jus publicum. The right of ownership of real property that is held in trust by a government for the benefit of the public (within the public trust doctrine).

Mootness. In judicial procedure, an issue or case that is no longer of relevance. A court will not usually hear or decide a moot case.

Navigable waters. Those waters over which commerce may be carried or that are used for transportation, including the territorial seas.

Negligence. The failure to exercise the care toward others which a reasonable or prudent person would do in the circumstances, or taking action which such a reasonable person would not.

Nonpoint source. A source of contaminants that is not a "point source" or associated with a discrete point of discharge. The contaminant enters the receiving water in an intermittent and/or diffuse manner.

Nuisance. Any unreasonable use that interferes with another landowner's quiet enjoyment of the land but falls short of a physical trespass.

Particulates. A criteria air pollutant comprised of small solid material. Particulates are produced as a by-product of the unburnable fraction of fuel, particularly coal.

Pendant jurisdiction. A court which has jurisdiction over one claim between the parties may, for the sake of efficiency, here other claims between the parties, even though it would not otherwise have authority or jurisdiction over this other claim. In such a situation, the court is said to exercise pendant jurisdiction over the second claim.

Point source. Any discernible, confined, and discrete conveyance, including but not limited to any pipe, ditch, channel, tunnel, conduit, well, discrete fissure, container, rolling stock, concentrated animal feeding operation, or vessel or other floating craft from which pollutants are or may be discharged.

Preemption. The rule of law that says if the federal government has enacted legislation on a subject matter it shall be controlling over state laws and preclude the state from enacting laws on the same subject.

Prima facie. Latin for "at first look," or "on its face," referring to a lawsuit or criminal prosecution in which the evidence before trial is sufficient to prove the case unless there is substantial contradictory evidence presented at trial.

Primary treatment. The most basic level of wastewater treatment, consisting only of physical processes. The function of primary treatment is to remove large suspended or floating organic solids (typically human waste), heavy inorganic solids such as plastics grit, and excessive amounts of oil or grease.

Private nuisance. A nuisance that affects only one or a few specific neighboring properties.

Public nuisance. A nuisance that affects a wide segment of the human population.

Public trust doctrine. The concept that certain resources that are too unique and valuable to be privately owned without restriction should be regulated for the public benefit. This typically applies to the land beneath running water and tidal lands are that below the mean high tide line.

Release. Any spilling, leaking, pumping, pouring, emitting, emptying, discharging, injecting, escaping, leaching, dumping, or disposing into the environment.

Reliction. A gradual change of the water line on real property which gives the owner more dry land.

Riparian. Owner of land abutting a water source.

Riparian rights. Water rights that spring from the ownership of property abutting a water source.

Secondary treatment. An entirely biological process of treating sewage water that relies on biological oxidation. Through a process of microbial oxidation of organic matter as the water passes through a gravel bed, the treatment purifies the water, in much the same manner as the self-purification action of a stream.

Silviculture. The care and cultivation of forest trees; forestry.

Species. A population of organisms capable of interbreeding healthy offspring under natural conditions.

Standing. The status of being qualified to assert or enforce legal rights or duties in a judicial forum because he or she has a sufficient and protectable interest in the outcome of the controversy.

Stationary source. An immobile facility, such as a power plant, that emits pollutants.

Statute of limitations. A statute establishing a period of time from the accrual of a cause of action (as upon the occurrence or discovery of an injury) within which suit must be filed.

Strict liability. Liability that is imposed without a finding of fault (as negligence or intent).

Surface water. Water on the land surface, i.e., oceans, lakes, rivers.

Take. Under the ESA, any possible conduct that could cause actual injury to an endangered or threatened species.

Technology forcing. Technology forcing is a strategy where a regulator specifies a standard that cannot be met with existing technology, or at least not at an acceptable cost. The idea is that this will force industry to develop new, better technology.

Threatened species. A species that is likely to become endangered within the foreseeable future throughout all or a large part of its range.

Toxic pollutant. A substance that poses a significant or unreasonable risk of hazard to the public health or welfare.

Water dependency test. A test determining whether a permit is issued for the discharge of dredge or fill material into navigable waters, depending on whether water use is a critical component of the activity.

Wetlands. Land areas that are inundated or saturated by surface or groundwater at a frequency and duration sufficient to support, and that under normal circumstances do support, a prevalence of vegetation typically adapted for life in saturated soil conditions. Wetlands generally include swamps, marshes, bogs, and similar areas.

COMMON ACRONYMS AND ABBREVIATIONS

AAEE: American Academy of Environmental Engineers

AANWR: Alaskan Arctic National Wildlife Refuge

AAP: Asbestos Action Program

AAPCO: American Association of Pesticide Control Officials

AARC: Alliance for Acid Rain Control

A&C: Abatement and Control

ACA: American Conservation Association

ACBM: Asbestos-Containing Building Material

ACE: Alliance for Clean Energy

ACEEE: American Council for an Energy Efficient Economy

ACL: Alternate Concentration Limit *or* Analytical Chemistry Laboratory

ACM: Asbestos-Containing Material

ACP: Air Carcinogen Policy *or* Agriculture Control Program (Water Quality Management)

ACQR: Air Quality Control Region

ACRES: The Assessment, Cleanup and Redevelopment Exchange System

ACS: American Chemical Society

ACTS: Asbestos Contractor Tracking System

ACWA: American Clean Water Association

ACWM: Asbestos-Containing Waste Material

ADA: Americans with Disabilities Act

ADABA: Acceptable Data Base

ADI: Acceptable Daily Intake

ADR: Alternate Dispute Resolution

ADSS: Air Data Screening System

AEA: Atomic Energy Act

AED: The EPA's Air Enforcement Division

AEE: Alliance for Environmental Education

AEERL: Air and Energy Engineering Research Laboratory

AEM: Acoustic Emission Monitoring

AERE: Association of Environmental and Resource Economists

AFA: American Forestry Association

AFCA: Area Fuel Consumption Allocation

AFCEE: Air Force Center for Environmental Excellence

AHERA: Asbestos Hazard Emergency Response Act

A&I: Alternative and Innovative (Wastewater Treatment System)

AID: Agency for International Development

AIHC: American Industrial Health Council

AIP: Auto Ignition Point

AIRS: Aerometric Information Retrieval System

AL: Acceptable Level

ALARA: As Low As Reasonably Achievable

ALJ: Administrative Law Judge

AMBIENS: Atmospheric Mass Balance of Industrially Emitted and Natural Sulfur

AMOS: Air Management Oversight System

AMPS: Automatic Mapping and Planning System

AMSA: Association of Metropolitan Sewer Agencies

ANC: Acid Neutralizing Capacity

ANPR: Advance Notice of Proposed Rulemaking

ANRHRD: Air, Noise, & Radiation Health Research Division

ANSS: American Nature Study Society

AOC: Abnormal Operating Conditions

AOD: Agron-Oxygen Decarbonization

AOML: Atlantic Oceanographic and Meteorological Laboratory

APA: Administrative Procedures Act

APCA: Air Pollution Control Association

APCD: Air Pollution Control District

APCO: Air Pollution Control Officers

APHA: American Public Health Association

APTI: Air Pollution Training Institute

APWA: American Public Works Association

AQCCT: Air-Quality Criteria and Control Techniques

AQCP: Air Quality Control Program

AQCR: Air-Quality Control Region

AQD: Air-Quality Digest

AQDHS: Air-Quality Data Handling System

AQDM: Air-Quality Display Model

AQMA: Air-Quality Maintenance Area

AQMP: Air-Quality Maintenance Plan *or* Air-Quality Management Plan

AQSM: Air-Quality Simulation Model

AQTAD: Air-Quality Technical Assistance Demonstration

A&R: Air and Radiation

ARAR: Applicable or Relevant and Appropriate Standards, Limitations, Criteria, and Requirements

ARB: Air Resources Board

ARAC: Acid Rain Advisory Committee

ARCC: American Rivers Conversation Council

ARCS: Alternative Remedial Contract Strategy

ARG: American Resources Group

ARIP: Accidental Release Information Program

ARL: Air Resources Laboratory

ARM: Air Resources Management

ARNEWS: Acid Rain National Early Warning Systems

ARO: Alternate Regulatory Option

ARRP: Acid Rain Research Program

ARRPA: Air Resources Regional Pollution Assessment Model

ARZ: Auto Restricted Zone

ASDWA: Association of State Drinking Water Administrators

ASHAA: Asbestos in Schools Hazard Abatement Act

ASIWCPA: Association of State and Interstate Water Pollution Control Administrators

AST: Advanced Secondary (Wastewater) Treatment

ASTSWMO: Association of State and Territorial Solid Waste Management Officials

ATERIS: Air Toxics Exposure and Risk Information System

ATS: Action Tracking System

ATSDR: Agency for Toxic Substances and Disease Registry

ATTF: Air Toxics Task Force

A/WPR: Air/Water Pollution Report

AWT: Advanced Wastewater Treatment

AWWA: American Water Works Association

AWWARF: American Water Works Association Research Foundation

BAA: Board of Assistance Appeals

BAC: Biotechnology Advisory Committee

BACM: Best Available Control Measures

BACT: Best Available Control Technology

BADT: Best Available Demonstrated Technology

BART: Best Available Retrofit Technology

BAT: Best Available Technology

BATEA: Best Available Treatment Economically Achievable

BCT: Best Control Technology

BCPCT: Best Conventional Pollutant Control Technology

BDAT: Best Demonstrated Achievable Technology

BDCT: Best Demonstrated Control Technology

BDT: Best Demonstrated Technology

BMP: Best Management Practice(s)

BMR: Baseline Monitoring Report

BO: Budget Obligations

BOD: Biochemical Oxygen Demand *or* Biological Oxygen Demand

BP: Boiling Point

BPJ: Best Professional Judgment

BPT: Best Practicable Technology *or* Pest Practicable Treatment

BPWTT: Best Practical Wastewater Treatment Technology

BSI: British Standards Institute

BSO: Benzene Soluble Organics

BTZ: Below the Treatment Zone

BUN: Blood Urea Nitrogen

CA: Citizen Act *or* Cooperative Agreements *or* Corrective Action

CAA: Clean Air Act *or* Compliance Assurance Agreement

CAAA: Clean Air Act Amendments

CAER: Community Awareness and Emergency Response

CAFO: Consent Agreement/Final Order

CAG: Carcinogenic Assessment Group

CAIR: Clean Air Interstate Rule or Comprehensive Assessment of Information Rule

CAM: Compliance Assurance Monitoring rule *or* Compliance Assurance Monitoring

CAMP: Continuous Air Monitoring Program

CAO: Corrective Action Order

CAP: Criteria Air Pollutant *or* Corrective Action Plan *or* Cost Allocation Procedure

CAR: Corrective Action Report

CAS: Center for Automotive Safety *or* Chemical Abstract Service

CASAC: Clean Air Scientific Advisory Committee

CATS: Corrective Action Tracking System

CAU: Carbon Adsorption Unit

CBA: Chesapeake Bay Agreement *or* Cost Benefit Analysis *or* Conservation Bank Agreement

CCA: Competition in Contracting Act *or* Candidate Conservation Agreement

CCAA: Canadian Clean Air Act

CCAP: Center for Clean Air Policy

CCP: Composite Correction Plan

CCTP: Clean Coal Technology Program

CD: Climatological Data

CDC: Centers for Disease Control

CDD: Chlorinated dibenzo-p-dioxin

CDF: Chlorinated dibenzofuran

CDS: Compliance Data System

CEA: Cooperative Enforcement Agreement

CEA: Cost and Economic Assessment

CEARC: Canadian Environmental Assessment Research Council

CEB: Chemical Element Balance

CEM: Continuous Emission Monitoring

CEMS: Continuous Emission Monitoring System

CEPA: Canadian Environmental Protection Act

CEPP: Chemical Emergency Preparedness Plan

CEQ: Council on Environmental Quality

CERCLA: Comprehensive Environmental Response, Compensation, and Liability Act

CERCLIS: Comprehensive Environmental Response, Compensation, and Liability Information System

CERT: Certificate of Eligibility

CFC: Chlorofluorocarbons

CFM: Chlorofluoromethanes

CFR: Code of Federal Regulations

CHAMP: Community Health Air Monitoring Program

CHESS: Community Health and Environmental Surveillance System

CIAQ: Council on Indoor Air Quality

CICA: Competition in Contracting Act

CID: The EPA's Criminal Investigations Division

CIMC: Cleanups in My Community

CIS: Chemical Information System

CITES: Convention on International Trade in Endangered Species of Wild Fauna and Flora

CLEANS: Clinical Laboratory for Evaluation and Assessment of Toxic Substances

CLF: Conservation Law Foundation

CM: Corrective Measure

CMA: Chemical Manufacturers Association

CME: Comprehensive Monitoring Evaluation

CMEP: Critical Mass Energy Project

CMP: Coastal Management Plan

CNG: Compressed Natural Gas

CPF: Carcinogenic Potency Factor

CPO: Certified Project Officer

CQA: Construction Quality Assurance

CR: Continuous Radon Monitoring

CRR: Center for Renewable Resources

CSGWPP: Comprehensive State Ground Water Protection Program

CSIN: Chemical Substances Information Network

CTG: Control Techniques Guidelines

CWA: Clean Water Act (aka FWPCA)

CWAP: Clean Water Action Project

CWTC: Chemical Waste Transportation Council

CZARA: Coastal Zone Management Act Reauthorization Amendments

CZMA: Coastal Zone Management Act

DCO: Delayed Compliance Order *or* Document Control Officer

DDT: DichloroDiphenyTricloroethane

DERs: Data Evaluation Records

DES: Diethylstilbesterol

DI: Diagnostic Inspection

DMR: Discharge Monitoring Report

DNA: Deoxyribonucleic acid

DO: Dissolved Oxygen

DOI: The United States Department of the Interior

DPA: Deepwater Ports Act

DQO: Data Quality Objective

DSAP: Data Self Auditing Program

DSCF: Dry Standard Cubic Feet

DSCM: Dry Standard Cubic Meter

DSS: Domestic Sewage Study

DWEL: Drinking Water Equivalent Level

DWS: Drinking Water Standard

EA: Environmental Assessment *or* Endangerment Assessment *or* Enforcement Agreement *or* Environmental Action *or* Environmental Audit

EAB: The EPA's Environmental Appeals Board

EAP: Environmental Action Plan

EAO: Emergency Administrative Order

EB: Emissions Balancing

ECHO: Enforcement and Compliance History Online

ECOS: Environmental Council of States

ECR: Enforcement Case Review

ECRA: Economic Cleanup Responsibility Act

EDB: Ethylene Dibromide

EDC: Ethylene Dichloride

EDF: Environmental Defense Fund

EDTA: Ethylene Diamine Triacetic Acid

EEA: Energy and Environmental Analysis

EER: Excess Emission Report

EERU: Environmental Emergency Response Unit

EF: Emission Factor

EHC: Environmental Health Committee

EHS: Extremely Hazardous Substance

EI: Emissions Inventory

EIA: Environmental Impact Assessment *or* Economic Impact Assessment

EIR: Environmental Impact Report *or* Endangerment Information Report

EIS: Environmental Impact Statement *or* Environmental Inventory System

EJ: Environmental Justice

EL: Exposure Level

ELI: Environmental Law Institute

ELR: Environmental Law Reporter

EM: Electromagnetic Conductivity

EMAP: Environmental Mapping and Assessment Program

EMR: Environmental Management Report

EnPA: Environmental Performance Agreement

EOP: End of Pipe

EOT: Emergency Operations Team

EPAA: Environmental Programs Assistance Act

EPA: United States Environmental Protection Agency

EPACT: Environmental Policy Act

EPCRA: Emergency Preparedness and Community Right to Know Act

EPI: Environmental Policy Institute

EQIP: Environmental Quality Incentives Program

ERA: Economic Regulatory Agency

ERAMS: Environmental Radiation Ambient Monitoring System

ERC: Emergency Response Commission *or* Emissions Reduction Credit *or* Environmental Research Center

ERCS: Emergency Response Cleanup Services

ERDA: Energy Research and Development Administration

ERD & DAA: Environmental Research, Development and Demonstration Authorization Act

ERL: Environmental Research Laboratory

ERNS: Emergency Response Notification System

ERT: Emergency Response Team

ERTAQ: ERT Air Quality Model

ES: Enforcement Strategy

ESA: Endangered Species Act *or* Environmentally Sensitive Area

ESC: Endangered Species Committee

ESH: Environmental Safety and Health

ET: Emissions Trading

ETS: Environmental Tobacco Smoke

EUP: Experimental Use Permit

ExEx: Expected Exceedance

FACA: Federal Advisory Committee Act

FATES: FIFRA and TSCA Enforcement System

FCC: Fluid Catalytic Converter

FDF: Fundamentally Different Factors

FDL: Final Determination Letter

FE: Fugitive Emissions

FEDS: Federal Energy Data System

FEPCA: Federal Environmental Pesticide Control Act; enacted as amendments to FIFRA

FERC: Federal Energy Regulatory Commission

FF: Federal Facilities

FFAR: Fuel and Fuel Additive Registration

FFDCA: Federal Food, Drug, and Cosmetic Act

FFEO: The EPA's Federal Facilities Enforcement Office

FIFRA: Federal Insecticide, Fungicide, and Rodenticide Act

FINDS: Facility Index System

FIP: Federal Implementation Plan (CAA)

FLM: Federal Land Manager

FLPMA: Federal Land Policy and Management Act

FMP: Financial Management Plan

FOIA: Freedom of Information Act

FONSI: Finding of No Significant Impact

FP: Fine Particulate

FPA: Federal Pesticide Act

FPEIS: Fine Particulate Emissions Information System

FPPA: Federal Pollution Prevention Act

FRA: Federal Register Act

FRES: Forest Range Environmental Study

FRN: Final Rulemaking Notice

FRS: Facility Registry System

FS: Feasibility Study

FSA: Food Security Act

FUA: Fuel Use Act

FURS: Federal Underground Injection Control Reporting System

FWCA: Fish and Wildlife Coordination Act

FWPCA: Federal Walker Pollution and Control Act (aka CWA)

FWS: U.S. Fish and Wildlife Service

FY: Fiscal Year

GAAP: Generally Accepted Accounting Principles

GEMS: Global Environmental Monitoring System

GEP: Good Engineering Practice

GHG: Greenhouse Gas

GIS: Global Indexing System *or* Geographic Information Systems

GLERL: Great Lakes Environmental Research Laboratory

GLP: Good Laboratory Practices

GPG: Grams-per-gallon

GPR: Ground-Penetrating Radar

GPRA: Government Performance and Results Act

GPS: Groundwater Protection Strategy

GR: Grab Randon Sampling

GWM: Groundwater Monitoring

GWPS: Groundwater Protection Standard *or* Groundwater Protection Strategy

HA: Health Advisory

HAP: Hazardous Air Pollutant

HAPEMS: Hazardous Air Pollutant Enforcement Management System

HAZMAT: Hazardous Materials

HC: Hydrocarbon

HCCPD: Hexachlorocyclo-pentadiene

HCP: Hypothermal Coal Process *or* Habitat Conservation Plan

HDPE: High Density Polyethylene

HEPA: High-Efficiency Particulate Air

HHE: Human Health and the Environment

HI: Hazard Index

HFC: Hydrofluorocarbon

HI: Hazard Index

HMIS: Hazardous Materials Information System

HMTA: Hazardous Materials Transportation Act

HMTR: Hazardous Materials Transportation Regulations

HOV: High-Occupancy Vehicle

HPV: High Priority Violator *or* High Production Volume

HRS: Hazardous Ranking System

HRUP: High-Risk Urban Problem

HSDB: Hazardous Substance Data Base

HSL: Hazardous Substance List

HSWA: Hazardous and Solid Waste Amendments

HW: Hazardous Waste

HWM: Hazardous Waste Management

HVAC: Heating, Ventilation, and Air-Conditioning system

IAG: Interagency Agreement

IAQ: Indoor Air Quality

IC: Internal Combustion

ICBN: International Commission on the Biological Effects of Noise

ICCP: International Climate Change Partnership

IES: Institute for Environmental Studies

IP: Inhalable Particles

IPM: Inhalable Particulate Matter

IRM: Intermediate Remedial Measures

ISO: International Organization for Standardization

ITC: Innovative Technology Council *or* Interagency Testing Committee

ITP: Incidental Take Permit (ESA)

IUP: Intended Use Plan

JAPCA: Journal of Air Pollution Control Association

JEC: Joint Economic Committee

JECFA: Joint Expert Committee of Food Additives

JEIOG: Joint Emissions Inventory Oversight Group

JLC: Justification for Limited Competition

JMPR: Joint Meeting on Pesticide Residues

JNCP: Justification for Non-Competitive Procurement

JOFOC: Justification for Other Than Full and Open Competition

LADD: Lifetime Average Daily Dose *or* Lowest Acceptable Daily Dose

LAER: Lowest Achievable Emission Rate

LAMP: Lake Acidification Mitigation Project

LCA: Life Cycle Assessment

LCD: Local Climatological Data

LCL: Lower Control Limit

LCM: Life Cycle Management

LCRS: Leachate Collection and Removal System

LD LO: The lowest dosage of a toxic substance that kills test organisms

LDAR: Leak Detection and Repair

LDIP: Laboratory Data Integrity Program

LEPC: Local Emergency Planning Committee

LEV: Low Emissions Vehicle

LFG: Landfill Gas

LFL: Lower Flammability Limit

LGR: Local Governments Reimbursement Program

MACT: Maximum Achievable Control Technology

MAPSIM: Mesoscale Air Pollution Simulation Model

MATC: Maximum Acceptable Toxic Concentration

MCL: Maximum Contaminant Level

MCLG: Maximum Contaminant Level Goal

MCS: Multiple Chemical Sensitivity

MDL: Method Detection Limit

MEC: Model Energy Code

MED: The EPA's Multimedia Enforcement Division

MEI: Maximally (or most) Exposed Individual

MEP: Multiple Extraction Procedure

MFS: The National Marine Fisheries Service

MMPA: Marine Mammal Protection Act

MOE: Margin of Exposure

MOS: Margin of Safety

MPI: Maximum Permitted Intake

MPN: Maximum Possible Number

MPWC: Multiprocess Wet Cleaning

MRBMA: Mercury-Containing and Rechargeable Battery Management Act

MRF: Materials Recovery Facility

MRID: Master Record Identification number

MRL: Maximum-Residue Limit (Pesticide Tolerance)

MSDS: Material Safety Data Sheet

MSW: Municipal Solid Waste

MTD: Maximum Tolerated Dose

MUP: Manufacturing-Use Product

NAA: Nonattainment Area

NAAQS: National Ambient Air Quality Standards

NACEPT: National Advisory Council for Environmental Policy and Technology

NADP/NTN: National Atmospheric Deposition Program/National Trends Network

NAMS: National Air Monitoring Stations

NAPAP: National Acid Precipitation Assessment Program

NAPL: Non-Aqueous Phase Liquid

NAPS: National Air Pollution Surveillance

NARA: National Agrichemical Retailers Association

NARSTO: North American Research Strategy for Tropospheric Ozone

NAS: National Academy of Sciences

NASA: National Aeronautics and Space Administration

NASDA: National Association of State Departments of Agriculture

NAWCA: North American Wetlands Conservation Act

NCWS: Non-Community Water System

NCP: National Contingency Plan

NDWAC: National Drinking Water Advisory Council

NEDS: National Emissions Data System

NEIC: The EPA's National Enforcement Investigations Center

NEPA: National Environmental Policy Act

NEPI: National Environmental Policy Institute

NEPPS: National Environmental Performance Partnership System

NESHAP: National Emission Standard for Hazardous Air Pollutants

NIEHS: National Institute for Environmental Health Sciences

NETA: National Environmental Training Association

NFRAP: No Further Remedial Action Planned

NICT: National Incident Coordination Team

NIMB: Not in My Backyard

NIMBS: Not in My Backyard Syndrome

NIOSH: National Institute of Occupational Safety and Health

NIPDWR: National Interim Primary Drinking Water Regulations

NISAC: National Industrial Security Advisory Committee

NMFS: National Marine Fisheries Service

NMHC: Nonmethane Hydrocarbons

NMOC: Non-Methane Organic Component

NMVOC: Non-methane Volatile Organic Chemicals

NOA: Notice of Arrival

NOAA: National Oceanographic and Atmospheric Agency

NOAC: Nature of Action Code

NOAEL: No Observable Adverse Effect Level

NCOD: National Drinking Water Contaminant Occurrence Database

NODA: Nevada Occupational Disease Act

NOEL: No Observable Effect Level

NOIC: Notice of Intent to Cancel

NOI: Notice of Intent

NOIS: Notice of Intent to Suspend

NOV: Notice of Violation

NORM: Naturally Occurring Radioactive Material

NPCA: National Pest Control Association

NPDES: National Pollutant Discharge Elimination System

NPHAP: National Pesticide Hazard Assessment Program

NPIRS: National Pesticide Information Retrieval System

NPL: National Priorities List

NPMS: National Performance Measures Strategy

NPTN: National Pesticide Telecommunications Network

NRD: Natural Resource Damage

NRDC: Natural Resources Defense Council

NSDWR: National Secondary Drinking Water Regulations

NSEC: National System for Emergency Coordination

NSEP: National System for Emergency Preparedness

NSPS: New Source Performance Standards

NSR: New Source Review

NSR/PSD: National Source Review/Prevention of Significant Deterioration

NTI: National Toxics Inventory

NTIS: National Technical Information Service

NTNCWS: Non-Transient Non-Community Water System

NTP: National Toxicology Program

O & M: Operations and Maintenance

OALJ: The EPA's Office of Administrative Law Judges

OAQPS: Office of Air Quality Planning and Standards

OCD: Offshore and Coastal Dispersion

ODP: Ozone-Depleting Potential

ODS: Ozone-Depleting Substances

OECA: The EPA's Office of Enforcement and Compliance Assurance

OECD: Organization for Economic Cooperation and Development

OF: Optional Form

OI: Order for Information

OLC: Office of Legal Counsel

OLTS: On Line Tracking System

OPA: The Oil Pollution Act

OPR: Office of Protected Resources (NMFS)

ORE: Office of Regulatory Enforcement

ORM: Other Regulated Material

ORP: Oxidation-Reduction Potential

OSHA: Occupational Safety and Health Administration

OTAG: Ozone Transport Assessment Group

OTC: Ozone Transport Commission

OTIS: Online Tracking Information System

OTR: Ozone Transport Region

P2: Pollution Prevention

PA/SI: Preliminary assessment and site investigation

PAG: Pesticide Assignment Guidelines

PAH: Polynuclear Aromatic Hydrocarbons

PAI: Performance Audit Inspection (CWA) *or* Pure Active Ingredient compound

PAM: Pesticide Analytical Manual

PAMS: Photochemical Assessment Monitoring Stations

PAT: Permit Assistance Team (RCRA)

PATS: Pesticide Action Tracking System

PCA: Principle Component Analysis

PCB: Polychlorinated Biphenyl

PCM: Phase Contrast Microscopy

PCN: Policy Criteria Notice

PCO: Pest Control Operator

PCS: Permit Compliance System

PCSD: President's Council on Sustainable Development

PDCI: Product Data Call-In

PFC: Perfluorated Carbon

PFCRA: Program Fraud Civil Remedies Act

PHC: Principal Hazardous Constituent

PHSA: Public Health Service Act

PI: Preliminary Injunction

PIGS: Pesticides in Groundwater Strategy

PIMS: Pesticide Incident Monitoring System

PIN: Pesticide Information Network

PIN: Procurement Information Notice

PIP: Public Involvement Program

PIPQUIC: Program Integration Project Queries Used in Interactive Command

PIRG: Public Interest Research Group

PIRT: Pretreatment Implementation Review Task Force

PIT: Permit Improvement Team

PITS: Project Information Tracking System

PLIRRA: Pollution Liability Insurance and Risk Retention Act

PLM: Polarized Light Microscopy

PLUVUE: Plume Visibility Model

PM: Particulate Matter

PM2.5: Particulate Matter Smaller than 2.5 Micrometers in Diameter

PM 10: Particulate Matter (nominally 10m and less)

PM 15: Particulate Matter (nominally 15m and less)

PNA: Polynuclear Aromatic Hydrocarbons

PO: Project Officer

POC: Point of Compliance

POE: Point of Exposure

POGO: Privately-Owned/ Government-Operated

POHC: Principal Organic Hazardous Constituent

POI: Point of Interception

POLREP: Pollution Report

POM: Particulate Organic Matter

POR: Program of Requirements

POTW: Publicly Owned Treatment Works

PPA: Planned Program Accomplishment

PPB: Parts Per Billion

PPE: Personal Protective Equipment

PPG: Performance Partnership Grant

PPIC: Pesticide Programs Information Center

PPIS: Pesticide Product Information System; Pollution Prevention Incentives for States

PPMAP: Power Planning Modeling Application Procedure

PPM/PPB: Parts per million/ parts per billion

PPSP: Power Plant Siting Program

PPT: Parts Per Trillion

PPTH: Parts Per Thousand

PR: Pesticide Regulation Notice *or* Preliminary Review

PRA: Paperwork Reduction Act *or* Planned Regulatory Action

PRATS: Pesticides Regulatory Action Tracking System

PRC: Planning Research Corporation

PRI: Periodic Reinvestigation

PRM: Prevention Reference Manuals

PRN: Pesticide Registration Notice

PRP: Potentially Responsible Party

PRZM: Pesticide Root Zone Model

PS: Point Source

PSAM: Point Source Ambiant Monitoring

PSC: Program Site Coordinator

PSD: Prevention of Significant Deterioration

PSES: Pretreatment Standards for Existing Sources

PSI: Pollutant Standards Index *or* Pounds Per Square Inch *or* Pressure Per Square Inch

PSIG: Pressure Per Square Inch Gauge

PSM: Point Source Monitoring

PSNS: Pretreatment Standards for New Sources

PSU: Primary Sampling Unit

PTDIS: Single Stack Meteorological Model in EPA UNAMAP Series

PTE: Potential to Emit

PTFE: Polytetrafluoroethylene (Teflon)

PTMAX: Single Stack Meteorological Model in EPA UNAMAP series

PTPLU: Point Source Gaussian Diffusion Model

PUC: Public Utility Commission

PV: Project Verification

PVC: Polyvinyl Chloride

PWB: Printed Wiring Board

PWS: Public Water Supply/ System

PWSS: Public Water Supply System

QAC: Quality Assurance Coordinator

QA/QC: Quality Assistance/ Quality Control

QAMIS: Quality Assurance Management and Information System

QAO: Quality Assurance Officer

QAPP: Quality Assurance Program (or Project) Plan

QAT: Quality Action Team

QBTU: Quadrillion British Thermal Units

QC: Quality Control

QCA: Quiet Communities Act

QCI: Quality Control Index

QCP: Quiet Community Program

QL: Quantification Limit

QNCR: Quarterly Noncompliance Report

QUA: Qualitative Use Assessment

QUIPE: Quarterly Update for Inspector in Pesticide Enforcement

RA: Reasonable Alternative *or* Regulatory Alternatives *or* Regulatory Analysis *or* Remedial Action *or* Resource Allocation *or* Risk Analysis *or* Risk Assessment

RAATS: RCRA Administrate Action Tracking System

RAC: Radiation Advisory Committee. Raw Agricultural Commodity; Regional Asbestos Coordinator. Response Action Coordinator

RACM: Reasonably Available Control Measures

RACT: Reasonably Available Control Technology

RAD: Radiation Adsorbed Dose (unit of measurement of radiation absorbed by humans)

RADINFO: Radiation Information Database

RADM: Random Walk Advection and Dispersion Model; Regional Acid Deposition Model

RAM: Urban Air Quality Model for Point and Area Source in EPA UNAMAP Series

RAMP: Rural Abandoned Mine Program

RAMS: Regional Air Monitoring System

RAP: Radon Action Program *or* Registration Assessment Panel *or* Remedial Accomplishment Plan *or* Response Action Plan

RAPS: Regional Air Pollution Study

RARG: Regulatory Analysis Review Group

RAS: Routine Analytical Service

RAT: Relative Accuracy Test

RBAC: Re-use Business Assistance Center

RBC: Red Blood Cell

RC: Responsibility Center

RCC: Radiation Coordinating Council

RCDO: Regional Case Development Officer

RCO: Regional Compliance Officer

RCP: Research Centers Program

RCRA: Resource Conservation and Recovery Act

RCRIS: Resource Conservation and Recovery Information System

RD/RA: Remedial Design/ Remedial Action

R & D: Research and Development

RD & D: Research, Development and Demonstration

RDF: Refuse-Derived Fuel

RDNA: Recombinant DNA

RDU: Regional Decision Units

RDV: Reference Dose Values

RE: Reasonable Efforts; Reportable Event

REAP: Regional Enforcement Activities Plan

REE: Rare Earth Elements

REEP: Review of Environmental Effects of Pollutants

RECLAIM: Regional Clean Air Initiatives Marker

RED: Reregistration Eligibility Decision Document

REDA: Recycling Economic Development Advocate

ReFIT: Reinvention for Innovative Technologies

REI: Restricted Entry Interval

REM/FIT: Remedial/Field Investigation Team

REMS: RCRA Enforcement Management System

REP: Reasonable Efforts Program

REPS: Regional Emissions Projection System

RESOLVE: Center for Environmental Conflict Resolution

RF: Response Factor

RFA: Regulatory Flexibility Act

RFB: Request for Bid

RfC: Reference Concentration

RFD: Reference Dose Values

RFI: Remedial Field Investigation

RFP: Reasonable Further Programs. Request for Proposal

RHA: The Rivers and Harbors Act

RHRS: Revised Hazard Ranking System

RI: Reconnaissance Inspection *or* Remedial Investigation

RI/FS: Remedial investigation and feasibility study

RIA: Regulatory Impact Analysis *or* Regulatory Impact Assessment

RIC: Radon Information Center

RICC: Retirement Information and Counseling Center

RICO: Racketeer Influenced and Corrupt Organizations Act

RI/FS: Remedial Investigation/Feasibility Study

RIM: Regulatory Interpretation Memorandum

RIN: Regulatory Identifier Number

RIP: RCRA Implementation Plan

RISC: Regulatory Information Service Center

RJE: Remote Job Entry

RLL: Rapid and Large Leakage (Rate)

RMCL: Recommended Maximum Contaminant Level (discontinued in favor of MCLG)

RMDHS: Regional Model Data Handling System

RMIS: Resources Management Information System

RMP: Risk Management Plan

RNA: Ribonucleic Acid

ROADCHEM: Roadway Version that Includes Chemical Reactions of BI, NO_2, and O_3

ROADWAY: A Model to Predict Pollutant Concentrations Near a Roadway

ROC: Record(s) of Communication

ROD: Record(s) of Decision

RODS: Record of Decision System

ROG: Reactive Organic Gases

ROLLBACK: A Proportional Reduction Model

ROM: Regional Oxidant Model

ROMCOE: Rocky Mountain Center on Environment

ROP: Rate of Progress *or* Regional Oversight Policy

ROPA: Record of Procurement Action

ROSA: Regional Ozone Study Area

RP: Radon Progeny Integrated Sampling *or* Respirable Particulates *or* Responsible Party

RPAR: Rebuttable Presumption Against Registration

RPM: Reactive Plume Model *or* Remedial Project Manager

RQ: Reportable Quantities

RRC: Regional Response Center

RRT: Regional Response Team *or* Requisite Remedial Technology

RS: Registration Standard

RSCC: Regional Sample Control Center

RSD: Risk-Specific Dose

RSE: Removal Site Evaluation

RTCM: Reasonable Transportation Control Measure

RTDF: Remediation Technologies Development Forum

RTDM: Rough Terrain Diffusion Model

RTECS: Registry of Toxic Effects of Chemical Substances

RTK **Net**: Right-to-Know Network

RTM: Regional Transport Model

RTP: Research Triangle Park

RUP: Restricted Use Pesticide

RVP: Reid Vapor Pressure

RWC: Residential Wood Combustion

S&A: Sampling and Analysis. Surveillance and Analysis

SAB: Science Advisory Board

SAC: Suspended and Cancelled Pesticides

SAEWG: Standing Air Emissions Work Group

SAIC: Special-Agents-In-Charge

SAIP: Systems Acquisition and Implementation Program

SAMWG: Standing Air Monitoring Work Group

SANE: Sulfur and Nitrogen Emissions

SANSS: Structure and Nomenclature Search System

SAP: Scientific Advisory Panel

SAR: Start Action Request *or* Structural Activity Relationship

SARA: Superfund Amendments and Reauthorization Act of 1986
SC: Sierra Club
SCAP: Superfund Consolidated Accomplishments Plan
SCLDF: Sierra Club Legal Defense Fund
SCRAM: State Consolidated RCRA Authorization Manual
SCRC: Superfund Community Relations Coordinator
SCS: Soil Conservation Service
SCSA: Soil Conservation Society of America
SCSP: Storm and Combined Sewer Program
SDC: Systems Decision Plan
SDWA: Safe Drinking Water Act
SDWIS: Safe Drinking Water Information System
SBS: Sick Building Syndrome
SEA: State Enforcement Agreement
SEA: State/EPA Agreement
SEAM: Surface, Environment, and Mining
SEAS: Strategic Environmental Assessment System
SEDS: State Energy Data System
SEGIP: State Environmental Goals and Improvement Project
SEIA: Socioeconomic Impact Analysis
SEM: Standard Error of the Means
SEP: Standard Evaluation Procedures
SEPWC: Senate Environment and Public Works Committee
SERC: State Emergency Planning Commission
SES: Secondary Emissions Standard
SETS: Site Enforcement Tracking System
SFDS: Sanitary Facility Data System
SFFAS: Superfund Financial Assessment System
SFIP: Sector Facility Indexing Project
SFIREG: State FIFRA Issues Research and Evaluation Group

SHA: Safe Harbor Agreement

SHWL: Seasonal High Water Level

SIC: Standard Industrial Classification

SICEA: Steel Industry Compliance Extension Act

SIP: State Implementation Plan

SITE: Superfund Innovative Technology Evaluation

SLAMS: State/Local Air Monitoring Station

SLN: Special Local Need

SLSM: Simple Line Source Model

SMCL: Secondary Maximum Contaminant Level

SMCRA: Surface Mining Control and Reclamation Act

SMOA: Superfund Memorandum of Agreement

SMP: State Management Plan

SMR: Standardized Mortality Ratio

SMSA: Standard Metropolitan Statistical Area

SNA: System Network Architecture

SNAAQS: Secondary National Ambient Air Quality Standards

SNAP: Significant New Alternatives Project; Significant Noncompliance Action Program

SNARL: Suggested No Adverse Response Level

SNC: Significant Noncompliers

SNUR: Significant New Use Rule

SO^2: Sulfur Dioxide

SOC: Synthetic Organic Chemicals

SOCMI: Synthetic Organic Chemicals Manufacturing Industry

SOFC: Solid Oxide Fuel Cell

SOTDAT: Source Test Data

SPAR: Status of Permit Application Report

SPCC: Spill Prevention, Containment, and Countermeasure

SPE: Secondary Particulate Emissions

SPF: Structured Programming Facility

SPI: Strategic Planning Initiative

SPMS: Strategic Planning and Management System *or* Special Purpose Monitoring Stations

SPOC: Single Point of Contact

SPS: State Permit System

SPSS: Statistical Package for the Social Sciences

SRAP: Superfund Remedial Accomplishment Plan

SRR: Second Round Review. Submission Review Record

SRTS: Service Request Tracking System

SSC: State Superfund Contracts

SSD: Standards Support Document

STALAPCO: State and Local Air-Pollution Control Officials

STAPPA: State and Territorial Air Pollution

STEL: Short Term Exposure Limit

SWC: Settlement with Conditions

SWDA: Solid Waste Disposal Act

SWIE: Southern Waste Information Exchange

SWMU: Solid Waste Management Unit

SWPA: Source Water Protection Area

SWTR: Surface Water Treatment Rule

TAG: Technical Assistance Grant

TAMS: Toxic Air Monitoring System

TAP: Technical Assistance Program

TAPDS: Toxic Air Pollutant Data System

TCDD: Dioxin (Tetrachlorodibenzo-p-dioxin)

TCDF: Tetrachlorodi-benzofurans

TCE: Trichloroethylene

TCRI: Toxic Chemical Release Inventory

TD: Toxic Dose

TDS: Total Dissolved Solids

TEAM: Total Exposure Assessment Model

TEC: Technical Evaluation Committee

TISE: Take It Somewhere Else

TITC: Toxic Substance Control Act Interagency Testing Committee

TLV: Threshold Limit Value

TOC: Total Organic Carbon/ Compound

TPED: The EPA's Toxics and Pesticides Enforcement Division

TPQ: Threshold Planning Quantity

TPY: Tons Per Year

TQM: Total Quality Management

TRC: Technical Review Committee

TRD: Technical Review Document

TRI: Toxic Release Inventory

TRIP: Toxic Release Inventory Program

TRIS: Toxic Chemical Release Inventory System

TRLN: Triangle Research Library Network

TRO: Temporary Restraining Order

TSA: Technical Systems Audit

TSCA: Toxic Substances Control Act

TSCATS: TSCA Test Submissions Database

TSCC: Toxic Substances Coordinating Committee

TSD: Technical Support Document *or* Treatment, Storage or Disposal (facility)

TSDF: Treatment, Storage, and Disposal Facility

TSDG: Toxic Substances Dialogue Group

TSI: Thermal System Insulation

TSM: Transportation System Management

TSO: Time Sharing Option

TSP: Total Suspended Particulates

TSS: Total Suspended (non-filterable) Solids

TTFA: Target Transformation Factor Analysis

TVA: Tennessee Valley Authority

TVOC: Total Volatile Organic Compounds

TWS: Transient Water System

TZ: Treatment Zone

UAC: User Advisory Committee

UAQI: Uniform Air Quality Index

UFL: Upper Flammability Limit

UIC: Underground Injection Control

ULEV: Ultra Low Emission Vehicles

UMTRCA: Uranium Mill Tailings Radiation Control Act

UNECE: United Nations Economic Commission for Europe

UNEP: United Nations Environment Program

USC: Unified Soil Classification

USDA: United States Department of Agriculture

USDW: Underground Sources of Drinking Water

USFS: United States Forest Service

UST: Underground Storage Tank

UTP: Urban Transportation Planning

UV: Ultraviolet

UVA, UVB, UVC: Ultraviolet Radiation Bands

UZM: Unsaturated Zone Monitoring

VCM: Vinyl Chloride Monomer

VCP: Voluntary Cleanup Program

VE: Visual Emissions

VEO: Visible Emission Observation

VOC: Volatile Organic Compounds

VP: Vapor Pressure

VSD: Virtually Safe Dose

VSI: Visual Site Inspection

VSS: Volatile Suspended Solids

WA: Work Assignment

WAP: Waste Analysis Plan

WAVE: Water Alliances for Environmental Efficiency

WB: Wet Bulb

WCED: World Commission on Environment and Development

WDROP: Distribution Register of Organic Pollutants in Water

WED: The EPA's Water Enforcement Division

WENDB: Water Enforcement National Data Base

WERL: Water Engineering Research Laboratory

WET: Whole Effluent Toxicity test

WHO: World Health Organization

WHP: Wellhead Protection Program

WHPA: Wellhead Protection Area

WHWT: Water and Hazardous Waste Team

WICEM: World Industry Conference on Environmental Management

WLA/TMDL: Wasteload Allocation/Total Maximum Daily Load

WLM: Working Level Months

WMO: World Meteorological Organization

WP: Wettable Powder

WPCF: Water Pollution Control Federation

WQS: Water Quality Standard

WRC: Water Resources Council

WRDA: Water Resources Development Act

WRI: World Resources Institute

WS: Work Status

WSF: Water Soluble Fraction

WSRA: Wild and Scenic Rivers Act

WSTB: Water Sciences and Technology Board

WSTP: Wastewater Sewage Treatment Plant

WWEMA: Waste and Wastewater Equipment Manufacturers Association

WWF: World Wildlife Fund

WWTP: Wastewater Treatment Plant

WWTU: Wastewater Treatment Unit

ZEV: Zero Emissions Vehicle

ZOI: Zone of Incorporation

ZRL: Zero Risk Level

ADDITIONAL READINGS

Anderson, Terry L. & Donald R. Leal, *Free Market Environmentalism* (Palgrave, rev. ed.2001).

Carson, Rachel, *Silent Spring* (Houghton Mifflin, 1962, 1987).

Case, David W., *Voluntary Corporate Environmental Regulatory Initiatives,* in *A Handbook of Global Environmental Issues* (Wil Burns & Joel Heinen eds., WorldScientific Publishing, forthcoming 2010).

- *Changing Corporate Behavior Through Environmental Management Systems*, 31 WM. & MARY ENVTL. L. & POL'Y REV. 75 (2006) (Symposium on Corporate Governance and Environmental Best Practices).

- *The EPA's HPV Challenge Program: A Tort Liability Trap*?, 62 WASH. & LEE L. REV. 147 (2005).

- *Corporate Environmental Reporting as Informational Regulation: A Law and Economics Perspective*, 76 U. COLO. L. REV. 379 (2005).

- *The Law and Economics of Environmental Information as Regulation*, 31 ENVTL. L. REP. 10773 (2001).

- *The EPA's Environmental Stewardship Initiative: Attempting to Revitalize a Floundering Regulatory Reform Agenda*, 50 EMORY L.J. 1 (2001).

- *Legal Considerations in Voluntary Corporate Environmental Reporting*, 30 ENVTL. L. REP. 10375 (2000).

- *Environmental Information Disclosure and Stakeholder Involvement: Searching for Common Ground*, 6 CORP. ENVTL. STRATEGY 415 (1999) (Mark Cohen, Mark Abkowitz, Susan Buck, and Patricia Drake).

Cunningham, William P. & Mary Ann Cunningham, *Principles of Environmental Science* (McGraw-Hill, 2005).

Encyclopedia of American Environmental History (Univ. of Houston Center for Public History ed., 2010).

Environmental Regulations and Policies (ICFAI University Press, 2009).

Ferrey, Steven, *Environmental Law: Examples & Explanations* (Aspen, 3rd ed. 2004).

Findley, Roger W. and Daniel A. Farber, *Environmental Law in a Nutshell* (7th ed. West, 2008).

Lomborg, Bjørn, *The Skeptical Environmentalist: Measuring the Real State of the World* (2001).

Mandelker, Daniel R., *NEPA Law and Litigation* (West: Environmental Law Series, looseleif, 2007–09).

Patton-Hulce, Vicki R., *Environment and the Law: A Dictionary* (Contemporary Legal Issues, 1995).

Practicing Law Institute, *Basics of Environmental Law* (1993).

Ruhl, J.B. *et al*, *The Practice and Policy of Environmental Law* (Foundation Press, 2008).

Rychlak, Ronald J., *Cards and Dice in Smokey Rooms: Tobacco Bans and Modern Casinos*, 57 Drake L. Rev. 467 (2009).

- *Understanding Visual Exhibits in the Global Warming Debate*, Heartland Policy Study No. 115 (March 2008), available in print and online <http://www.heartland.org/xxx>.

- *Ocean Aquaculture*, 8 Fordham Env. L.J. 497 (1997).

- *Changing the Face of Environmentalism*, 8 Fordham Env. L.J. 915 (1996).

- *Swimming Past the Hook: Navigating Legal Obstacles in the Aquaculture Industry*, 23 Environmental Law 837 (1993) (Lewis & Clark) (with E.M. Peel), *reprinted online* by the National Agricultural Law Center at the University of Arkansas School of Law (2009) <<www.NationalAgLawCenter.org >>.

- *Coastal Zone Management and the Search for Integration*, 40 DePaul U.L. Rev. 981 (1991).

- *The Humorous Origins of the Green Movement: The Three Stooges as Early Environmentalists*, 48 Okla. L. Rev. 35 (1995).

- *Common Law Remedies for Environmental Wrongs: The Role of Private Nuisance*, 59 Miss. L. J. 657 (1989).

- *Thermal Expansion, Melting Glaciers, and Rising Tides: The Public Trust in Mississippi*, 11 Miss. Col. L. Rev. 95 (1990).

Salzman, James,. with J.B. Ruhl & John Nagle, *The Practice and Policy of Environmental Law* (Foundation Press, 2008).

- *Concepts and Insights in Environmental Law and Policy* (Foundation Press 2003, 2d ed. 2007) (with Barton Thompson, Jr.).

Sanera, Michael & Jane S. Shaw, *Facts, Not Fear: A Parent's Guide to Teaching Children About the Environment* (Regnery Press, 1996).

Simonsen, Craig, *Essentials of Environmental Law* (3rd., 2006).

Vaughn, Jacqueline, *Environmental Politics: Domestic and Global Dimensions* (2003).

SUBJECT INDEX